THUNDER AT 1AM
Copyright © James Dean Divine - 2019

First published in Scotland in 2019 by Jim Divine.

All similarities to actual characters —
living or dead — are purely coincidental.

Cover Design: Jim Divine

Other books by James Dean Divine:

The Lost Tornado (2015)

DEDICATION

Steve, Richard and Nancy. I smile when I remember you.

My family and friends.

My writing mentor, the brilliant author Tony Black.

And last but not least, the woman who's put up with me for the past few decades. Thank you Trish.

Enjoy with laughter and tears.

Foreword by Philip John

When you read Jim's' books, you get the sense that life has singled him out for a good kicking. But he rises above it all. These are the stories of every working-class kid who dared to take the road less travelled.

Jim's first book, 'The Lost Tornado', is a devastating yet inspirational tale of personality overcoming adversity.

'Thunder At One AM' picks up where the first book left off. I implore you to buy both books and start at the beginning.

Jim knows a thumping good story and thrills in the telling of it. Defiant, and funny as fuck, Jim's' crazed dispatches from his extraordinary life will keep you spellbound, and leave you with a big goofy grin on your face.

PHILIP JOHN, DIRECTOR: Downton Abbey, Outlander, Moon Dogs, Marvel's Iron Fist, Being Human, New Tricks, Mistresses.....

Prologue - Thunder at One AM

In my youth I spent a lot of my time writing; songs, poetry and letters to Jim'll Fix It. I hoped that this artistic output would bring me girls, flocking like bees to honey, desperate to know this New Romantic god. Let's face it. That didn't go to plan. At weekends I'd go up town to discos. Inevitably I returned home crestfallen, collar-up against the cold and the rain of the ruthless Scottish climate. I looked a sight, trudging along Princes Street, it seemed I'd been singled out by fate for a life without the love of a good woman.

After one of these, particularly wet and downbeat nights, I returned home at around one in the morning and set up my synthesizer. Thunder at 1am came calling, and it seemed to sum up my little world perfectly, then.

WE SIT AND STARE THROUGH SEASON'S THOUGHTS
IMPROVING IN OUR MINDS
REFLECTING ON THE TIMES, WE LEFT BEHIND
THEY SAY A YOUNG MAN IN HIS PRIME
AND WOMEN FROM NOVEMBER
SHOULD NEVER GET TOGETHER

HOPE DISAPPEARS. IN THE WINDS OF REJECTION
THERE'S SOMEONE LIKE ME
TO SEE ME THROUGH, YEAH WE'LL GET THROUGH WHEN
HOPE DISAPPEARS IN THE WINDOW'S REFLECTION
THERE'S SOMEONE LIKE ME
TO TAKE ME THROUGH THE DAY

I SEE THE SKY AND WATCH THE WORLD GO BY
THESE VERY MODERN TIMES AND I
ARE WAVELENGTHS FAR APART
I HEAR THE THUNDER CRY AT ONE AM
THE LIGHTNING STRIKES ME BLIND AGAIN
A SILHOUETTE INSIDE

LONDON DECEMBER 2012

AS I'M COMING TO, slowly awakening, I get the awful stench of days-old urine. My nostrils are stung with the same intensity as smelling salts. My head jerks upwards, I recoil as I realise I've been sleeping with my head on a homeless man's shoulder. There's absolute silence, save the mechanical drone of a diesel engine somewhere in the distance. The side of my face, nose and lips are covered with frozen saliva, I've got a horrible metallic taste in my mouth. My cheek aches, I dab my finger to it, there's blood, I look at the guy's shoulder, there's blood there too, and I realise that my jaw must have frozen to his coat during the night and my sudden awakening must have torn it.

Thankfully with the cold conditions, the blood has congealed quickly enough for me not to have to do anything about it for the moment.

I'm frozen to my core, shivering uncontrollably, I look around in a daze and find I'm sitting in Charing Cross station in London on a cold steel bench. There is a pile of Metro newspapers under my arse, I'm wearing a thin designer shirt and jacket, the shirt has vomit down the front, I button my jacket up to cover it as if that'll make any difference to the state I'm in. I look at the time and temperature on the departure board. It's 3.04 and -7 degrees, four days before Christmas. I lean forward on the seat to dig up any residual energy that I can summon.
I attempt to stand up, but an aching from several parts of my body forces me back down. I try to identify where the aches are coming from, starting with what hurts most. My

feet. I look down at my shoes and notice no socks are visible. I painfully pull the left shoe off. It's in hell of a state, and I curse as I slowly peel it from my skin. Trish'll go mental as she just bought me these beautiful, or used to be beautiful, Italian leather shoes for Christmas and there are still days to go before I'm even meant to open the bloody present. My heel is several different shades of red, there's blood all over the rim of the shoe. A big gory blister the size of a golf ball sits there daring me to puncture him. My right heel is exactly the same, but at least I can sense a sock there, hidden somewhere in the well of the shoe, which offers me a strangely comforting feeling. I pull it up, curse my luck as it reopens a bloody crevasse and I attempt once again to stand up.

This time I'm expecting the pain and manage it, enough to manoeuvre myself to an upright position. I look down at the guy, and he's still out of it. I have a sense of admiration and jealousy in equal measures and wish I could sleep as soundly as him. God knows I'm desperate to shut my eyes, but I know if I do I'll never wake up again, there's a wee phantom hanging around me telling me to keep moving. I pull the thin jacket around me to try to get warmth from somewhere. It's impossible. As I shuffle towards the station doors, I can feel my coccyx throb, and the previous night's encounter begins to unfold...

'...How in hell's name did I get to this point in my life?' I ask myself......

George Street, Edinburgh, Summer 1985

THE ELEVATOR TRAVELS LANGUIDLY toward the fourth floor, my heart's in my mouth. It's beating so hard against the wall of my chest, and the drawl of the sexy transatlantic voice calling out every floor only adds to my excitement. The anticipation of starting my new job as a Junior Art Director had been consuming me all weekend. I'm itching to sit down at my desk in my very own office with a pad, a pencil and a chance to prove how good I am at this advertising game. I'm burning with an intensity and energy more powerful than anything I'd felt in my entire life.

As the lift passes floor three, I prepare myself. I do my jacket up, make sure the top two buttons on my shirt are unfastened, I run a hand through my newly cut hair and take a deep breath. I'm ready to attack my new career like a Rottweiler' teeth spoiling for a postie's arse. The lift stops.

Ping!

The door slid open into unexpected darkness. It took a second or two for my eyes to adjust, a red neon sign fizzed on and off intermittently, pulsing the name 'MARR ASSOCIATES' against the stark black material wall, casting a long, dark shadow. I had only ever been here when it was alive with people and daylight, it now looked like a scene from a Gary Numan video. Everything was red and black; furniture, carpets, lights, signs, Sofas. It was awesome.

Boom. I'd arrived. In more ways than one.

I walked towards the imposing pre-reception desk and

plonked my bum on the curved sofa next to it, awaiting the arrival of the receptionist, looked at my watch and only then realised I'd arrived half an hour early. Still, it was a great place to hang out. After a minute or so sitting fidgeting, my arse was getting numb, these sofas were quite plainly only for show, form over function, Bauhaus, if I remembered my history of art correctly. I stood up, thought I'd try the doors that led into the main office. They were closed. I rummaged in the plant pots for a key, just in case, although god knows what would've happened if I'd found it, opened the door and the alarm had gone off? What then, made an arse of myself for the umpteenth time in my short life. I went back to the sofa, wiped my hands on it as they were now covered in an ash-like substance from the fake plant's fake soil. I sat in one of the hollows of the curved sofa, it was not as comfy as the high point, so I lay back on the crest of a wave and chewed on the croissant I'd picked up downstairs, it was cold but tasted as lovely, as free food always does.

As I settled down in the darkness, my senses ramped up.

What was that horrible smell?

Fish?

I was sure I could smell fish.

I thought I'd imagined it, but it got stronger and stronger the more I sniffed. I walked back over towards the desk, there was a pile of mail on it, one package, in particular, looked like it was leaking oil. I leaned down, put my nose close to it and pulled back instantly. It was disgusting, definitely the source of the smell. I had to disperse it somehow. I looked around and spotted a fire door, I hoped it wouldn't set the alarm off as I pushed the bar.

Light flooded in, and the whole room changed into something a lot less glam than before. I wafted the door a few times it helped get rid of the pong a bit. I closed it again. As darkness returned, I heard something in the corner of the room. It sounded like somebody sobbing. I opened the door again, entirely flooding the place with brightness and made my way to the corner where the noise was coming from. There was a fat guy in a dark suit cowering in the corner with his eyes closed. His wet cheeks glinted in the semi-darkness, his forehead was as wrinkled as an out of date turnip.

'Who's there?' I said.
He put his hands up to protect himself as if I was going to hit him.
'Please. Don't?' He said. In a broad Glaswegian accent.
'I don't know anything about the Blue Gorilla?'
'The Blue Gorilla? What are you on about?' I said
'Are you carrying?'
'Carrying what?'
'A chib, a gun, a pair o cement wellies?'
'What are you on about?' I repeated, shaking my head, confused by this unwelcome and frankly confusing start to my new career.
'I'm just starting my first day here.' I said, extending my hand.
'Jim Divine. Junior Art Director,' as I said this, he changed instantly.
'Almost caught ye out there didn't I wee man?' He said, even though I was a good five inches taller than him.
He dragged a sleeve across his wet face, drying his cheeks with the material. A sudden assertiveness came over him.
'Ye'd better shut that door, or you'll get pelters from Carol, and by the way, I was only yankin yer chain' he said, see what yer made o.'
'OK?' I said, wondering what the hell I'd come into.
'It's an act I do wi all the new starts, see if they're up for a giggle an that,' he said. Faking a laugh.

As I tried to figure out if he was kidding or not, the lift sprung into action, somebody was on their way to the fourth floor. He returned to his previous state and ran to where he was before, hiding in the corner. I stood there with hands-on-hips wondering if this was some kind of Jeremy Beadle set up.

The lift opened, and Carol, the receptionist, stepped out carrying a couple of pints of milk and a mass of flowers. She flicked a switch, and the place turned into the vibrant, hip place I'd seen before.

'Morning Mr Divine' She said. She was dressed in a cracking looking red mini skirt and low cut top, no jacket I noticed.

'Morning Carol' I said. I think I unintentionally raised my eyebrows a couple of times as I looked at her cleavage. I then looked around to see where the fat guy was. He coughed, pretended he was tying his shoelace. 'Morning Scott' Carol said.

'Ahem, morning Carol, you OK?'

'Perfectly. Forget your keys again did you?' She said teasingly.

'Nah, I was meant to be in Glasgow this morning, but something came up' He said.

When he walked out into the light, I noticed he was wearing white slip-on shoes that had clearly been re-whitened that morning.

Carol opened the main door and hit about a hundred light switches, a concert pianist would have been proud of her moves. The whole place kicked into action, It reminded me of my first ever concert, Ultravox - The Vienna tour at Tiffany's. Lights everywhere, lasers bouncing all over the dance-floor, the glitter balls that hung like diamond earrings on the lobes of Joan Collins. The sheer excitement of it all made me want to dance like an electro-pop diva.

Carol put the coffee percolator on the boil and turned all of the reception computers on. The place was literally buzzing. The guy Scott disappeared quietly into one of the offices at the back of the building.

'I guess you'll be dying to get started' Carol said.
'You've no idea' I said, 'I'm champing at the bit'.
'Follow me,' she said.
As she led me through to a beautifully appointed office, I couldn't help noticing her hand-crafted curves, she was the perfect 'boy's night-time squidgy-squirty-pyjama-bottoms fantasy secretary.'
We got to my office; black teak furniture, a bright red carpet that matched the décor throughout the office and a set of blinds on three internal windows, the fourth wall was a massive built-in library. She opened one of the shades.
'This is your room I'd suggest you keep this blind open. It was the blind that looked right onto her desk.
'It'll let you see what's going on throughout the office'. She said.
I kinda hoped she meant that she'd be revealing certain aspects of her person in my direction, but again that could be put down to an over-active and very underused libido on my part.
'Wow,' I said, 'This is perfect.
As she walked out, she shouted over her shoulder.
'Tea or coffee?'.
'Tea, please'.
'Always tea? Or just today?'
'Always tea please Carol,' I said as I removed my jacket and put my brand new portfolio onto the desk. I felt like a movie star.
She shouted through from the kitchen.

Thunder At One AM

'Milk and sugar?'
'Just a little milk please'. This was brilliant.

I sat down on the plush leather armchair, which was now MY plush leather armchair, swivelled around in it a few times, ground my arse in it to see just how soft it was, (and to mark my territory). I looked in all of the drawers, there were four sets of them in my office and a big desk with a pile of Letraset sketch pads and a full set of Pantone pens. This was the stuff of my wildest dreams, well, that and the secretary of course but I'd give it a while before pursuing her.

As I relaxed and grew more comfortable, I got to looking around the place. I couldn't believe my luck. The library's shelves were filled with designer magazines and reference books on all kinds of stuff, art, history, geography and a hundred other subjects. I also had my own phone for the first time in my life, there was a briefcase with my name on it sitting in a corner and a congratulations on your new job card from Colin and Wilma, the owners.

This kind of thing didn't happen to people like me. I kept looking around waiting on Jeremy Beadle to jump out. My heart was ramped, I subconsciously did up one of my shirt buttons. After all these years of wishing and dreaming, here I was. Exactly where I hoped to be, this was another first in my life.

As the day progressed, the office became more alive, clients, suppliers, staff, maintenance guys buzzed like bees all over the place. This was way beyond dream-time for me.

I was called into a few client meetings, asked my opinion on a few things and felt really comfortable doing this, which surprised me. A brief or two landed on my desk, and I lost myself in them for the whole day, nobody came in to ask me to hurry up or questioned anything I was doing. It was magic. Colin popped in a couple of times to look at my ideas, and his encouragement was incredible. Even when I thought I was producing crap, he still kept me going.

'You'll produce far more crap than good stuff in your career,' he said.

'But hopefully your good stuff will be great, and that's what pays the bills. Don't worry about it, you're doing well.'

As the days and weeks went by I became more familiar with my surroundings and felt I belonged. I'd met everyone in the team and had sussed that Scott, the Glaswegian and Colin, were the people I'd be working closest with.

One day I felt comfortable enough with him to ask Scott about that first day.

'So Mr MacPhail, tell me what you were on about that day, the Blue Gorilla?'

He laughed for a good five minutes, was about to tell me but burst into a fit of giggles. Eventually, he said.

'It was one of your type, some creative wee bastards. A couple of young guys, a team from London. Wee shits just about gave me a fuckin heart attack' that morning.

'Why were you crapping it from the Blue Gorilla though?'

'The fish' he replied.

'I don't get it, Scott,' I said.

'The fish' he repeated.

'International gangster language. It means you're going to be swimming with the fishes'.

'Scott' I said, 'What in hell's name are you talking about? I do not understand what you are trying to say, what have fish got to do with a Blue Gorilla'.

He took a deep breath and stood with his hands in his pockets, jingling the loose change within.

'Well,' he said. 'A few months previously we'd done some advertising and design for a company based in deepest Manchester. They were allegedly gangsters, and they'd decided that we were the guys who could get their big project 'The Blue Gorilla Discotheque' off to a flying start. We had created a great campaign, which had a four-week countdown idea, and it had ticked down to perfection. By the time the launch date had come and gone, the numbers of visitors had been twenty per cent over target. What more could a client ask for? We waited three months for payment, but it never arrived. We took them to court, and they let us know in no uncertain terms that we had made a bad move. That's what freaked me out. I'd picked the mail up that morning and shit myself at the fish parcel, being a Glaswegian I've more experience of gangster dealings than you Edinburgh saps. Every day that week, I hid behind the screen, waiting to make sure that it was a 'friendly' who was in the reception area. I was genuinely expecting the Manchester Mafioso to walk through the door with machetes or machine guns. Man, it's been a long time since I've shit ma breeks like that'.

'Really Scott? Mafioso?' I said. I shook my head at the guy and walked on.

 The following Monday at about ten o'clock. I got a phone call from a guy called Phill Clark in London.

'Did you get my teaser campaign?' He said.

'I have no idea what you're talking about Mr Clark' I replied.

'What?' He said.

'For the past few weeks, I've been sending your company parcels to get a 'plaice' in your agency,' he spelt out the word p-l-a-i-c-e.

'A Plaice, as in fish?' I said.

'Yeah. Do you get it?'

'Of course, I do, it's pretty rubbish though,' I said.

"I know, it was a last-minute idea' He said.

'So it was you,' I said. 'Do you realise that the police are waiting to speak to you, and your accomplice?'.

'What are you talking about' he said totally flummoxed. I explained to him about the hidden meaning and how Scott had kacked his pants.

He burst out laughing.' Shit.' He said, 'I can't believe that. Does that mean I won't be getting an interview then?'

'On the contrary' I said,

'Next time you're in Edinburgh give me a shout, and we'll meet up, I owe you one. That twat has been doing my box in for weeks, I could do with another idea to scare him into silence. The beers are on me if you can come up with something.'

KIRK

I'D BEEN RUNNING WITH the athletics squad for many years by now, generally training five to six days a week, speed, endurance and interval sessions. I was getting to a reasonable level at 800 Metres. One of the guys at Meadowbank, Paul Forbes, had recently reached the final of the Commonwealth Games 800 metres. He was leading after more than halfway through the race; unfortunately, he faded towards the end, but I was so proud of that guy. I'd heard he had a tough upbringing and felt an affinity with him. I'd bumped into him, and his training partner Peter Hoffman, who also regularly battled it out with Seb Coe, and they'd offered me nothing but encouragement. 'You actually run like a young Steve Ovett,' Paul used to say. Which pleased and irked me as I was a massive Seb Coe fan.

The problem was nowadays, I was working full-time at the ad agency and the hours were a pain in the arse. Agencies are notoriously known for their lack of sympathy to anything other than the deadline. The deadline dictates your life.

In the mid-eighties, there was a lot of great work up for grabs in Scotland, which meant there was a lot of pitching of ideas and a lot of hours put into those pitches and much of the time spent was in the early hours of a morning. One of the most intense pitch scenarios I was working on involved me working three full days on the trot with barely an hour's shut-eye between the days. This had a catastrophic effect on my training and consequent races, it always seemed to happen around the time of the Scottish Championships. It took days to recover from intense periods like that. Jogging was OK, and probably a good thing, but if I tried to up the ante to sprinting or high-intensity training, it was a no-no.

I had made the decision to be a designer and knew that it was something I could win things at whereas laterally athletics was always just a passion that would stand me in good stead for health and getting rid of a lot of pent up energy.

As the squad grew, we were getting more distance guys in, which meant that my brother John, Tracy and I were the only two middle-distance runners and the rest were long-distance. One day when we turned up for training, Fred told us Kirk Smith would be joining the squad.

'Why?' I said. 'All he does is moan'.

I'd raced against this guy Kirk three times over the past three months, all 1500m races, this was not my distance yet I beat him, just, in all three races. In the last of them he ripped his number off and threw it onto the track in a real strop, the officials were straight over to him, reprimanding him for his unsporting behaviour, I think he got some kind of warning. I laughed to myself, smirking at the vision of him with his angry face hating me as I crossed the line.

Fast forward a few months, and we were best of friends. Isn't life strange?

Sitting in his car, eating fish n chips, talking about our future and women. He'd had his eye on this wee blonde thing, Linda, an 800m runner from Dalkeith. I knew who she was, seemed a good prospect and not a bad lass.

'Her friend Trish fancies you,' he said, 'apparently thinks you've got a tidy arse'.

I could not think who she was.

'You must have seen her,' he said. 'Red hair, sprinter, her dad helps coach her'.

I'd no idea who she was.

'Is she attractive?'

'Yeah, I think so, but you know me, I only have eyes for Linda'.

I kept an eye out over the next wee while and eventually

spotted this girl Trish. She was a fast wee bugger, no doubt about that.

I hadn't really got a chance to see her up close and didn't want to hang around too closely in case her dad thought I was perving. Our athletics squad were mainly middle-distance runners while hers was sprint based.

'How do you fancy a double date with them' He said one day.
'I'm not sure what age is she?'
'I think she's nineteen'.

I was twenty-five at the time, and she was younger than three of my sisters, seemed a bit creepy, 'baby snatcher' they'd call me.

'I'm not sure Kirk', I said.

'You know I've just been dumped by a virtual schoolie, and I think now's the time for me to go after an older woman, somebody more mature, somebody who knows her way around the bedroom. When were you thinking of this double date?'

'Our squad night out is in two weeks so we could do that, if you don't fancy her then you can just hang with the rest of the group,' he said.

I'd only really seen her from a distance in the flesh, but Kirk had shown me some pictures of her in the papers, she was 'One for the future' according to the Scotsman and 'Little Miss Dynamite' according to the Evening News. I liked the look of her, she looked focussed and determined, but she was also ginger (perhaps she'd say she was, redhead, strawberry blonde, auburn summer or whatever. I liked to say, ginger). Weirdly enough, unlike a lot of guys, I was into redheads before they became the new blondes. I liked the general demeanour of them, (not that I'm lumping all redheads into the same box here). They were treated as a minority and outsiders a lot of the time, but for me, they, or at least the ones

I'd fancied over the years, had something feisty about them. A passion, a determination that you didn't get from run-of-the-mill chicks and to be honest if any bird showed more than a passing glance at me I was in there. And with this wee hottie thinking I had a tidy arse I was willing to let her get a closer look.

'OK,' I said. 'Let's see what happens'.

We arranged to meet them outside the Conan Doyle at the top of Broughton Street at eight. We'd suss them out and see if they came up to scratch, if not we could make our excuses and head to the night out at the Loon Fung on our own, maybe pick up a bird after our meal. Yeah, like that was the norm, my mind wandered: A few drinks, a nice Chinky and a wee burd to go home with for a bit 'How's your father', kick her out afterwards and roll over and sleep and await your bacon sandwich and a cuppa in the morning. I wished.

Kirk and I met up in the Claremont hotel, had a pint or two of Heineken for Dutch courage. This was my first ever blind date, even though I knew sort of what she looked like. Kirk was anxious, he'd been planning this for a long time, me on the other hand, I wasn't too fussed. He kept looking at his watch.

'Take it easy pal', I said to him a few times, 'Lassies are always late, in fact, if we turn up early, we could appear as a wee bit too eager and if that doesn't say I want to be under the thumb, then nothing does. We'll have another bottle of beer then take a slow stroll up the road,' I could sense his unease, but I guess he thought my experience of girls counted for something.

As we approached the pub, the two girls were outside looking at their watches. They looked hot, very hot. They were talking to an old guy in a raincoat. He seemed to scuttle off as we approached.

'What was the old perv after?' I said.

'He was asking how much we were, wanted to pay us both for a fun night out,' Trish laughed.

I was definitely interested now. How in hell's name had I managed not to notice this stunning wee ginger chick, was I blind?

They passed the test, big time, and we allowed them to join us for the squad Christmas night out. It was great fun. Turned out John and Trish have the same birthday. His chat was pretty pish, but it made an impact.

'How many brothers and sister's do you have?' He said.

'None, only me,' she replied.

'You'll be the spoiled brat then?' He said, slurring his words after a few beers.

She laughed at him.

'Try telling my mum and Dad that' she said.

I liked her a lot.

By the end of the night, John was crawling on the restaurant floor with a plastic rose in his mouth singing 'Some enchanted evening' to her. I kind of knew this was his subconscious or unconscious approval.

After a very unexpected great night out Kirk and I walked them to the bridges and were rewarded with a peck on the cheek. We gave them some money to get a taxi home, as the taxi pulled away our cash was thrown out of the window, I ran after it, a fiver was a lot in those days. Kirk was in heaven, and I was too, as I'd caught the money before it blew down the windy north bridge.

As the days and months proceeded Kirk, the girls and I became closer. It had developed into something I'd never experienced before. A relationship, a settled relationship. The nearest I'd had to that was a few months dating a girl who was still at school but was almost finished sixth year, so technically

in my book, she didn't count as a 'schoolie.'
In the end, she dumped me because she said I got on better with her mum and dad than I did with her. That was true. I was going to end it anyway as she was continually covering her boobs with baby powder, every time I got close to being amorous with her, (first base was the closest I'd ever got), I'd end up with a floury mouth, dry as a baker's table.

I liked the way this new thing was progressing. Trish was working at the Royal Bank, and her running was really taking off, I was also doing very well at Marr, life was brilliant.

TRISH - EDINBURGH 1985

I WAS SETTLING DOWN at Marr, getting used to having a wage every month, being able to think about what I was doing with my life and generally beginning to feel like an adult. I had also been going out with Trish for a long time, longer than I'd ever gone out with anyone. My Mum was glad, I think she thought she had me forever. I'd bumbled along just getting on with life and had never thought about anything further away than next week's pick 'n' mix.

This was different. Trish and I hit it off big time, she was way more mature than I was and I didn't give a shit what anyone else thought.

About this time, I'd become friends with a young guy, Tom Hanlon. We became friends on a trip to London as we both ran for Edinburgh Southern Harriers Athletics team, we found that we both had a lot in common, art, music, design, architecture. It was refreshing for me. Tom was one of the best athletes ever to come out of Scotland and the UK, and he was more than capable of making a living from the sport. We met more and more and eventually, I was able to recruit Tom into Marr as a production manager. We had some of the best laughs of our lives there. The fall guy was Scott MacPhail, the head of production, Tom was his junior.

Kirk also knew Tom and had known him for many years as they were in all in the same running groups as they grew up, Trish and Linda looked a bit younger than Kirk but I was the oldest by a long shot, I never felt or looked any older than them, and we all just got on. After we'd been going out for over a year, Trish was hoping I'd come up with a plan. 'What did the future hold for us?'

'Were we going to live together?'
'Did I want to keep this relationship going?'

I'd never ever thought about that kind of thing, like most guys
I was happy going along with life. Just seeing what happens,
looking no further over the horizon than possibly next week
but Trish is a planner, and for good reason; you don't plan,
you don't achieve anything and to be honest I hadn't achieved
anything. Ever.
She was bang on there. I'd landed a job, but that was it.
We were sitting in Niko's cafe at the east end of Princes Street
when she asked if I'd thought about what she'd said.

'Sure I have,' I said, looking deep into her lovely green eyes.
'Should we live together?'
I think this took her aback. Shocked her perhaps.
At this point, I could pretend that I remembered her every
detail and expression, the way we fed each other sausage and
beans over the paper tablecloth with interlocked arms and
forks, like Lady and the Tramp, but I can't. The only thing I
remember was how beautiful their mince pie, sausage and
beans were.
The outcome was that we decided to get engaged on her
birthday and we'd agreed to find somewhere to live together.
After lunch, I went back to work, and for the first time ever, I
had a plan for the next few years.

It worried the shit out of me.

Thunder At One AM

Six miles

EIGHT THIRTY IN THE evening on a Friday night and here I am savouring what is supposed to be the prime steak of my life. I've just finished a tough project at work and need to go for a run. I train every day and to miss a day is so guilt-ridden that it is not worth the mental hassle that I give myself and the fight with my coach, so I keep the sequence going. This particular Friday is a damp, dreich affair, the air is full of rainy mist. The standard Edinburgh lamppost light is being diffused, making the scene a very grey and orange affair. I plan to go a six-mile run, through St. Mark's park, along Ferry Road, down by the Colonies at Stockbridge, back up by the hilly Dundas, Queen and Broughton Streets and finally down Leith Walk. From there, along Great Junction Street, up Ferry Road and back through St. Mark's park to sprint over the wooden bridge and home to Claremont Court.

After the first couple of miles, I feel excellent, I'm on for a brilliant time, I can sense it. I'm running well under five-minute miles, and it feels comfortable. I'm floating along effortlessly. At times like this, it's so difficult to explain to those who have never experienced it. You feel like you're on a cloud, it's like your body, mind and the world are at one. An understanding between them that allows you, the person at the centre of this thrill to sit there like a passenger and enjoy the ride. It's probably the closest humans get to an out-of-body experience without having to go all Yogi or Booboo for that matter.

The rain and dampness are actually helping to keep me fresh for a change and because I'm concentrating on not slipping on the shiny cobblestones or dead leaves, the time flies by. I feel superb.

Into the third mile and I'm coming along a little street near to Glenogle baths. I'm running past the small colonial houses when I spot a young woman probably in her early twenties about half a mile ahead of me. It's a long straight road, and it's now quite dark. There are intermittent pools of orange light cast by the lamp posts.

As I'm approaching the woman, I begin to think about her. Will she get a fright?

Should I make as much noise as I can by slapping my feet a bit to alert her to the fact that a runner is coming behind her? Should I stay as quiet as possible and give her a quick fright as I zoom past her?

This is a real dilemma.

I get to within a couple of hundred yards of her and decide that the best tactic is to be as quiet as I possibly can and figure that just as she turns around, I'll go at full pelt past her and leave her to deal with her shock or uneasiness or embarrassment or whatever.

I slow down to quieten my splashing footfall, and just as I've slowed down enough, she turns around. She looks at me, horrified and begins to run along the quiet road. She puts her hands to her head and starts to scream. She's now screaming at the top of her voice.

'Somebody help me, somebody help me.'

I stop, freeze. What should I do? I can't turn around and go another way as I am halfway through the run and to turn back would be uphill all the way, and I don't like the sound of that.

By this time, the woman is approximately a hundred yards ahead of me, and it is about half a mile to the end of the road. I decide to carry on running, and as I approach her, she picks up the pace.

She's running amazingly quickly, especially as she's wearing high heels, I am now racing her.

We're both running for different reasons. I have to get to the end of the road first as I know there is a police box there and usually, there are cops there at weekends. She's running for her life, or so she imagines. I picture myself being arrested for some sort of sexual crime attempt and this thought fuels my burst of speed. I have to get past her. When I'm almost alongside her, she starts to scream and cry hysterically.

'Don't hurt me, please'.

This really makes me think 'fuck, I really have to get out of this situation', I decide that the best thing to do is to try to comfort her and let her know that I'm a good guy.

'It's OK ' I say as I jog alongside her.

'I'm not going to hurt you'.

As soon as I say it I know, it sounds like the very phrase a creep would use.

'I'm only out for a run' I shout. She pays no attention to this whatsoever as she's so manic with fright, and carries on running and screaming.

Just before the end of the road, I catch up with her. I'm shoulder to shoulder with her, and as I pass her, I look at her. I'm now cruising and in complete control. I'm surprised that I have the temerity to take her running technique into account and judge it. Her arms are all over the place, and her feet are splayed and pointing outwards.

I run straight past her. I now have no concern for her in the slightest. I decide to ignore the whole scene. I've been through a few emotions in the last half mile. I tried to be sympathetic, but she was too hysterical to see that. I tried to be cunning and cruise past her, but she had stupidly turned around at the wrong moment. I'd wanted to pacify her, but her frenzy and panic made her blind. I washed my hands of the whole incident.

As I passed the police box, two coppers are standing

sheltering from the rain eating a chippy.

'Did you hear anything unusual sir' says the small one, wiping brown sauce from his mouth as I jog past them.

'There's a woman down the road who got a bit of a fright when I ran past her' I said.

'Is that right sir?' He says, clearing his throat of chips, trying to sound authoritative. 'Would you mind stopping here for a moment until we verify your story,' 'sorry, it's too cold and wet to hang about here,' I really wanted nothing to do with that stupid cow. I was not responsible for her insecurities. Why should I care?

'Hold on right there sir' said the wee cop. Now getting ready for some kind of action.

I completely ignored him.

'This is a free country, I've done nothing wrong and can't be bothered with this insignificant incident,' I said.

This may well have been the most exciting thing that they had to deal with tonight, but I'd no intention of being part of it. I run on, knowing full well that I can outrun them. I can if necessary, go through the graveyard or over the river. Getting away from them will be no problem.

I feel like a hedgehog that has inadvertently wandered into a condom factory and is baffled at all the commotion when it's spotted just going about its business.

I know I've done nothing wrong, but they didn't know if I had or hadn't and were treating me as if I was guilty.

'Pricks' I thought.

The thrill of them chasing me actually appeals to me now. I feel like taking the piss out of them. Just to prove that I am fitter and faster.

I look around trying to make them angry. It works. They're both adjusting their uniforms and putting their hats on getting themselves ready to pursue me. I feel superior and in effect, more righteous.

Thunder At One AM

One of them heads down to Glenogle road, where the woman was last seen, and the wee fat one comes after me.

'Oi, you' he shouts.

I stop and turn around. I can see that even though I've just run three and a half fast miles and he has run a slow hundred yards, I am still in better shape than him. He's struggling for breath. I am appalled at the lack of fitness in our Police Force. Shame on them.

I shout to him.

'Listen, pal, I'm on a good run just now, I've done nothing wrong and just because you and your pal are bored stiff don't expect me to join in with it'.

'I advise you to stop' he shouts puffing heavily.

'Go back to your Tardis and finish your chippy or give that lassie a lift back to her house' I reply.

'I know what you look like' he shouts, knowing fine that he has no chance of catching me.

'If you've done anything we'll Identikit you'.

By this time I've really had enough of the whole situation. It's been blown entirely out of proportion. I'm only out on a run. I've done nothing wrong. I try to understand what the hell's happening.

I stop suddenly with a bravado that I've only ever felt once before with those two scumbags on the way to college years ago, I drop my shorts and shout 'Identikit this ya wee fat tosser' showing him my arse.

He's infuriated and pulls out his walkie talkie.

'We're on to you' he shouts.

'Why don't you piss off you wee fat bloater, try helping somebody instead of wasting my time'.

As I run away, I feel every stride is cleansing me of that whole stupid situation.

A minute or two later a police car passes me, it does a full three hundred, and sixty-degree turn in the road like a scene from the Sweeney, two cops get out and head towards me. I simply vault the wall take three long strides over the shallow river at Canonmills and jog in parallel alongside them on the opposite bank. They know that if I can get to the bridge before them, I'm home and dry.

As they jog alongside me they keep looking back at their car, which is sitting there with the keys in the ignition and the door open, getting further away, they know there's a good possibility that it will get nicked in this area. The wee fat one arrives on the scene, picks up a couple of stones and throws them at me, I move away from them easily.

'Not only are you a little fat shit but you throw like a girl' I shout. I leap with ease onto the bridge a good hundred yards ahead of them, sticking the Vickies up and jog the rest of the way home through the park hoping that Pie Ross or Ronnie Duke will be somewhere nearby and perchance be on-hand to nick their panda car.

TRISH HALF BOTTLE

BY THE TIME TRISH and I decided that we could each be
the 'One', I had at long last gained employment and a positive
outlook on my future. Hers was never in doubt. Being a bright
cookie with all the personality to go with it as well as being
a beautiful young redhead meant that we could now look to
the future with a bit of hope. After we'd agreed to get engaged,
I thought I'd take her out and at the same time visit a part of
my past to see how far I'd come. In terms of distance, it was
actually a ten-second walk. In terms of experience and belief
in myself, it was a thousand miles.

I was now working opposite the George Hotel, in fact, I was
looking down on them from a great height. Marr had an office
in George Street, a real fancy looking ad agency that thumbed
its nose at the stuffy old establishment over the road where
I'd spent a miserable time learning to understand hierarchy,
lowerarchy and how to avoid being hit by flying pots and pans
from angry fat chefs.
Since those early days, I'd learned a hell of a lot about life. I'd
started there as a Commis Waiter and looked about twelve.
People bullied and ridiculed me for many things, but since
then I'd gone off to college and gained a few qualifications and
accolades, and most of all, I now had a great job.

I called the hotel up one day and by his voice, knew that it was
Louis, one of the head waiters on the other end.
I put on a really posh accent, which I knew would butter this
guy up just nicely. The posher you spoke, the further up your
arse these arse-lickers would try to stick their tongues.
'May I reserve Una Tabluea para Samedi ' I said. Sounding
like a real posh twat. Later learning that I was mixing French,

Spanish and Italian.

'Certainly, seer, how menny and for what time?' He said in his Italian accent, which grew thicker with the thought of the tips he thought he was going to make.

'Two peepil. Sevahn Thiiity' I said, throwing the 'R' away and hoping to sound like the poshest of twats. I thought I was doing a grand job of impersonating Maggie Thatcher. I could hear him salivating at the thought of another tenner snuck into his back pocket that no-one else would see, including his bloody minions those poor wee commis Waiters.

'Certainement' he said.

'Pahdon?' I said.

'Certainly sir, we'll see you then'.

I pissed myself laughing. I hadn't told Trish where we were going as it was a surprise, she'd never been to a posh hotel before. Even though her mum was head of Catering at Surgeon's Hall, one of the most prestigious places to dine in the whole of Scotland. Royalty had been there many times, including the Queen, Princess Anne, Charles, etc.

Sandra, Tricia's mum later told me about a time of great embarrassment to her. One evening she was in charge of a massive event, the guest list sounded more like a night at Buckingham Palace than a hall in Edinburgh. There was Princess Anne as the chief guest and more Sirs than Arthur's Round Table.

Sandra had sent wee Jeanie in to inquire who would like what for starters. Minutes later she returned with a list on a scribbled bit of paper.

'What's that?' Sandra enquired.

'The list' said Jeanie a bit perplexed.

'Where did you get the list' Says Sandra.

'I wrote it down. I just shouted at them, hands up who wants soup and who wants Pâté'.

Sandra's face turned ashen.

'So you asked Princess Anne to put her hand up to ask for soup?'
'Aye? Was that wrong'.
'Get bloody well back to that sink now you're not going back in there again.'

The Saturday night arrived, and I could not wait to get into that place that held such misery and pain for me all those years ago. When we walked into the dining area, I recognised all of the head waiters and a couple of the commis waiters. Thankfully, not one of the head waiters remembered me. It might have been that by then I'd become more sophisticated, but in truth, it was probably the fact that I'd grown at least six inches taller and was now approaching six feet, I was a tiny five foot six waiter back then.
We were shown to our table by John; a little crawling insect who I'd liked initially but had gone off him when he made me work Christmas and New Year with the promise of 'Big Rewards', I ended up getting a fifty pence share of the tips while he and the other three head waiters made hundreds of pounds.
I played along, it was great being unrecognised, I felt a real sense of power, Batman-like. I had a bit of money to spend tonight, and there was no way he was getting a tip. In fact, I'd thought about creating some kind of situation where I'd get the meal free, but at the same time, as it was a special night for Trish, I didn't want to act all humpty and arrogant just to get a discount. I decided to play it cool, see what happened.
We ordered a lager for me and a G&T for Trish to start, then had Pâté' and Melba toast for starters and decided on steak and Chips for mains. As I ate the melba toast, I remembered Alex, an old friend and down-and-out who had worked with me at the George way back in time. He was tasked with mainly menial kitchen jobs but also with the making of the

melba toast. I remember watching how skilfully he toasted the bread, then carefully sliced it through the middle of the crust. He then toasted it again finally delivering two slices of thin toast from one piece of bread, I bet my mum wished she knew how to do that way back when she struggled to feed us ten kids in the house. It was mesmerising.

A sudden voice interrupted my thoughts.

'Woulda you lika some Vino Seer' John said in his pathetic Italian accent which had come all the way from that ancient, historic Italian outpost of Wester Hailes.

'Can we have a look at your reds?' Trish said.

'A half bottle or full bottle madam' he said.

'Let's go for a full bottle' I said.

We've no training tomorrow'.

'OK. Sounds good' she said.

We sat and chatted about the future, how our training was going, we were training with different athletics squads at this point and didn't always have the time to keep each other updated as we worked five days and trained six days a week. All this time the creepy little turd John was trying hard to ingratiate himself to us, I could see him look at me a couple of times as if the penny had dropped, but thankfully it never did. It was almost as if someone had farted, but he wasn't sure where the stench was coming from, something inside him knew that he knew me, but he just could not get the definitive link. He did so many double-takes I was sure he'd have a sore neck at the end of his shift.

The first course passed and was excellent, we had by then started the wine which was flowing rather nicely. As we finished our main course, John came up to fill our glasses again.

He lifted the bottle and immediately Trish stopped him, thinking he was taking the bottle away.

'We ordered the full bottle' she said.

He wiped the top of the bottle with the white cloth and poured into her glass. Looking at her quizzically.

He then filled mine and walked back to his place at the service area.

I looked at her with a smirk.

'Did you think he was going to take that bottle away because he thought we'd only ordered a half bottle?' I said to her, laughing.

She started pissing herself laughing as the realisation of her naivety dawned.

'You thought he was going to wait until he thought we'd drunk half a bottle and was then going to whip it away' I said pissing myself.'

'How did you think he was going to measure when we'd had exactly half a bottle', with a ruler?'

By this time, the two of us were killing ourselves laughing.

At the end of the meal, the little shit was hanging around for his reward. Asking if we wanted complimentary liqueurs. We took them. He then offered us more After Eights. I had absolutely no sympathy for this grovelling little bastard that had made my life a misery. As we left, he held his white-gloved hand out. I put the After Eight wrappers into it and closed his fingers around them without him seeing what was there. I hoped he thought it was a bundle of notes. It felt brilliant. I didn't tell Trish what I'd done as she would be mortified.

It felt so good.

As our relationship grew, we spent a lot of time walking around the area I grew up in my teenage years, Broughton, Claremont Court, Warriston. There was a lot to see and do. The park was pretty good, three football pitches, a river, a big woodland area and a whole load of different animal and birdlife. One evening after we'd had tea at my house we wandered over to the park, it was a beautiful spring evening. As we walked towards the gates of the park, there was a real burning smell in the air. I knew fine well that it was Redbraes Bakery, when they got a new baker in, there was always burning as the ovens were extremely hot and the new guys struggled with getting the 'burnt rolls' just burnt enough and not so burnt that they were inedible. I saw Trish sniffing.

'What's the burning smell?'

'I'm not sure I should tell you' I said.

'Why not?'

'Because I don't think you'll like what you hear'.

'What are you on about?'

'I'm telling you,' I said.

'You won't like it'.

'I honestly do not have a clue what you're on about, how could I not like a burning smell?'

'OK. It's the crematorium,' I said, keeping a straight face.

'Yeah, sure?' She said.

I pointed over to where we were heading and showed her the road signs to Warriston Crematorium.

She put her hands over her mouth.

'I feel sick,' she said.

I couldn't keep my laughter in any more.

'What are you laughing at' she said

'That isn't funny'.

'Of course, it is' I said.

'It's hilarious'.

I tried to take her hands away from her mouth and nose to let her smell what she thought was burnt flesh, but she resisted.

'This really isn't funny' she said storming off.

I laughed again and pointed over to the bakery where smoke was billowing through the open door.

It took a few seconds to register, and as it dawned on her, I started moving away, laughing.

'You little shit,' she said, eventually getting the joke and chased me through the path to the park.

We were getting on really well by now and what I loved about her was the fact that she knew more about football and sport in general than any female I'd ever known.

Before long, we were meeting virtually every day. I'd see her training at Meadowbank with her squad most nights. I knew her dad helped to train the team and had to be on my best behaviour as I didn't know what he was really like.

It took a while for me to find out what age she really was. Initially, when we'd first gone out on our date at the Conan Doyle she'd told me that she was nineteen and I believed her, girls are so much more mature than guys and Trish had more sense and class about her that I could ever hope to muster.

It was months later before she told me the truth. We were lying kissing on her single bed.

'What, you're only seventeen?' I said, pretending to be shocked.

'I'm almost eighteen though' she said.

"How near?' I asked, not really caring to be honest as I'd decided that we were good together.

'Next month'.

'When, next month'.

'October twenty-first' She said.

'That's the same date as John's birthday' I said.

'Must be a good omen'.

'When's your birthday' She asked.

'October first'.

'What age will you be'.

I tried to change the subject as I'd figured out that on my birthday I'd be nine years older than her at least for twenty days.

She was having none of this avoidance lark.

'Come on then. What age?'

'I'll be twenty-five'.

'Oh my god, that's ancient!' She said, laughing.

I think that was the last time we discussed our age difference and the great thing was that it didn't matter to either of us. I think she was so advanced mentally that I was now just catching up.

We'd both been working and training hard for the past six months, and it was now coming to the end of the Athletics season. Trish had been picked for the GB squad to compete at the European Juniors in Germany (along with a few good friends including Tom Hanlon, Elliot Bunney, Dawn Flockhart, as well as Colin Jackson, John Regis, Roger Black, Dalton Grant and so on). We decided that when she returned we'd go on holiday somewhere glamorous and warm.

When she got back, her coach had decided to bring winter training forward this year, and she'd be starting again in three weeks. This gave us hardly any time to plan a break. In the end, after flicking through my Mum's Sunday Post, we decided on a holiday for a week to Wales. We'd never been before, and the ad made it seem so much fun. Bloody Rhyl.

We'd only ever spent a single night away since we met so this would be a real test.

We got the National Express down there, and when we arrived, it was not what we'd been expecting. It was grey, damp and thoroughly miserable.

After making our way to the guest house which turned out to be a pretty bog-standard looking terraced house on an everyday street, we were met at the door by a small moustachioed man in a mustard cardigan. He opened the door to show us into the basic suite which comprised a mattress on the floor of a single room, a two ringed cooker and a chair in the corner with a woollen blanket. He pointed

Thunder At One AM

to it, and in a thick Welsh accent said.

'If it gets too cold, feel free to use the extra bedding'.

He handed me the keys, and that was the last we saw of him.

I'll be honest, it was not glamorous or warm, or for that matter even clean, but all I had on my mind was getting to know Trish a bit better and to be frank the colder, the better. This way I'd have a great excuse for keeping her nice and warm under the covers on the mattress.

We spent the week walking along the beach, watching the miniature railway trains steam by and generally going to cafés for tea and cake. The thing that sticks with me most is the evenings we were there. There was an almighty screaming from upstairs in the house. It was not the terror kind of scream but that of intense pleasure. On the third night of this, I was getting annoyed, it was keeping us up.

The following morning our door was knocked. I opened it to a woman of about four feet six inches.

'Could I borrow some milk?' She said.

'Yeah, sure' I said. I gave her a jug, and she toddled upstairs. About an hour later, the door knocked again.

This time I opened it to see a six-foot-six black guy standing there with our milk jug.

He popped his head in, said hi to Trish and headed back up. We looked at each other and laughed.

'Well I think I know what all that noise is about' I said.

Sadly that's as eventful as the holiday got.

The following year we planned our first proper holiday abroad. I'd never been on a plane and was so excited sitting there at the travel agents booking a holiday to Spain.

We decided on a place called Calella. This time it was a real hotel, and I was hoping it would have sun and heat like I'd never experienced before.

I could not stop looking at the brochure, those blue cloudless, skies, the swimming pools that made you want to dive in, even if you couldn't swim, the golden beaches, the big double beds, the exotic food, the whole thing was going to be amazing. We only had nine months to wait.

When it came around, I'd never been so excited in my whole life. All of these new experiences were making me giddy, I really could not wait. As we stepped onto the plane I wanted the window seat, just to see how high we were flying, up to this point the highest I'd ever been was on top of Arthur's seat, approximately two hundred and fifty metres high, we were now heading for about thirty thousand feet. I had no idea what this would look like. I must have looked like an absolute moron, pressing every button and acting like this was the first time anyone had flown. Trish took it all in her stride as she'd flown many times with her mum and dad over the years.

I sat there through the whole flight, mesmerised by the beauty of the clouds and the blueness of the sky. It had a vibrancy and intensity of colour that I'd never seen, I could also feel the heat seeping through the body of the plane. It was magical. Experiencing it at my age, I guess I was about twenty-six or twenty-seven was a real bonus as I'd been able to take it all in. I was able to rationalise the wonder of it all whereas most people had now gotten so used to it that they took it for granted and could no longer see or appreciate what a fantastic thing flying was.

When we arrived at the other side, the door opened, and this gust of hot air drifted in, there was an odd smell as well, it was like warm olives or palm oil. I felt myself purr like the cat that got the cream.

After a bus journey that saw me take in every single thing that we passed, the advertising billboards in Spanish, the windmills, the lack of green fields, driving on the other side of the road, the Spanish chatter on the bus, the heat that

Thunder At One AM

permeated. It was all new and so thrilling for me.

When we got to our hotel, Trish signed us in like a pro, as Mr and Mrs Divine. I was so impressed with her

We got to our room, and it was exactly as we'd seen it in the brochure. Before we'd even put the suitcases down, I was on the balcony overlooking the pool and getting ready to get my trunks on.

'I think we'll put all of our things away before we go out' Trish said.

She opened the suitcases, and within minutes, her stuff was hanging up, in drawers and totally ship-shape. I wanted to leave it until we'd been outside merely because I was so excited. Trish made me put all my stuff away, and after I'd finished, I could see her point. I immediately put on my new trunks and headed down to the pool.

The white sun-beds were all over the place, and the heat was magical, I spread my hotel towel onto one of the beds and lay down with my hands behind my head. I was in paradise. That heat was one of the best things I ever experienced. I could now understand why so many people came to Spain for their holidays.

When I was younger, I used to plant myself in front of the electric fire in the house. There was something about the heat that I loved. A cosiness that made me feel safe and protected. The downside with the fire was that my legs got burned, fireside tartan Mum used to call it.

As I lay there, I gradually became accustomed to my surroundings and started to look around. My eyes just about popped out of my head when I looked to the sun-bed on my left. There were a beautiful pair of tits facing at me. Jeez, I looked away quickly. This was the first time I'd ever seen a topless woman in public. She smiled at me, and my embarrassment must have been obvious. I looked away only to see many other lovely women around the pool in the same state of dress. I started to worry about getting up from the sun-bed as my wee felly was trying to introduce himself. I could now understand why so many guys came to Spain for their holidays.

I lay back down and closed my eyes, took a deep breath of satisfaction and fell into a slumber.

I was rudely awakened by a cold sensation. I opened one eye to see what was happening. Rain.

Bloody rain. Everyone was in commotion, grabbing their towels and books and heading towards the reception area.

No. Surely this was a bad dream?

It wasn't. After that warm, false start it rained consistently for three whole days. I must have been an absolute nightmare to Trish. I moaned for the entire three days. After being shown a brief glimpse of the promised land it had now being cruelly taken away. I must have been in some kind of depression. All those months of wishing and hoping had come true for me but had been snatched away after only an hour or so. There was nothing to do in this place when the rains came except drink, beer and coffee. As we were on a training break, we did a bit of both. I sat with my beer and watched the torrents of rain flow down the narrow streets like a river, wondering if that was all of the sun that I'd see. Typical Scot, looking on the downside. That day I'd decided to see how many drinks I could have from the vast array around the bar. I thought I was doing quite well, reaching number fifteen and sixteen, which were the Sangria and the chocolate brandy liqueur. After that, I remember nothing except getting into the lift to our room on the fourteenth floor. As the elevator went up, so did my stomach. The contents found their way into a bin in the corner. A single eruption straight in, no hitting the sides or any other part, I remember how chuffed I was at my accuracy. The next day I felt like Chicken Licken: The little chicken that thought the world was going to fall on his head.

On the fourth day, we'd met another Scottish couple who were in our hotel. Brian and Sonya. They seemed quite nice, they were from Glasgow, and both were Celtic supporters. As we got to know them, it was evident that the only thing we had in common was that we were Scottish. I'd never spent much time with Glaswegians before, and this was now becoming a problem. They wanted to hang about with us, but all they ever spoke about was Celtic and how they'd throw pint glasses 'Begbie Style' into a crowd of Rangers fans with not so much as a second thought. When we ended up at a Celtic pub with both of them dancing on the tables singing Irish paramilitary songs we'd had it. We kept out of their way and made sure that we would not go out together ever again. Around day five, the sun made its way back onto the scene. I was so grateful, I'm not sure if I said a short prayer, but I was now happy again.

Trish suggested spending a day on the golden beach, I'd only ever experienced Portobello beach, and although it was quite lovely to walk on, you'd never, ever contemplate lying there in your trunks unless you wanted the second-hand Kennomeat tan from all the effluent that flowed in from the burst pipes at Seafield.

'OK,' I said.

'Show me what it's all about'.

It was lovely, lying on the soft, warm sand on our hotel towels, listening to the waves and sounds of the people. In the distance, there was an old woman selling fruit.

'Manzana, uva, piña, Naranja' she shouted as she approached us.

I looked at her scrumptious tray with ice and all of this lovely looking fruit.

She made her way along the beach and back again. As she approached us for the second time, I said to Trish that I was going to buy some.

'Don't be stupid' Trish said.

'You'll get ripped off.'

'What, from an old woman' I said laughing, letting her know that I knew how to read people and this poor old dear could do with some sympathy.

I stuck my hand up and waved her over.

'How much?' I said, pointing to the mango.

'Ocho pesetas' she said in broken English.

'Too expensive' I said. Waving my hand to let her know it was a no-sale.

She put two fingers up. 'Two, Dos' she said.

'Ah, two mangoes for a few pesetas' I said.

'That sounds more like it'.

She held her hand out for the money which I gave her.

She bent down and stuck two grapes in my mouth.

'Ah, that's nice' I said to Trish.

'She's also giving me a couple of grapes. Didn't I tell you I know how to read people?'

The old bugger then headed away, almost running down the beach.

'Eh.' I said, lying there on the sand spitting out the grape seeds, not quite knowing what the hell was going on.

Trish lay there reading her book, sniggering to herself.

'Told you,' she said.

'I'm not having this' I said.

'What are you going to do?' Trish said.

'Go after her of course' I said.

'All she'll do is pretend she doesn't speak English and complain to the locals that you're hassling her and knowing you, you'll get hassled yourself and maybe beaten up by some young Spaniards who'll think you're bullying the poor wee Spanish pensioner. Just treat it as a life lesson'.

Trish was right, as usual, but I lay there fuming, feeling hurt

Thunder At One AM

and ripped off by the old bat. What would they think back in the Court if they heard that one? After a while, I appreciated that it was a good lesson. I still wanted to go after the old bugger and planned to get her back the next day but somehow never got around to it.

As the holiday went on I got sunburnt all over, I got drunk another couple of times, but overall it had been brilliant. We found that we could comfortably live in each others company, no problem at all. It was a nice feeling. The Spanish weather was changing from summer to autumn hence the rain.

On the way home, the plane went through a massive thunderstorm. It was shaking and dipping all over the place. There were a lot of folk screaming, holding their heads and crying. As I'd never flown before I took it all in my stride, thinking this must happen all the time. I couldn't help but notice that Trish had her nails firmly embedded into my thighs. She wasn't saying a word.

Threading the Needle - George Street 1987

SCOTT MACPHAIL, OUR PRODUCTION manager was one of the funniest characters I ever worked with. He landed on his feet the same as I did. He was from a rough Glaswegian background and had no class whatsoever. He attempted to mix with the upper echelons of the advertising elites, but as soon as he had a drink he would resort to dropping his pants and asking the females if they'd like to dance with the 'Black Mamba,' although I'd no idea what the black mamba was, if he'd been a black guy or even well-tanned I'd have guessed, he was as white as the cross on the Scottish flag.

I found him to be the perfect foil for my wicked sense of humour. He was in a position of power – Production Manager with one of the top creative agencies in the UK. He also knew he should never have been there. He did not have the upbringing, neither did I. The difference was Scott tried to carry-off the pretence that he'd been born with a silver spoon in his gob.

He came in one day with a brand new navy blue pinstriped suit. I'll give him his due, he looked smart. I felt the need to bring him down a peg or two as he'd been acting up recently, really doing my nut in. I had always been a collector of wee nick-knacks, and I noticed that in my little jar, I had a purn of thread that was an exact match for the blue material in his suit. I had a quiet word with Tom when we were on our lunchtime run about a great idea for a wind-up. When we got back to the office, we swung the plan into action. Tom pretended that he had to speak to Scott about a job.

They went to the board room to discuss the intricacies. While they were away, I looked out the thread and got a needle. I threaded the needle with the navy blue cotton, then threaded it through the seam of the arm of his new suit. I then dropped the whole purn of thread into his inside pocket and pulled about six inches of cotton to the outside of the jacket to make it look like a very long loose thread. When Scott and Tom returned, I gave it a few minutes. Scott was sitting in an alcove area, and his jacket was, with a couple of desks in the way, about twenty seconds away from him. I pounced over to the jacket.

'Looks like you've got a loose thread on your jacket Scott, I'll get rid of it'.

I jumped up and proceeded to pull the thread, of course, I knew it was attached to a whole 100metres of thread on his inside pocket. I picked and pulled until there was a pile of thread on top of the jacket shoulder. Scott screamed, jumped up.

'What the fuck are you doing with my new jaiket ya silly wee bastard?'.

He ran over to me and grabbed the jacket. He began to cut the wasted thread delicately like a brain surgeon with a scalpel.

Tom came over.

'Here Scott, let me get that'.

He reluctantly handed the scalpel over to Tom and eyed him carefully, worried that he might do more damage to the suit. Tom pretended to be sympathetic.

'I think there's a bit more loose thread here'.

He pulled as fast as he could, managed to pull out a good twenty metres of thread. Scott put his hands to his head,

'What the fuck are you doin' wi ma new jaiket, geez it now'.

Tom ran around the other side of the desk, still pulling at the thread. Scott was incandescent with rage.

'Geez it here ya bastard,' his head was bright red. By this time, a few of the other members of staff had appeared at the door and were looking on with great amusement.

It was clear that Scott was picturing the arm of his brand new jacket falling off at any second. Tom was laughing so much that Scott caught him. He took the jacket and scalpel and managed to snip off the thread at the nearest point to the seam.

'You bastards' he said you're going to buy me another jacket if that arm comes off.

'That's what you get for buying a suit from Poundstretcher' I said.

'Piss off ' he said furiously, concentrating on tucking in the last two millimetres of thread back into the small hole it had come from.

'Here Scott old pal, let me do that' Tom said.

'Fuck you, Hanlon, I'm not falling for that one again' he said, 'No I'm serious, I think I can fix it'.

Scott foolishly handed the items over to Tom, more in hope and desperation than anything else. Tom acted as if he was trying to be serious then all of a sudden pulled out another great wad of the thread.

'I knew it ya dirty little bastard, ah'm gonnae fuckin kill ye'. He ran over to grab the jacket from Tom. Tom threw the jacket to me, and I pulled another twenty metres out and then threw it back to Tom. By the time Scott got his jacket back, there was a full handful of thread hanging from his new jacket. He sat at his desk and put his head in his hands again. 'I just cannae believe this' he said.

'Look what you two have done to my new jaiket'.

We were pissing ourselves laughing, Scott just sat there shaking his head at us. He knew something was going on but didn't know what. After a good ten minutes laughing, I felt sorry for him.

Everybody from the office was now in the room all curious as to what it was that Tom and I were pissing ourselves at.

Thunder At One AM

I walked over to the sad figure of Scott and asked him for his jacket,

'Fuck off' he said, putting his hands through his hair, dropping dandruff onto the desktop.

'Come on Scott, I said,

'It was only a joke'.

'It might have been a joke to you but this jacket cost', he said.

'It was a practical joke' I said,

'Practical fuckin joke was It? He Said.

'You two are a fuckin practical joke, and you'll be buying me a new jaiket.'

I grabbed the jacket and pulled the purn of thread from the inside pocket. He stopped and looked up.

'You bastards' he said, 'you fuckin dirty Bastards. You had me so fuckin worried. 'Bastards…' he began to laugh and eventually he had doubled over. He grabbed both of us and gave us a big bear hug.

'Don't ever do that to me again or fuckin' I'll kill you.'

It was fantastic entertainment. Scott was an overweight Glaswegian. He had a big fat belly and Tom, and I often joked with him, asking when was the last time he'd seen his knob.

A couple of weeks previously, some company had sent me a small toilet pan shaped coffee cup as a promotion for their up and coming 'don't flush your money down the toilet' advertising campaign. It was so awkwardly shaped that it was impossible to drink from so it just lay there gathering dust, pencils and pens on a shelf.

Tom and I went for a run every day, and we would warm up in the toilets as there wasn't a lot of room to stretch anywhere else. Every time we went in, there was always a small puddle of pish on the floor in front of the toilet pan. We suspected that it was Scott as he couldn't see his tackle. This went on for weeks and weeks with Scott denying it was him. Tom and I decided to prove it was him for once and for all.

We monitored everybody who went into the toilet, including clients and visitors. We would make sure that the floor was completely dry before and after every visit. If there were a tiny bit of residual spill, we would wipe it up with toilet paper, preparing the trap for the big pisher. After Scott had pissed twice that day, there was no question who the culprit was. Each time he came from the toilet, there was a big puddle lying there. There was a stain on the front of his trousers. He still denied it. The next day I took my small toilet pan cup, and when I knew Scott was about to go into the loo, I nipped in ahead of him and placed the cup right at the base of the toilet pan and put a hand-drawn sign on it.

' For the Glasgow overspill.'

He came in a few minutes later, not looking too happy. 'Who's the wise cunt then?' He said. Holding the cup and sign in his grubby paw. He still denied it, even though the words were all blurred and dripping.

'Fuck off Scott, it's obvious' Tom said.
'Prove it?' He said defiantly.
'In a Court of Law, could you prove without questionable doubt that it was me that pissed oan the flair?' He said eloquently.
'Scott, look at the fucking front of your trousers, you're zip's down, and there's a dark stain,' Tom said, putting his hands in the air and shouting.
'Case closed'.

THE CARPET WHALE

TOM AND I HAVE just got back into the office after doing yet another hard lunchtime run: From work, down to Abbeyhill then up Arthur's Seat, around Queen's Park, past Holyrood Palace, up Regent Terrace and all the way up to Princes Street, then St. Andrew's Square before bombing as fast as we can along George Street and back to work again. I always thought we were getting close to hurting some unfortunate bystander as we sped along at a real rate of knots, dodging in between all of these people walking for their lunch.

We do a quick warm-down, get washed and changed in the loo's as always and head back to our office for the sandwiches that Tom's Mum, Agnes, makes for us every day. Always Salmon, and always too much butter for me, which I have to scrape off, but they taste brilliant.

As I walk through to my room, I know something's up when I hear Tom absolutely pissing himself with laughter. I go through to the production department, and Scott's there just looking at Tom.

'What the fuck are you laughing at Hanlon?' He says.

Tom can't say a word, he's just laughing and pointing at Scott.

'You are a fuckin' weirdo Hanlon' he says dismissively.

I can see what the problem is and don't have the heart to laugh. Scott has just got in from a trip to one of our biggest clients, and he's wearing what he thinks is a trendy Miami Vice, Don Johnson type of suit. It's evident to anyone looking that he actually has a scientist's lab coat on and a pair of white Chef's trousers, this alongside a pair of white slip-on shoes and no socks are what has put Tom over the edge. Scott always tried to do fashion on the cheap, thinking he was even cooler than the fashion gurus by getting the look without paying the price. The problem was the look he was getting was more medical student than Miami Vice.

'Classic Scott' is all Tom can say between fits. Rolling on the floor and clapping his hands.
Scott goes back behind his desk and sits there, pulling at his curly hair watching dandruff float onto the desktop.
'Come on Scott, he doesn't mean anything by laughing' I say, trying to cheer him up.
'Fuck off you. Always trying to solve other people's problems. Smart cunt that you are'.
I'd no idea what he was on about and shook my head a bit.
'Come on Scott, no need to be like that' Tom chipped in.
Scott grabbed his stapler and threw it at me, I had to duck; otherwise, it would have hit me on the head.
I shouted out the first thing that came into my head.
'Fuck off ya carpet whale'.
Phil came out of his room, laughing.
'What did you call him?'
'I don't know, a carpet whale?'
'What in fuck's name is a fuckin carpet whale,' Scott said.
'I don't know' I said.
'Come on' Phil repeated, 'tell us'.
I always used to make up nicknames for people, I did this as a defensive act in case they ever said or did something to me, and I had to retaliate quickly with words. I'd been caught out on many occasions and decided to create some and store them up for the right time. This was one of them.
I'd heard the phrase 'Couch potato' a thousand times and wondered what you called folk who'd gone past the couch potato phase and could no longer get onto the couch because they were so fat. I decided on the name 'Carpet Whale', and this was the first time I'd used it. There was no way I could tell Scott what it meant as the heat of the argument had now

cooled, and I was back to being in control which meant I'd now have to make something up to pacify him.

'It's a Beluga' I said.

'What the fuck is a Bellooguh?' He said, trying to mock me.

'A white whale,' I said.

'I saw one on a rug down at Behar Carpets in Seafield. You looked like it with your white kit on'.

'Are you calling me a fuckin whale Divine? Ya skinny wee fucker.'

'You're missing the point' I said and walked into my room, slammed the door for effect, which seemed to do the trick.

A wee while later, Phil came in.

He was pissing himself with laughter.

'That was brilliant' he said.

'Carpet whale. Do you mind if I use that?'

'Feel free, I'm just glad I didn't have to explain to him what it really meant. Otherwise, I think he might have tried stapling my head to the wall,' I said. Laughing.

The Ratskeller

I'M JUST ABOUT TO leave the office for the evening. I'm packing my things into my rucksack ready to head to Meadowbank to train with the squad. As I close my door, Scott shouts something out to me. The agency is about to pitch for a new continental lager account, it's called Ratskeller and is reported to be one of the most potent brews available. We've all been working on it for a few weeks and are only now starting to get somewhere.

'Sorry Scott, what were you saying?' I say, putting my bag over my shoulder and heading into his room.

'Get the lads round for a Ratskeller. What do you think?' He says.
'Eh?' I say, caught unawares.
'Get the lads round for a Ratskeller.' He repeats.

'It's not really saying a great deal Scott' I say to him shaking my head.
'It's inviting all the boys round tae have a wee party,' he replies. Pulling his jumper over his head and looking around as if it's a secret party.
'I know that' I say but what is its USP?'
'What dae ye mean' he says.
'Its Unique Selling Proposition? It could be Beck's or Stella or any other premium lager or beer' I say knowledgeably while at the same time, knowingly irritating the shit out of him.
'What makes the phrase 'GET THE LADS ROUND FOR A RATSKELLER' a USP?' I say to him.
'Up yer fuckin arse Divine.' He says, 'You're just jealous that I've got a great idea.'

'Do Tim and Phil know your working on this' I ask him.
'Naw' he replies, 'I thought I'd surprise them with an award-winning campaign. Who would've thought that me, a production manager, could come up with such a great creative campaign, eh?'
'I'm not too sure Tim and Phil will be too happy about you working on their pitch' I say to him, really meaning that I know for a fact that Tim and Phil will be pissed off about the production manager working on a creative idea, and more to the point I know it's an absolutely crap idea, and they'll take the piss out of him for a very long time.
It's after seven in the evening. 'I'm leaving now Scott' I say. 'Are you staying long?'
'I'll just stay on a bit longer and finish this campaign idea' he says excitedly. 'Think they'll like it?' He went all starry-eyed at the prospect of impressing the creative team.
'Do you want honesty Scott, or do you want to hear what you want to hear?
'Honesty please'.
I honestly think they'll hate it'.
He laughs, genuinely believing that I'm jealous. 'Fuck awfff.'
'See you in the morning Scott' I call, as I go out of the door. There's no reply from him as I look through the window and see that his tongue is busily working its way around his lips as he scribbles on Tim's big expensive Letraset pad with a thick black pen.

I walk to work the next morning, it's a beautiful sunny day in Edinburgh, and it feels brilliant to be part of the advertising fraternity, it is at times the most exciting business in the world. We have a pitch for the Ratskeller account (an imported lager from the Balkans or some eastern province like it). The pitch is in two days, and we still have to crack the concept, hence Scott's activity. I'm first into the office and pop the coffee percolator on, put in some Mayan blend, walk through to my room and am almost snow-blinded by the glare from Tim and Phil's office. I walk through next door to where the light is emanating and am astonished by the vast array of white sheets hanging from every available space on the shelves, desks and even the chairs. I'm impressed by the amount of paper that Scott had produced. Unfortunately, it's all crap. Tim and Phil will go mental at him, wasting all of their expensive Letraset paper.

Scott hasn't travelled the paths of other art directors or designers in our office, or the general industry for that matter, in his mind he's gone straight to the top. He has not gone through the time, pain and heartache of making an idea work, he has bypassed the usual stress of tying up a lot of loose ideas and somehow bringing them together in a brilliant flash of inspiration, he has not required the standard research procedures into the product or even thought about photographic or illustrative styles. He has gone straight to the top of the podium. In his mind, these ideas are going to win International Awards. I can only imagine Tim and Phil's reaction when they find their sacred creative space so rudely, crudely, insultingly, and disparagingly abused by a glorified 'Barras white sock salesman', it sounds cruel, but I can't wait for the fun to begin.

'Good morning Jim' Tim says as he breezes healthily through the main door with the sun streaming in behind him. He lifts his Ray-Bans onto the top of his sunburned head and walks to the kitchen where he carefully unloads two bottles of sparkling Perrier water from his bright orange leather briefcase and places them precisely into the fridge. He then goes to the toilet, and by the time he's finished, Phil has arrived.

'Morning Jimbo', he says in his usual cheery Yorkshire way.
He removes the bicycle clips from his brown cords, folds his
little bike in two and grabs a glass from the kitchen cupboard
and fills it with tap water. He wanders to his room.
'Did you see that show with Frank Sidebottom last night it
wa...'
'What the…' He says as he splutters water all over Tim's desk.
At that very moment, Tim walks in.
'What the…' he repeats.

'Get the lads round for a Ratskeller?' Phil shouts, laughing
cruelly.
'The boys will love it?' Howls Tim.
'Pull the head off it lads?' Screams Phil.
I'm astonished at how they're taking it. I expected them to
be pissed off, but they're both leaning against their desks
laughing. I find it really funny as well, but the Libran in me
can somehow 'feel' for Scott knowing that he'll be slaughtered.
He is, after all, trying his best and really wants to be a creative.

He comes in a bit later that morning, and when he sits at his
desk, there's a big pile of crumpled paper sitting dejectedly on
it.
He sits for a moment then wanders through to their room.
There's nobody there, they've both gone into the boardroom
to work on the idea for the campaign.
'What d'you think o my ideas lads,' he shouts hopefully,
excitedly, through the door.
I can hear the tension and expectation in his voice, I listen
to it most Mondays when he hasn't heard the result for his
favourite team, the anticipation of the result, the hope that
there will be good news, the elation of finding out that they've
hammered the opposition. Unfortunately for Scott, Celtic are
more competent at what they do than he is at being a creative.

'It's a NO from me,' shouts Tim. 'Not good enough, sorry'.
'What d'ye mean, not good enough ya tosser?' Scott says
adamantly.
'There's no real depth, no USP to it' Tim says, trying
desperately to control his laughter.
'Fuckin posh wanker' says Scott.
'Phil?' He shouts, hoping that Phil at least will sway the
opinion.
'It's a no from me, Scott,' Phil says. 'No real USP'.
'USP. That's what that wee fanny was goin on aboot last night',.
He says, pointing to my office.
 'What the Fuck's a USP anyway?'
'Listen Scott' says Phil 'If I were you I'd stick to production,
being a creative really is a hard job, we just make it look easy'.
'Fuck you two' he says, pulling at the curly fringe on his head,
piling up a neat little stack of black curly hairs and dandruff
onto the stack of papers that sit there.
'Jealous bastards,' he says to himself, he heads to his desk.
He sits for a while sulking and muttering. Eventually forming
his frustrations into words. He shouts through to Tim and
Phil's room.
'When the big man comes in I'm going to present them to
him, you two'll be so fuckin jealous when ah get the nod'. He
skulks off to the kitchen and pours coffee into the cup that's
been sitting on his desk from the night before. He slopes back
to his desk and flattens out all the sheets and puts them into
some kind of order.
'The big man'll see what I mean, just you wankers wait, I'll get
an Award'. He says muttering in a barely audible tone.

He waits all day for Colin, who doesn't actually come in until
way after five-thirty in the evening, Colin, being the boss,
catches up on his meetings and messages, progress from the
creative teams and everything else that keeps the boss of one

of the country's best creative advertising agency busy. All the while, Scott sits outside of his office on the small red stool, waiting on the opportunity to pounce and present his ideas. Five hours later he's still waiting, but at last, when everyone except me, has gone home, he gets his chance to sit with the boss and explain his ideas. Colin nods and shakes his head at the right bits of the explanation, asks a few probing questions, Scott's hands are waving around as if he's got manic, naked glove puppets, and he seems to be relishing his chance to shine. He comes out of the office after a good half hour, beaming and flushed as if he's just done a good gym workout. He winks at me knowingly, puts on his white jacket and heads for the door.

I decide that I've had a long enough day, turn out my office lights and go through to say goodnight to Colin.
'Well? Get the lads round for a Ratskeller?' I say.
Colin shrugs as if to say what can you do.
'Night boss' I say and head home.

As I head out I spot a big pile of crumpled white papers in Colin's bin, he's poured cold, black coffee on top of the pile to ensure it never sees the light of day.

Poor Scott.

THREE Y'S MEN

IT'S CHRISTMAS TIME AT Marr Associates in Leith.
The new MD is a tiny wee guy with an ego as big as Santa's
'Pilton bad boy list,' we've been working pretty hard, but not
as hard as I've ever worked, in fact, it's relatively painless
by comparison to some of the stuff I've put up with in my
thirteen years here. Anyway, Colin's at long last graced us with
his presence in the Engine Room, and now the party can start,
even though it's now twenty past seven on a working day.
Liz, Colin's PA, claps her hands to get everyone's attention,
she'll do anything for a bit of limelight will Liz.
'Right folks, before we all get too drunk, we're going to have
the Secret Santa'.
I'm quite looking forward to it as I got our new MD in the
draw and got him a pair of 'Invisible Liftee Pads,' you put
them into your shoes and are immediately three inches taller
without anyone knowing, this would no doubt embarrass
him, but I was sure he'd wear them later.
Eventually, a present with my name on it was drawn out.
It was a bottle of something. Too big to be wine or beer, I
thought as I weighed it in my hands.
'Rip it open' they shouted.
I did and found to my surprise a litre bottle of baby oil?
'I could see everyone looking around at each other, trying to
guess who'd bought me that.
I had no idea. 'Lynsey?' 'Nope.'
'Wilma?' 'Nope'
I went through all the girls but got the same answer.
Eventually, Brian piped up. 'It was me. And I'd like to rub it all
over your body'.
'Er, that's not going to be happening' I said.
'You're such a wee fucking tease,' he said.

I was shocked. Did he think I was gay? I thought back to see if I could remember any time that I'd given him that impression, I couldn't, why would I? Everyone was laughing, I was confused. Brian was a strange guy, I never trusted him. There was always something dodgy about him. A sense that he'd do something untoward if you let your guard down.

He and Richard had appeared from somewhere, I've absolutely no idea where they came from, but one day in Marr, they were a team, copywriter and art director. Just like Phil and me.

Richard was a lovely guy. Salt of the earth, his sense of humour was so subtle that you had to know him to get it. He was from a place called Oswestry, near Wales, I think. His illustrations and cartoons were so succinct and to the point that I felt he had missed his vocation. He detested Brian and hated the fact that they'd been thrown together in some cruel, twisted advertising mixer. They were polar opposites in every way. You could feel the strong magnetic repelling as they stood next to each other when presenting their work to Colin or when they were sitting opposite each other in the office. Richard did not have a single positive thing to say about Brian, ever.

Brian's personality and behaviour were summed up succinctly. One day Richard came into the office as always. Kettle on, an excellent strong coffee and a read of his paper.

'How's it going Richard'

'Yeah good Jim, you?'

'Good' I said.

'I don't think Brian will be in today'.

'Why's that?' I said, not really caring.

'You know Cath, his girlfriend?'

'Not really, I think I met her once, seemed quite nice, I was surprised at how attractive she was, all things considered' I said.

'Exactly' Richard said.

'Well, last night, Brian called me just after midnight asking if he could sleep at mine'.

'Why...?' I said, beginning to get into the story.

'The silly fucker had arranged with another couple to come around to theirs for dinner and some extracurricular activity'.

'What do you mean?' I said.

'Swingers?'

'Spot on' Richard said.

'Did Cath know this was happening?'

'Nope.'

'What a twat' I said'. He invited a couple round to shag his girlfriend and didn't even tell her, what a dick'.

'That's not the worst of it though' Richard said.

After she beat him about the head with something substantial and stormed out, the other couple just sat there eating their tea. I'm not sure what the hell he did with them, but when Cath came back in after a couple of hours simmering, she found the three of them in bed.

'Seriously? I said disbelievingly', 'that's just mental. Sick, Christ, what goes through that guy's head?'

'Exactly', Richard said. 'Now you know what I have to go through when we work together'.

'Come on then Jim' Wilma shouted. Bringing me back to the moment.

I looked at the bottle of oil, must have been expensive.

'Thanks Brian' I said. 'I appreciate the thought, but the nearest you'll get to putting oil on me is if you get a job as a chef in your next life and I come back as a side of spare ribs'.

'Good enough for me' He said, smiling.

'Right guys, enough of this 'man love' said Liz.

'Let's get the hell outa here, and into the big taxi, they're all waiting for us downstairs'. ....

LEAVING THE COURT

AFTER TRISH AND I had agreed to get married it put my world into a spin. Everything was going to change. I mean everything. I'd grown up in a two-bedroomed house in Pilton with nine siblings. Moved to a five-bedroomed house in Claremont Court, got used to a wee bit more space but still sharing with John. As the years passed, the kids moved away, the father walked away, and all that was left was me, Gordon and Mum. Three refugees in a land that had been incredibly noisy and populated twenty-four hours a day, seven days a week, three hundred and sixty-five days a year was now quiet and desolate, and it would be even more so when thirty-three per cent of that populous disappeared in the next few weeks. I'd never contemplated having my own place. I could not think that far ahead. My furthest thought was about what sweets to get from the Tuck shop when I next got paid. Buying a flat was way off my radar until Trish came along.
I honestly think that I'd still be on my Mum's coat-tails if I hadn't met her.
I'd spent a bit of time looking after John and Karen's flats in the past, but now having the responsibility of my own apartment was overwhelming. I'd have to give up the pick n mix and other things and put the money towards buying a house. Something that massive was beyond my comprehension so I basically ignored the thought and went into autopilot seeing where it would take me, a bit like an out-of-body experience, I guess it was my only coping strategy. We'd looked at a few properties and ended up with a top floor, one bedroomed flat just off Easter Road, convenient for the footie.
As we'd both been living at home all of our lives, we never had any real material things except for clothes and a couple of

knick-knacks that we felt were part of our history, photos and records, that kind of thing.

I remember my last night vividly in Claremont Court. I'd been there for around eighteen years, from ten until twenty-eight, a seriously long time. By now I had a room of my own, the fungus was still on the walls. The rain and condensation pooled on the window sill, making me wary not to lean on it when I looked one final time out onto the view over Leith and the old school buildings that had played such a massive part in my life.

I had packed all I owned into a single box if this is what my life had achieved to date it all added up to nothing more than a pile of plastic and paper that would one day fade and deteriorate into the wind, leaving not a trace of what I was or had been. It was a poignant moment of reflection that really made me think about what I was about to do. I had to do better than I'd done in the past. I never thought I was a loser, but in no way did I think I was a winner, creating that mindset would take a bit more time.

Trish's dad, Eric, had brought his car into town and was picking me up along with my stuff. Trish had a few bits more than me and was looking forward to independence although her Mum had insisted that there was no way we were moving into a flat together until we were married. I was gutted at this but as always went along with it as I only wanted to be with Trish. As I was heading out of the court for the last time as a 'Courty', I felt elated but also sad. Everything that had happened to me over all these years had led to this moment. I waved to a couple of the boys as I exited under the entrance canopy. I wound down the window when I saw Alex.

'Zat you oaf then?' He said.

'Yip, that's me'.

'Still, gonnae see ye at Easter Road though eh?'

'Of course, you are,' I said. 'Just because I'm leaving the court doesn't mean I'm dumping my team. In fact,' I said. 'If anything it'll be even better, Trish and I will only be a five-minute walk away'.

'Ya dancer.' He said.

'Make sure you let me know where you'll be before the game, and we can hook up,' I said.

'Sound,' he said. He leaned over, we shook hands.

'Good luck with the new flat.'

'Thanks Alex. See you around'.

I wound the window up, and we headed towards Leith.

I sat there in the car not saying a word to Eric, I was caught up in all the things that had gone on in the past, my mind raced back to the first time I'd ever come to Claremont Court.

PENRITH 1970

THE PILTON GANG WERE really upset that John and I were heading to a new house. We'd grown up together since we were toddlers. It seemed like another planet away even though, in reality, it was only twenty minutes on a bus along Ferry Road, a walk through St Marks park and you were there. Claremont Court stood in all her Post-Modernist glory. Gary Gilchrist and his wee brother Frankie were the closest friends John and I had, Snottery Beak, Keith Stewart and Mikey McDaid were part of the gang as well, but the four of us stuck together more, probably something to do with the fact that we were two sets of brothers roughly the same age. We'd had all kinds of adventures over the years but mostly good stuff, the bad stuff was buried deep within us all, and it stayed that way. We'd known for a long time that we would be heading into the City centre and as the days ticked away, we got closer and closer. The fear of losing such an integral part of who we were was terrifying, and the bond grew to a level that had never been there before.

One day I came in from school and mum told me that Hilary, Gary's mum had decided that I would be allowed to go to visit their gran and granddad in Penrith, England. I was gob-smacked. I'd never been anywhere (except Kinross), and that counted as a torture trip rather than anything to do with pleasure.

'When?' I said.

'Your bag's packed,' Mum said.

'You're leaving tonight, Gary's granddad will be here in half an hour to pick you up'.

I could not believe my luck. 'How far is it, will they understand me, where will I sleep...' A hundred questions still to be answered but there was no time for that.

I grabbed a slice of toast, said cheerio to the gang. John and Frankie were sitting on the stone steps at the stair door, faces tripping them like they weighed a ton. 'How come we're no allowed tae go?' They moaned. Nobody paid them any attention. Including me, all I wanted to do was get into that light blue Hillman Imp and head for the big open road.

The stair echoed with noise as Gary, his granddad and gran all trundled down from the top landing with the other kids pulling at the skirt tails of their mum. It seemed every single person that lived in the stair was out to see us off, there was a sense of carnival about the place, I was ecstatic. I remember Gary's gran had a fag hanging from her bottom lip the whole time, she never inhaled, the cigarette bounced around like a conductor's baton as she spoke.

Gary had a lovely brown suitcase, it was one his mum owned when she was wee, and she'd kept it pristine all this time. I had a blue sports bag that dad had borrowed from one of his pals.

We jumped into the back seats of the car, I guess nowadays it would be absolutely minuscule, but to a couple of young kids, it was perfect. I'd hardly ever been in a car and this journey into the unknown, over the border had me scared and excited in equal measures. I guess it must have taken a few hours to drive to Penrith, but it flew by. When we got there, we stopped at this fantastic big house. There was a lovely rockery in the garden, and some rose bushes. I remembered trying to grow flowers in our backyard in Pilton and had imagined them looking like these, I wanted to give my mum a present and had decided to dig the garden for her. It was a disaster. I could make only lumps of cracked mud.

We walked up the half a dozen or so steps and headed into the house. It had a really clean smell about it. There was thick carpet all the way up the hallway and up the stairs. Stairs. I'd never been in a house with stairs before, I was gob-smacked, they were beautiful.

'On you go lads,' Gary's granddad said. Gary, you're in the room to the left and Jimmy to the right'.

We ran upstairs, and as I opened the door, I thought I was in a dream. There was a massive bed with lovely crisp white sheets, two pillows and some cushions at the end of it. There was a window with some net curtains and red velvet curtains with a band around them to keep them open. The view was incredible, I was overlooking a big field with what looked like cows in it. I think that was the first time in my life that I'd ever been ultra excited.

I ran through to Gary and was about to tell him when I remembered it was his Granny and granddad's house and he'd been here plenty of times before.

'Well, what do you think?' He said.

'This is going to be the best holiday ever,' we jumped up and down hugging with excitement.

The next morning I woke from a fantastic, peaceful sleep, probably one of my best ever. I lay in bed, wondering what to do. I'd never been in anybody's gran and granddad's house overnight before and was confused. I was ravenous but had no idea what the protocol was in such situations. Did I lie in bed until someone came to the door? Did I get up, head downstairs and hope that someone would be around to guide me to breakfast? In the end, I just lay there, listening to the summer sounds outside my English window. Birds were singing, there was the gentle hum of what I imagined were Hillman Imps going up and down the winding streets of Penrith. Something happened to me that morning, I was unsure of what it was. The stress and pressure that I'd felt throughout my life, even though I was unaware that I'd been feeling anxiety and tension simply dissipated. I was somebody new that morning. I was fresh, I was energised. I didn't realise it at the time, but I was onto stage two of my life.

As it turned out, I fell into a deep sleep and was awakened by a gentle knocking on the door from Gary's granddad. I washed, changed into a clean T-shirt and headed downstairs, examining and being awed by the thickness of the carpet. When I walked into the breakfast room, there was a round table with a white cotton tablecloth covering it. There were two teapots, a pot of coffee, plates, knives and forks and a bowl of fruit. I'd never seen this. Gary's gran held a seat out for me and pushed it closer to the table as I sat down. She poured a pile of cornflakes into the bowl in front of me and asked if I wanted a banana in it. I was bewildered. A banana in cornflakes. 'Yeah, that would be nice' I said. She chopped the banana into little slices and spread them all over the cornflakes.

'Sugar?' She said'.

I nodded. She spread it over the whole plate and then poured ice-cold milk on top.

The first bite was like nothing I'd ever experienced. It was magical.

That was followed by a few cups of hot sweet tea, some toast and blackberry jam (which to this day, I still have for breakfast when I'm away anywhere). After all of that food, I was ready to go for a nap, but no. They tidied up and said we had ten minutes to get our stuff together as we were heading to Lazenby.

'What's that?' I asked Gary

'A swimming pool, outdoors, it's got slides and a diving board as well'.

I was never any good at swimming so wasn't as excited as Gary. I'd excused myself from swimming lessons for years as I never had trunks, I'd been offered a pair of my sister's navy blue knickers and told that nobody would notice that they weren't real trunks. But gratefully declined the offer, so I had no idea what this swimming thing was all about. Gary was basically a fish.

We got to this fantastic location in the countryside, as we stepped out of the car I could smell lemons, as we approached the entrance I could see the outdoor pool was surrounded by these beautiful trees covered in bright yellow fruity lemons. I'd never seen a fruit tree before, and this was a sight that had me baffled. I never really appreciated that fruit grew on trees until this moment. Fruit was something that you bought at supermarkets or greengrocers. I was awestruck and wandered around, looking at them.

'Can I pick one?' I said to Gary's Granddad.

'Yeah, of course, you can,' he said

'But go for the small ones as they'll be the sweetest'.

'I walked around until I saw what I thought was the ideal lemon. I'd never had a real lemon before, only lemonade and lemon ice lollies. I thought this is how they would taste.

I picked it off the tree and sat down on one of the sun loungers, as I peeled it the zesty, tangy taste nipped my lips. I got the peel off and took a couple of segments and stuck them into my mouth.

Definitely not what I was expecting.

I looked around, and the three of them were laughing at me. I joined in, throwing the remaining bits at Gary, who dived into the pool to avoid being hit.

I ventured into the shallow end and just spent hours paddling around, enjoying looking up at the clear, bright blue skies and the colour of the lemon trees.

I went into the changing room to get changed back into my shorts. When I got there, I saw a man undressing. He stood there, drying himself with a towel in the nude. He dropped the towel and looked at me.

'Hello,' he said.

'Where are you from'.

I couldn't say anything. I was shocked. This was the first time I'd ever seen a naked man, and he had hair all around his big Willie and up to his belly button. I thought there was something wrong with him and I bolted out of there without looking back, still dripping.

Gary's grandparents had a newsagents shop in the town centre. Every morning they'd drive to the shop, we'd get out of the car, go into the shop and were allowed to choose any two things in the shop. I always went for the same things. A packet of fish & chips flavoured crisps and a Bounty bar.
From there we would be told to be back at the shop for lunchtime. This gave us the whole morning to explore the place. There was a castle, a forest, a hill with Beacon Pike on top and a lot of Gary's pals, who he'd grown up with on his countless trips here over the years. I was introduced and felt I had to show these guys how tough I was. Mum had bought me a couple of new things for my trip, including a brand new pair of Clark's Tuff shoes. I proceeded to show them how 'Tuff' the shoes were by kicking the front of them against a wall. I got the other kids to join in, and pretty soon we were all doing our damnedest to kick down this stone dyke wall. After a while, we stood back to admire that mess we'd made of both. My shoes were surprisingly unscathed while everyone else's were no longer black or the colour they started out as. They were cut and chopped, and some were showing socks through the front of them. We agreed that my shoes really were 'Tuff' and the boys would go home and ask if they could get the same shoes. The wall was demolished as well.
There was a knock on the door later that night, some of the parents had come around to have a word about The Scottish Boy,' thankfully my pretending to be sound asleep act worked a treat. I heard Gary's granddad say to the people 'We'll talk to him in the morning about it'.
Thankfully, they never did.

Going Dutch - Claremont Court 1970

THE SMALL AD IN the Dandy had really got John, and I excited.

'REAL AUTHENTIC COLOUR TV FROM YOUR BLACK AND WHITE SET.'

How could this be? We said to each other as we looked at the small print. But there it was in black and white. There was no doubt about it this was the real thing.

'TURN YOUR BLACK AND WHITE WORLD INTO A WORLD OF FULL COLOUR WITH THE AMAZING NEW COLOUR CONVERSION KIT, 'AS SEEN ON TV'.

We studied the ad for ages, looking for the mistake or the rip off evidence, we went through the details; it cost £5, it was easy to install, it said in bold letters, GUARANTEED COLOUR. This was too good to be true? Surely?
Was this too good to be true?
We looked at the outlet list. It was available in Leith, Iona Street, Robert Creamer, TV and Radio repair specialist. Perfect. All we had to do now was find the money.

We did various jobs for a few weeks; a bit of car washing, cutting grass and cleaning windows, and stealing a bob or two from Mum's Purse. We'd now saved up enough money. We opened our joint piggy bank (in reality John had put in about ninety per cent of the capital, I'd squandered mine on sweets and ironing, my wee sisters Ironed my shirts for a fee). The purchasing day arrived, and we were gushing with excitement, it was all we talked about the night before, just imagine real colour TV, in our house.

We speculated about how amazing Star Trek and Scooby-Doo would be. How, at last, we'd be able to see the football in colour, admiring the vibrant yellow and green of Brazil's strip, gasp as we witnessed the bright dawning of a new era.

One of my school pal's, Billy Sheridan, had a large house in Great King Street, I think his mum and dad owned all five floors, Billy had a basement to himself, and in their living room, there was a big oak cabinet with a colour TV inside. I distinctly remember Star Trek was on and when Spock fired his phaser at a rock it glowed bright orange. This was the first time I'd ever seen colour on a screen, I was smitten. I now thought back to that day and could not wait to feast my eyes. My cartoon future lay before my very eyes, my heart pumped like a Scooby-Doo Janny after being unhooded.

We ran towards Iona Street as fast as our legs would carry us. There was a film on in half an hour, a western, we wanted to know how the wild west would look in colour. When we got there, the shop was closed.

Disappointed doesn't even come close. We were gutted. We looked for a sign, closed for lunch or something along those lines, but there was nothing. We decided to go back in a couple of hours and trudged home like a couple of sad sacks. We held on an hour or so and went back. When we got there, the shop was still closed. We went again at four o'clock, it was still closed. I looked through the letterbox and saw a whole box of colour conversion kits sitting next to the till in a large plastic bag, I tried to think of ways to get one: a coat hanger opened up and stretched to hook a prize? A magnet on the end of a stick? I wanted one so badly.

The following week we went back to the shop. Still nothing,

then again every two days with no luck, it was always shut. We asked the butcher next door when the shop opened, and he shook his head and laughed.

'The guy just opens the shop when he feels like it. In fact, the only way you can guarantee that you'll get him is if you get a sleeping bag and camp outside the shop, he's so unpredictable,' this was not what we wanted to hear.

On our third Saturday of trying we turned up again at ten-thirty in the morning, as we got a hundred or so metres from the shop we saw a guy at the door, he was about to lock up. John shouted.

'Mr. Can we buy a colour TV set.'

He looked around, keys jangling on his belt.

'A colour TV Set?' He said.

'How can you afford a colour TV set?.'

'He means a colour TV conversion kit', I said.

'We've been coming here for a couple of weeks to try to get one, but the shop was always shut'.

'Don't tell anyone' the guy whispered looking around ', but I'm actually a spy'.

'Really' said John, eyes opening widely.

'Don't be fuckin' stupid' he said.

'Do you think I'd be workin' in this shithole if I was a spy?'

He opened the door up reached inside and grabbed a box.

'That'll be Six quid' he said.

'It's only five pounds' I said, 'It was in the paper'.

'How much money have you got' he said.

'Five pounds and thirty pence' I said.

'Right, it's yours for five pounds and thirty pence' he said.

I handed him the cash, and he handed over me a very light box.

We were so excited at actually getting the thing that we didn't care about the extra money. We took shots of carrying the box between us and walked as fast as we could towards home. As we got into the living room, seven kids were sitting around waiting for us to conjure up our magic with the TV conversion kit. We carefully opened the box, pulled out all of the paper and packaging, there was tons of it. Eventually, after a lot of digging we got down to a little package at the bottom of the box, it was wrapped in a plastic bag and felt quite flimsy. We thought the guy had sold us a dummy. We searched through all the packaging again, looking for all this new technology. There was nothing to be found. We packed it all back into the box and went back to the shop. As usual, it was locked.

We got back home disconsolately and opened up the box again. This time I pulled out the plastic bag and noticed that there was something inside it. There was a bit of acetate and an instruction sheet. John grabbed it from me, He opened it up and read it.

'Congratulations' it said. You have just purchased the latest Black and White to Colour technology'.
'Please follow the instructions carefully and you will enjoy the mind-bending, high-octane thrill of colour TV'.

1. Take the Colour Conversion Kit carefully from its protective wrapping, ensure that the wrapping material is disposed of sensibly as it may be misused by children under three years of age.

2. Use the plastic gloves provided to handle the Colour Conversion Kit.
(There were no plastic gloves).

3. Feed the string (not supplied, we had to use shoelaces) through the pipe at the top of the Colour Conversion Kit and tie in a firm knot.

4. Follow this procedure with the pipe at the bottom of the Colour Conversion Kit.

5. Find a shoe, paint tin or any similarly heavy object and bend the top pipe around the object.

6. Unroll the Colour Conversion Kit acetate and tie a weight to the bottom pipe.

By this time, we were both feeling like complete donkeys. All of the kids sitting around were none the wiser.

7. Switch on the TV and enjoy colour TV in your own home.

We were completely dumbfounded. It was shit.

After all that time and effort, all we had to show for it was a stupid bit of red, clear and blue acetate hanging from a paint tin on top of the TV. It looked like we were watching Telly through a flippin' translucent Dutch flag. You could barely see the black and white image through the thin acetate. In fact, the only time we would see real colour as it should be was if they showed a full-screen picture of the Dutch flag.

Suckers.

Cheese & Onion

AFTER DUMPING THAT SHITTY plastic colour acetate crap in the bin, I grabbed my ball and headed outside, back to my reality, the all-encompassing reality I always seemed to turn to; kicking a ball about the streets. I was gutted, the promise of colour cartoons and football had disappeared like the steam from a boiled kettle. I tied my shoelaces that I'd taken back from the Colour Conversion Kit, tucked my trouser legs into my socks and shut the door, fuming. I knew that when I had a ball at my feet, that was all that mattered. I'd recently started tucking my trouser legs into my socks as I was learning new football tricks. It was annoying when the bloody flares got in the way. I'd learned from lessons past how painful hitting the ground with your face, using your teeth as a crash mat could be.

 Claremont Court was deserted, my pals were in having their tea, I had eaten some toast on beans after school and wasn't hungry. Underneath the part of the Court where we lived there was a separate kind of building with four houses, it seemed to be an afterthought of the architects, a place to earn extra revenue. This was where Sandy and Bobby lived. As I walked towards the wall where I kicked the ball against I noticed an overflow pipe was letting out hot, steaming water. I kicked my ball underneath the stream of hot water to see what would happen. After maybe thirty seconds or a minute I took it from the overflow and to my amazement, the ball bounced about five times higher. I kicked it against the wall, and it was like I had turned into Superman. The ball travelled a hundred miles an hour. I took it into the grassy area near the pensioner's houses and must have kicked it a hundred feet into the air, it was magic. The effect wore off after a couple of minutes, so I kept putting it under the hot overflow. I booted the ball until my legs hurt and the effect was becoming tiresome. Just as I was getting ready to go elsewhere, I heard a shout.

'Jimmy Divine, is that you?'
I came out from under the sheltered area I was playing in and looked up, shielded my eyes from the summer sun. Spud Thomson was hanging over his balcony.
He waved me over. 'Are you busy just now?'
'No, just kicking my ball around'.
'How would you like to earn fifty pence?'
My eyes lit up, a bit of saliva escaped from my mouth, I wiped it with my sleeve.
'Sure, what do you want me to do?' I said eagerly.
'It's wee Bob's birthday in the morning and Betty, and I have been too busy to get him his present. Would you mind running down to Leith Athletic and getting him a Rangers strip?'
'No problem Spud'. I said, will you look after my ball, I dinnae want to risk losing it tae the Pilrig boys?' (It was always a risk when any of us left the safety of our own district, there was always someone after you, wanting to fight you for something you'd done or said, or just simply wanting to pagger you because you came from the Court).

He nodded. I threw it up to him, their balcony was much lower than ours, you could almost dreep from it onto the ground.
He missed it the first two times but caught it on the third.
'I dinnae think McLoy's got anything to worry about eh?' He said.
He threw down a white envelope, and I caught it before it hit the ground.
'Now there's potential'. he said.

I'd no idea what he meant.

'What size?' I said.

'Probably a small' he said. 'I can't ask Betty as she's sitting with the boys having their tea.'

'OK, I'll ask the guy if we can swap it if it doesn't fit.'

'Good lad, just hide it at the back of old Mr Carnie's house, then come up here and knock on the door for your ball, and I'll take it from there, clear?'

'As crystal' I said.

I ran the half-mile to the shop in no time, it was next door to my Grannies house in Leith Walk. As I passed her stair, I decided to go up for a drink of juice, maybe a biscuit and also to see her, the sad thing was, I think that was the order of priority. She was always happy to see all of her grand-kids, all eighteen of them but not at the same time. Number 226 Leith Walk was an old scary, high rise tenement built in the late 1800's it had dark corners and no lighting on any of the floors. There was a pointed, spiked metal fence that looked onto an area that was open to the elements. The abyss below was full of old rubbish, and the floor area was covered in moss from way back in time. It smelled awful. The drop from Granny's landing to the bottom looked a hundred feet, it terrified me, I used to try to stick to the safe side, well away from the fence just in case it gave way. The smell of rubber was always present, due to the India Rubber Company being situated at the back of the tenements. My Granny worked there, making the material that eventually became wellies and trawler-men's Macintoshes. The whole place had a darkness about it that always clung to me until I reached Dryden Street on my run home. The broader streets and bigger horizons seemed to let me breathe a bit easier, cleanse my lungs a bit.

I sat with Granny, and we watched Crossroads and drank tea.

She always put out a small plate of biscuits for me knowing fine well that I'd eat every last one of them.

'Did you just come here to eat my biscuits' she said.

'No I wasn't even coming to see you, I'm buying a football strip from the sport's shop,' she wasn't put out in the slightest by my unintended brush off. I was forever turning up for five minutes, getting something to eat or drink and then disappearing, still do the same today with my Mum.

'You better hurry up they close at six tonight.'

'What time is it?' I said, alarmed.

'Five minutes to six,' she said.

I gulped down the last of my tea, grabbed the last of the biscuits and stuffed them in my pocket.

'Cheerio Granny' I said gave her a quick hug and ran out of the house, slamming the door behind me.

I ran down the stairs as fast as I could, singing loudly so that if there were a bogeyman waiting to pounce, I'd frighten him off.

As I approached the shop, the guy was just about to lock up. I looked at him, putting on my best puppy dog eyes. It worked,

'You were lucky there, pal,' he said.

'If you'd been a minute later'.

'Aw, thanks mister, you're a lifesaver,' I said.

'Now pal, what can I do you for? He said, rubbing his hands together.

Shit. I had a panic attack. I'd forgotten what Spud had asked me to get Wee Bob, was it a Celtic or Rangers strip?

To me, they were both Glasgow clubs, and I thought they were much of a muchness. The two biggest clubs in my world were Hibs and our deadly rivals Hearts, all other clubs merged into a mass of non-importance.

I tried to remember, Celtic or Rangers. I tried to picture Spud as a packet of crisps talking to me, Cheese and Onion - green for Celtic, or was he Salt and Vinegar - blue for Rangers. I stood there, trying to remember as the guy started jangling his keys.

'Better hurry up pal a cold beer and a hot woman is waiting for me'.

I couldn't think. Spud was turning into a mixture of the two. I did an eenie meenie.

The Cheese and Onion was the winner.

'Can I have a small boy's Celtic strip please'.

The man walked into the storeroom and brought back a small cellophane packet with the Celtic crest on it.

'That'll be five pounds sixty' please. You can have it gift-wrapped for thirty pence,' he said.

'Yeah, that would be great' I said. Thinking that I could make an extra ten pence. Spud had given me six pounds, not including my fifty pence. I was sure he'd tell me to keep the change for having such a good idea.

I ran all the way home on a wave of satisfaction, what a great day it had turned out to be.

I got back to the Court and walked to the pensioner's houses, there was a row of charming wee cottages specially designed for the elderly with small gardens and nicely manicured lawns. I used to call it 'Deaf Row', every time they asked you a question you had to repeat the answer three or four times, infuriating, they were also well up the stairway to heaven.

I nipped into Mr Carnie's back garden and put the gift-wrapped strip under a bush.

I then went up to Spud's house. Sandy opened the door.

'Can I have my ball back Sandy? Your Dad was looking after it while I had my tea'.

As I was talking, Spud walked through from the living room with the ball in his hand.

'Here you are pal, Good tea?' He said, winking at me.

'Very good, and there was a wee surprise'.

'A wee surprise? Did you get a seat at the table? He said, laughing.

Sandy looked scoobied.

Spud threw the ball to me, and I trapped it under my left foot, kicked it down the stairs. I handed him the ten pence change.

'Surely yer a wee bit short there pal?' He said.

I checked to see that Sandy had gone.

'I got it gift wrapped with the change.' I said.

'Great thinking pal keep the ten pence,' Spud said, rubbing my hair.

The next day I was out and about kicking the ball as usual when my mate Weldo appeared.

'Spud Thomson's looking for you'.

'Spud? What for?' I said, thinking he was going to thank me for the beautiful gift wrapping.

'He was going mental, something about you taking the piss, buying Wee Bob a Celtic strip. Apparently, he opened up his present in front of everybody and as the green and white hoops emerged from the wrapping there was total silence. Thankfully for you, Wee Bob just sat there, oblivious and moved onto the next gift, but Spud's on the warpath, said he's going to boot your arse until you know the difference between Celtic and Rangers.

I shit myself. I'd obviously picked the wrong flavour of crisps. The last time I'd seen Spud as furious as this was when Tigger ate his lunch.

Tigger, our severely scruffy and battered ginger cat, had sneaked into Spud's asphalt lorry through the half-open window and polished off his salmon sandwiches.

Spud was furious. He'd only popped up to his house for a pee. He saw the cat in his van from his balcony and shouted at Tigger. 'I'm going tae boot yer arse ya little ginger bastard.'

Apparently, at the same time as he was shouting this, Alan

Tipton, a little ginger-haired boy from number 57only caught the end of the rant and ran screaming up to his house to tell his Mum Spud was going to batter him'.

'I went through my memory bank. 'I was sure Spud had said Cheese & Onion,' I said out loud.
'Cheese & Onion, what the hell are you on about?' Weldo said.
'Nothin,' I said, walking away, biting my nails.

Every time I ate a bag of crisps, my throat tightened slightly. I'd have to hide for a long time until he calmed down.

A few weeks after that I felt sorry for Wee Bob, he'd 'loaned' me his prized Wembley Trophy ball. I remember kicking it to John who blootered it into the barbed wire above the garages. It hissed like a rabid python and died a slow, painful death. I took it up to our house, turned a ring of the cooker on and tried for ages to close the hole with a hot knife to no avail. All I did was make the hole bigger. I was shitting myself, hoping he wouldn't tell Spud when he found out I'd burst his ball (I'd heard on the grapevine that Spud was still after me, I'd avoided him stealthily for weeks almost straining my neck at every corner whilst making sure I wasn't walking into a Spud trap). Wee Bob was still pretty young, and I decided the best way to move on was to bluff him. I bought a fifty pence ball from Woolworths and drew the words 'Wembley Trophy' onto it with a felt pen, hoping to god that he was fooled.

I got John to deliver it to him. I convinced myself that it was his fault in the first place.

BIG SONYA - POWDERHALL 1976

ALEX, PAUL AND A load of the other guys kept
disappearing. I must have wandered around half a dozen of
our usual haunts with a ball tucked under my arm looking
for the buggers, I was dying for a kickabout. This had been
going on for weeks, and I was utterly clueless as to where they
were going. They'd turn up around teatime, and none of them
would say anything about what they'd been up to.
'Were sworn to secrecy' Paul said.
'If we break it the game's a bogey, nae mair ridin,' he said,
moving his hips back and forward in a pathetic attempt to
convey sex.
'Shut yer pus' O'Neil,' Alex said.
'What are you lot on about, secret shaggin? Sure, ah'll believe
ye,' I said.
'It's true,' Paul said.
'I told you, shut it, Paul' Alex said again.
'Fuck off Chambers, ya sap, ah'm starvin. Aw that pumpin
away gie'd me an appetite, see ye aw aboot seven,' Paul said.
And they all buggered off leaving me with the ball still tucked
under my armpit.
So, at least I knew what they were up to but what I didn't
know was where and more importantly who with. And to be
honest, it sounded kind of creepy to me.
A day or two later, I hid down at the buckets, there was a
small recess where you could hide without being seen, the
only danger was that if somebody threw their rubbish down
the rubbish chute and missed, it was all over you. It had
happened to me a couple of times before, old fish, teabags
and the occasional used sanitary towel all over my head.
Absolutely disgusting but this time I felt it was worth the risk.
I was spot on. Five, ten minutes later, Alex, Sean, Higgy and

McCowan arrived at the grass verge in front of the main square. I could hear faint mumbling but didn't really care that I couldn't hear them, I was going to follow them.

They headed into East Claremont Street, down Broughton Road, along Logie Green Road and stopped at a stair door. They collectively rung the bell, waited and as a crack in the doorway appeared, all four of them piled in quickly. I hid for a few seconds then nipped over and had a good look at the nameplate, it had about a dozen names on it, but I didn't recognise any of them.

I thought the best thing to do was to just sit on the wall opposite and wait, practising my footie skills with a tennis ball I'd brought along for company.

I must have been there a good half hour before anything remotely interesting happened. A window near the top floor opened up, and I saw McCowan lean out, he was obviously looking for somebody. He shouted something back into the room and pulled the window shut.

It was a while later when the window opened again. This time a topless fat lassie was leaning out smoking, her tits were saggier than the bags under Lionel Blair's eyes, and her hair looked like it hadn't seen shampoo since Lionel was an 'A-Lister,' as I looked closer, I got a fright. Jeezus Christ. I said to myself. It was Big Fat Sonya.

Jeez, she had about four kids all under the age of three. What the fuck were they doing up there with her? This was dangerous territory. Her husband was a bit of a gangster and had a criminal record longer than Princes Street. I'd seen enough, I headed back to the Court and had a game of two-a-side long-bangers, me and Woody versus Jimmy and Stevie Maxwell.

'Where's everybody else?' Woody said.

'Yeah' Stevie said. I haven't seen them for a long time.

I was reluctant to tell them. For about two seconds.

'They're all shagging Big Fat Sonya'.
The ball bounced to a standstill, and three jaws fell open.

'What? That big fat lassie doon the road wi aw the bairns?'
Jimmy said.
'Yip. That's her' I confirmed. The three of them all pulled faces
of disgust after I reported the vision I'd witnessed.
'What's all that about' Woody said.
'No idea' I said. 'They were keeping all Secret Squirrel about
it, but I followed them this morning. I saw her hingin oot
the windae with her tits on show to everybody. Not nice, big
floppy things,' I said mimicking as well as I could. 'If you can
imagine those guys that throw the pizza dough around before
applying the tomato base, that's her tits'.
'Who's all there?' Stevie said.
'Alex, Sean, McCowan, and guess who else?'
'Paul O'Neil' the three of them said in unison.
'Yip'.
'Dae they ken her husband's a fuckin nutjob?' Woody said.
'No idea, but I'm sure they'll find out soon enough if they
keep this up,' I said.
'Fuckin idiots' Woody said 'Fuck them. Gies the baw Jimmy,'
Woody and I beat the Maxwell's 34-32.

Later in the afternoon, Jimmy, Stevie and Woody had headed
home. I went up to the house for a bite and then came back
down and spent a bit of time booting the ball against the
garage doors as a little change from the wall.
I heard the 'Four Shagateers' as they were now calling
themselves, coming into the Court.
'Fuckin hell, did ye see the way ah wis shagging her wi her
tights on?' Paul was saying.
There was laughter, but it stopped when they saw me.
'So?' I said.

'So what?' McCowan said.

'Have fun shaggin?'

'What's it tae you?'

'Nothin, and it never will be wi that big monster,' I said

'Ye dinnae even ken whae it is'.

'It's Big Fat fuckin Sonya,' I said.

'A pin dropped somewhere in the distance.

'How dae you ken whae it is?' Alex and Sean said.

'Well for a start even inspector Clouseau could track you muppets doon'.

'You better no tell anybody' McCowan said.

'Why would ah tell anybody that you lot are shaggin a big fat ugly cow? She's mingin,' Jeez, I hope your wearing Johnnies, yer likely tae catch VD or something'.

'Jealous' Sean said.

'Sure' I said. 'I really fantasise about putting ma meat and two veg near something that's likely tae take a bite. What are you all playing at? Her husband's a mental case. He'd rip your heeds off'.

'He's away at sea,' Paul said.

I laughed. 'Aye, right, pull the other one'.

'No seriously, he's away for a couple of months, Merchant Navy'.

'I'll believe ye,' I said. 'More like the good ship Saughton Prison.'

I was a couple of years older than them and wanted to give them the benefit of my wisdom. I was still a virgin, and they thought I was jealous because they'd all popped their cherries on the same night, in the same hole. There was something in me that wanted the experience, but the thought of someone like her putting her toilet parts near to mine filled me with dread and disgust in equal measures.

'Honestly guys, I'm not being funny, but this could get really dangerous'. They walked away.

A week or two later the gang bang gang had grown to eight. They were going down every day and all getting a shot at her. Sean explained how it worked.

'She stays in the bedroom, and we're all given numbers. She'd shout a number from one to eight, and generally, only three or four of us would get their ends away. '

Wee Stevie had gone down a dozen times, but his number had still never been called. He tried paying McCowan to swap numbers, but it never happened. The deal was that the guys whose numbers weren't called had to babysit and feed her kids while she was getting pumped into oblivion.

It eventually became so dull and routine to her that she was no longer getting her kit off, she lifted her skirt, and they had to shag her with her tights still on.

'Fuck sake, man' Paul said. "I was shagging her, and every time I stuck my dick intae her, her taes curled up. It was shite'.

I reckoned that over the two or three month period when it had all happened, there must have been at least a dozen guys from the Court and Broughton Road who'd lost their virginity, I just wondered how many of them would be scratching their bawbags at BB camp in Lilliesleaf this summer. They may have lost their virginity but at what cost?

I was sure my time would come soon.

Fairy in Fairyland - Portobello 1980

JOHN AND TAM KEPT disappearing, this had been going on for several days now, and I'd no idea where they were going. They both worked as roofers for the same company and as soon as they got home from work they'd get cleaned up and within ten minutes, they'd disappear into the wild blue yonder on their 100cc motorbikes. Every time I asked them about it, they'd tap the side of their noses with their index finger and wink.

One evening I decided to follow them. I got my mate Jimmy to give me a backie on his bike. We followed them for about twenty minutes and after a few twists and turns and a few quick diversions to avoid them spotting us, ended up at Portobello beach. I watched from behind the amusement arcade as both of them padlocked their bikes up and went into a house, which was right behind the promenade, virtually ten steps from the beach of golden sand and pure blue water. I made my way up the path towards the house, and John turned around, catching me red-handed. I dived into a bush at the side, trying to hide. John walked over to me, pulled up a couple of branches and took a deep breath. He looked so disappointed.

'What are you doing here', he said, as if I've discovered his secret gang hut.

'I followed you to see what you were up to, I was worried that you were meeting a drug dealer or something.' I lied.

'Don't talk shit' Tam said, 'you know we're no that stupid'.

'How did you get here anyway?' John said.

Just at that very moment, Jimmy walked into view.

'Jimmy gave me a lift on his bike.'

John explained that he's looking after our sister Karen's new flat and that she doesn't want me to know about it in case I bring down all my pals and get the place into a state.

'I'll tell you what' John said, 'since it's Friday, you can go back to the house, get a few things and then come back and stay until Sunday night. How does that sound?'.

' It sounds great' I said, knowing that I wouldn't have to spend another Saturday night listening to the auld man getting pissed and trying to play his two-stringed guitar at two in the morning, then arguing with mum and the neighbours.

'Can I bring a few pals'... before I can finish the question I realise that I am falling into the predicted version of me, and stop abruptly.

Within the hour, Jimmy had taken me home and dropped me back at Karen's flat before heading back to the Court on his own.

'What's the plan guys?' I said, as I threw my overnight plastic carrier bag into the corner of the living room.

'We're going for something to eat, probably a Chinky or pizza, after that, we were going to dander along to the shows and then get few cans for a cairy oot' Tam said. 'Maybe let you hear the new OMD album if you play your cards right'.

'Ah'm no sleeping in a bed wi you if that's what ye mean?' I said. Half-jokingly.

'Fuck off you.' Tam said.

I suspected he'd like me to go to bed with him, he'd mentioned my long flexible legs a few times, and it rankled a bit. But he'd have no more chance of losing his virginity than me. Surely?

'Superb' I said, really chuffed. I mean REALLY chuffed. I was sick of spending weekends with the auld man getting hammered and making everyone's life a misery.

We strolled onto the beach-front into a really splendid

summer evening, there were lots of people about, and the air and atmosphere were delightful. Tam popped into the chippy and picked up three fish suppers and three cans of Irn Bru. We just sat on the wee stone promenade wall saying nothing. Thoroughly enjoying the whole freedom thing.

'Are we still getting a Chinky later?' I asked.

'We'll see' John said.

Karen was the first one to escape from the house; she'd landed a job as a nursery nurse.

'Now she takes an interest in children,' I said to mum sarcastically, when I found out what her job was. It's ironic because Karen, although the eldest of the ten of us, spent the least time with us. After she'd hit thirteen, she spent most nights with her friends the Twins and stayed over at theirs, a lot, something we were never allowed to do. Probably because nobody would want us to stay over or ever offered for that matter.

Her new job allowed her to flee the nest, I had no idea where she was staying, and this was the first time I had been aware of the flat.

Just sitting there knowing that I'd escaped from the auld man's four-can-Saturday-night was absolute bliss.

We threw our chip papers into the bin, drank our juice and headed for the shows.

They're not the biggest shows, if Las Vegas were the world cup, Portobello Shows would be a blow football game between two asthmatic pensioners with wilting paper straws.

After a bit of time I'd spent three quid, one of my own and two that John had given to me. I was annoyed with myself. I'd blown the whole lot on the grabber arm thingy. I was trying to win a fluffy toy for my youngest sister Catherine, she'd not been feeling too well recently. If I'd looked up, I could have bought one from the shop and still had enough money to get some candyfloss. That's the problem with me; my eyes are bigger than my belly. If I see something that I want, I just go for it and don't think about the consequences, money literally burns a hole in my pocket. In fact, the first wage that I ever got from the George Hotel was handed to me on a Friday morning, and within ten minutes of getting back to the house, I had all of the kids over to the Tuck Shop letting them pick any sweets that they desired. I got so carried away that I had no money left to pay my mum dig money. She let me off until the following week.

By this time, John and Tam were getting bored, so we decided to head up to the flat to drink the six cans of lager that had been chilling in Karen's fridge. Just before we got to the flat, we heard a commotion in one of the arcades. As we walked through the plastic rainbow ribbons draping the door, a wee Glaswegian guy was removing his jacket.
There's a small crowd watching him.
'What's going on here?' John said to a guy, standing, laughing at the scene.
'This wee Weegie punter's had a few goes at the 'test-your-strength' machine, and he's come off second-best every time. He is not a happy holidaymaker.
As everyone watched, the wee guy rolls his sleeves up and shouts at the top of his voice.
'No bastard gets to call me a fuckin fairy'.
I looked at the machine and saw that there were five strength bars, the harder you hit, the higher the 'dinger' travels, and if you're very strong you hit the 'superhuman' bar, and the bell rings. I saw that the dinger was flashing at the 'Fairy' setting, this was what was upsetting him. Every time the light went on a loud, camp, Larry Grayson type voice said;
'Ooh, who's a big fluffy fairy then?'

The boy was getting really wound-up by this machine and intended to knock the bell off the top of the device to show the gathering crowd how unfairylike he is. He did a couple of practice swings, and to be honest, he looked quite tough with his completely tattooed arms and neck. He swung the oversized wooden mallet 360 degrees in a perfect arc. It crashed down on the pad, and the dinger went up, only as high as 'Fairy' again. He was raging,
'Ya fucking bastarding stupid fucker of a machine' he shouted. 'Nae bastard gets to call me a fuckin fairy,' he lets fly again, and again and again. The crowd around him were laughing their tits off, and this forced him to keep trying. He was quite clearly running out of energy, and his attempts were not even reaching fairy now. The dinger eventually only reached the 'Donkey' level and began to make donkey calls. The guy lost the plot completely, he started kicking the machine but still the 'hee-haws' come. I nudged John as I spotted a wee wifie in the corner of the arcade with her hand covering as much of her face as possible.
'That must be his wife'.
With the crowd laughing at the guy and his head getting redder and redder he picked up the whole machine, ran from the arcade and fell, flat on his face, as the electric plug cable pinged and stretched as it reached its limit, it reminded me of the dog reaching the limit of his tied leash in the Tom & Jerry cartoons. He grasped the cable, ripped it from the wall and threw the machine from the arcade onto the beach. 'That'll teach you ya fuckin bastard,' he said as he unrolled his shirtsleeves.
'Mary' he shouted, 'let's get the fuck oot o here'.
The woman slipped quietly out of the back of the arcade with a bigger beamer than him. By this stage there must have been a hundred folk laughing their heads off, it was a classic.

We went back to the flat, got the lager and strolled along to Joppa, taking in the sun, it really felt like a holiday. I took several deep, satisfying breaths but at the same time felt sorry for Mum and the rest of the kids who would have to suffer another shitty weekend of the auld man getting drunk on his four cans of Cally Special and bursting into the rooms to argue with everyone.

After we'd walked enough, we headed back to the flat, but not before stopping at the Golden Star to get a portion of chicken fried rice with curry sauce (no onions for me).

We got into the flat, all jumped onto the big sofa and stuck a video into the machine. Tam tried to put his arm around John. John looks at him like; do that again, and you're likely to be eating your cornflakes with a straw.

'Only fuckin wi ye big man' he said. Faking a laugh. He got a lot more space from us both after that.

As we were sitting enjoying the film, we heard sirens outside. There was a cop car at the arcade. John opened the big sash window, and we leaned out, the wee Weegie guy was standing just in front of the arcade in handcuffs.

He looked totally spent and his wife was nowhere to be seen.

A strange kind of melancholy comes over me as I look at him. It doesn't seem as funny now.

THE FATHER MUST DIE

I WAS IN THE FRONT garden of our house in Pilton with
John and a couple of my friends. I was the leader of the gang,
mainly because I was the oldest. Gary Gilchrist was second
in command and John was third. Frankie, Gary's wee brother
and Snottery Beak didn't even figure in the pecking order. We
were trying to invent some TV advertising jingles and had
chosen Kellogg's cornflakes as the product to work on. After a
while, we'd come up with the words:

We like cornflakes, cornflakes, cornflakes.
We like cornflakes early in the morning.

The words were OK, but we argued about how the word 'early.'
Should be pronounced.
I thought it should be ER LIE
But the others didn't agree. Snottery beak and Frankie
wandered off, bored by the whole thing, and I eventually
persuaded John and Gary to go with my line of thinking. We
proceeded to go up and down the street singing the jingle. As
we were heading back down to our house from the top of the
road a Police van closely followed by an Electricity Board van
whizzed past us and stopped outside our stair. By the time
we got there, my auld man was being led out and put into the
police van.
I was eight or nine, and this was the first time I remember the
Police coming to the door. I knew nothing of it at the time,
but this was his first time in the clink, I think the judge took
pity on him because he was unemployed and had eight kids
and twins on the way.
The second time, however, was more memorable as I was
older, probably around twenty, and I was involved - up to an

extent.

'In 1979 forester Robert 'Bob' Taylor returned home from a trip to Dechmont Law, near Livingston, dishevelled, his clothes torn and with grazes to his chin and thighs, he claimed he'd encountered a 'flying dome' which tried to pull him aboard. Due to his injuries, the Police recorded the matter as a common assault and battery, and the incident is popularly known as the 'only example of an alien sighting in Scotland becoming the subject of a criminal investigation'.

It was all over the papers, and the guy seemed to believe that he was Scotland's first genuine alien abductee. He was slated wherever he went, the tabloids gave him miles of column inches, mostly slagging the poor guy off. However, there was one man who believed every single word of the story.
My auld man.

He had suspected that there were aliens on the planet since the late fifties, he'd read every single word that was ever written on the Roswell incident. After he'd bottomed out a few cans of Cally Special, he'd take me out on really dark nights and show me all the planets and constellations. It was an education that I really shouldn't have had. His room was full of conspiracy theory books, and he'd drawn symbols and diagrams of pyramids, alien craft, mathematical equations on the wood-chip wallpaper that proved there was a tenth planet and all kinds of things that would have his hero, Erich von Däniken applauding in approval. I mainly went with him to get him out of the house, give mum and the other kids a bit of peace and quiet. Mum looked on me heroically from time to time for doing this.
One particular night he was really getting on mum's nerves, so much so that I thought she would either walk out on us or do

him some severe damage. She'd put up with his crap for years and had grown tired and weary from him, from looking after us and having three jobs to cope with. In all our time as kids, we'd never been for a holiday, which meant neither had she. The nearest we got was that shitty retreat at Kinross with those pathetic students that scared the shit (and piss) out of me. I could see Mum was at the end of her tether and decided to do something about it. I had put with his drunken Saturdays for years now and his Carlsberg Special nights were getting the whole family down. Week after week, month after month he'd promise John and I that he wouldn't drink tonight. I was always so happy when he said this, knowing that we could all sit down, relax and enjoy watching TV and having something nice to eat. The tension I carried around with me disappeared, and I felt happy, ecstatic even. As always, he never kept his promise. I'd catch him sneaking tins of beer into his room under a towel or in a bag, pretending they were something else, I'd challenge him, but he'd always deny the charge. He'd lock himself away, and hours later he'd reappear pissed and incoherent. Another night ruined and tension returned to me like midges around a freshly delivered Loch Lomond tourist. I figured out that the only way for us to be happy was to get rid of him.

I decided I would kill him.

This was something I'd thought about for a while. Definitely pre-meditated. Even if I had to serve a jail term, it would be worth it as we'd all have peace, eventually. I'd have it on my release from Saughton. For years and years, he'd been getting pissed every Saturday night. Sometimes he'd take John and me to Easter Road to watch Hibs, we'd beg him not to get beer on the way home, he promised. We'd be so happy, but he was not faithful to his word. He always ended up getting four cans of Cally Special and sometimes a half bottle of whisky. As we waited on him outside the off licence, we got that horrible sinking feeling in our stomachs. I'd put up with this for years. John went out most Saturday nights, but I had no money, so I stayed in, drawing or reading, something like that. When I knew he was in one of his angry moods, I'd sit at the top of the stairs for hours, crying to myself, waiting to rush down in case he attacked mum. The final straw came one Saturday night, it must have been one or two in the morning when I heard a scream from Mum and Dad's room. I rushed down and found the drunken old bastard trying to strangle her. I jumped on him, and eventually, he lost his grip and stormed off in a huff. I decided the time had come.

It was around eleven-thirty on a really snowy and wild winter's night when after all the usual shouting and arguing that he spouted had been spouted, I challenged him to a race around the football pitches at St. Mark's park. He accepted, I knew he couldn't resist as he still thought he could beat me, even more so when he was pissed. I was training pretty hard and was at an excellent fitness level, so how he thought he could even get near to me said a lot about his grasp on reality. My plan was quite simple, I would get him to run around the football pitches as many times as I could and get him so knackered that he would either collapse and die of hypothermia or have a massive heart attack and pop his drunken clogs on the spot. Billy agreed to help me get rid of the old bugger, and we formulated a plan. Unbeknown to the auld man, Billy and I were dressed in the same gear, a blue tracksuit top with black bottoms and white running shoes. He had no idea that Billy had sneaked over to the park before we got there. There were actually two football pitches side by side, making it a vast area to run around.

I got down to my marks, let the auld man say go. I had no

intention of holding back, I was committed to this and bolted off, along the long straight and continued to push it around the first corner, he was way behind already. I then jumped behind a small snow hill, and Billy emerged to carry on at the same speed. The auld man had no idea what he was up against, and after a few minutes, we'd lapped him. All credit to the old bugger, he tried to run faster and faster, but every time I passed him, I would show him I was in complete control and hardly out of breath. As I passed him for the third time, I patted him on the head to rub salt in. After six or seven minutes of this torture, he collapsed into a heap.

I stopped. Looked over to the opposite side of the field, Billy had started to walk towards me. I immediately felt so guilty. I ran over to the collapsed heap in the snow, the plumes of white breath were being thrown into the air with a rapidity that scared me. His face was as red as a London bus, and the wheezing sounded like he had a rattlesnake under his dandruff laden polo neck. When I got close to him, I could see his eyes were shut. As my feet crunched on the hardening snow as I approached him, he opened his eyes, gestured to me that he wanted to say something to me. I knelt down next to him, waiting on his last words.
'I never realised you could run so fast.' He whispered in broken, laboured words and shut his eyes again.
Billy emerged from the far side of the park, and we gave each other a 'what the fuck have we done' look.
'Is he?...'
Billy said.
'No, but he's in a bad way' I said, obviously worried.
'What are we going to do?'
'We should just leave him,' I said.
'What if he dies?'
'There's nothing we can do now, you knew that was the plan'.

I said, trying to sound convincing. I was anything but. If he died, nobody except Billy and I would know what had happened. If he lived and had some kind of disability but could still communicate, he'd grass us up. There was no question of the best outcome for us.

We both looked down at him, he was still rasping like a punctured whoopee cushion, eyes tightly shut.

We left him lying there and went back to the house, trying to act as normal as possible.

After an hour had passed, there was no sign of him.

'You two are awfy quiet,' Mum Said.

'What are you up to?'

'Nothing, just waiting on Higgy,' I lied.

Billy looked at me. He was cacking himself, I was too but couldn't afford to show it.

After another ten minutes or so I couldn't stand the pressure.

'Fancy a cuppa Mum?' I said.

'I've got one here' she said, looking at me, shaking her head. 'You just made it for me'.

'You two are up to something.

'Cuppa Billy?' I said.

'I'll chum you' he said. We slunk out of the living room.

We put our warm jackets and gloves on, walked back over to the park slowly, either to give him time to take his last breath or to give ourselves more time to come up with a plan if he really had kicked it, it served us well. We'd agreed that if he was gone, we'd pretend that we were out looking for him as we'd seen him walking in this direction and were worried that the poor old fellow had wandered out on such a cold night without a coat. As we got to the bridge at St Mark's, our pace slowed, it was like going into a room for an exam, there were no winners. At least in my case, all exams I'd ever done just proved to me how stupid I was. We walked over with great trepidation to where we'd last seen him and really were starting to panic as we could see something lying in the dark where he'd lain. He was moving in a strange way, unlike a human being. The hairs on the back of my neck stood on end, It was like an animal had possessed him. I didn't know whether to run towards or away from him. Just as we were closing in, he jumped at us on all fours, we both shit ourselves and fell over onto our Backs. I had automatically put my arms over my eyes, and when I removed them, a big black dog appeared above us, it had something in its mouth, looked like the auld man's polo neck. We Laughed involuntarily for a wee while more at the relief and a bit in sympathy with the poor dog, he had that dandruff ridden jumper in his mouth.

This of course only lasted until we realised that he was gone, nowhere to be seen, but the dog had his jumper so what the hell had happened?

We looked around the wider area, by this time the moon was bright and allowed us to see a lot more than before. The snow had melted under him, we saw clearly the shape of a person and lots of footprints where he'd stumbled and fought to get up. The footprints led to the bridge and melted to nothing, on the warm wooden slats that formed the walkway.

'Well at least he's still alive and able to walk' I said. Sixty per cent relieved.

'Billy closed his eyes and breathed a huge sigh.

'Where can he be?'

'No idea,' I said.

We spent a bit of time looking around, trying to figure out where he'd go without money and only dressed in a T-shirt and dirty breeks. After a bit more searching, we headed home.

Back at the house, I could see through the kitchen window that the auld man was washing the sweat from his forehead,

he was using the sponge for the dishes and drying himself
with a tea towel.

We walked in.

'How do you fancy coming tae Livingston wi me?'

'There was no mention of what had gone on earlier like he
had no idea.

'Livingston?' I said.

'Why?'

'I'm gonnae see that boy that was abducted by the aliens'.

'It's almost morning' I said.

'How can you go and talk to someone at this time, and you're
drunk'.

'I'm goin,' he said.

Billy and I sat on the stools in the kitchen, had some tea and
toast, knew that we'd got incredibly lucky.

'Phew!' I said, half smiling at him.

His raised eyebrows and shake of the head told me he was
more relieved than me.

As we sat there silently, the auld man had wandered away into
his room. He emerged with some warmer clothes on and his
donkey jacket over his shoulder. He popped his head into the
kitchen.

'Well?'

'Well, what?' I said.

'Are you coming?'

'Get lost, you're pissed, if you get into that heap of a car and
try to drive it in the state you're in, you'll get lifted.

He turned around, headed for the front door. Billy and I went
onto the balcony and looked on as he climbed into his car and
drove off.

Within the hour he was back in Edinburgh, Gayfield Square
Police Station to be specific.

In Livingston, some drunk had been pestering Mr Robert

'Bob' Taylor, so much so that he'd ended up calling the Police. Just before they arrived, the inebriated man had fled the scene in a blue Robin Reliant, and in his desperation to get away he'd wrapped the bloody fibreglass excuse of a car around a lamp post.

SILENCE

ONE OF THE THINGS I loved to do was lie in my kip on a
Sunday morning when the night before had passed without
incident; no screaming, shouting drunkenness from the old
man. This was a rare event, and so I enjoyed it all the more. I'd
lie there just taking in the peace and tranquillity. Tigger would
be lying, purring on my bed somewhere and I'd be under the
covers lapping up the warmth and silence. The window was
always slightly open as the condensation on the terribly inept
windows in the house would pool on the window sill and drip
onto the floor like an Alfred Hitchcock leaky tap, opening
them stopped It. I'd listen to the sound of a distant motorbike
or car and imagine that I was driving, heading to somewhere
remote, beautiful and carefree. The sound gave me a sense
of freedom and I'd listen to the engine with all of my might
until it faded and echoed away into the distance. As it did I'd
hook my imagination onto the back of the vehicle, wherever
it was going, and travel in my mind to the Highlands or Loch
Lomond, even the Broon's But n Ben. It was a magical feeling.
In truth, I'd never been further north than Kinross. I longed
to escape somewhere, I had no idea where but the thought of
all that fresh air and peace sounded like heaven to me. I guess
I'd spent my whole life surrounded by people, lots of them and
the thought of going somewhere, where you could get time to
think and breathe really appealed to me. Sadly the mechanics
of achieving it were well out of my reach. I used to draw and
paint pictures for the kids, but the truth was, I was painting
them for me.
I'd create a hilltop forest or a tranquil river meandering into
an Autumn sunset, as strange as it seems I was there, right
in the image. I remember one of the first books I ever read
was Thomas Hardy's The Mayor of Casterbridge. I was ten or

eleven at the time and had gone through my Mum's collection of Reader's Digest hardbacks. Initially, I thought they were dull, old people's boring stories but as soon as I had read the first chapter of that book I was hooked. The day before, I'd gone up to Lawson's with my Mum. Lawson's was the only place that would give her any kind of credit to buy us kids school clothes, beds or any other necessary equipment. I'm sure she was paying ten times the value for the stuff, but at least it was her choice, not like the previous help we were getting from the church, the St. Vincent De Paul's charitable foundation.

We'd get a notification that there was a piece of clothing or some new shoes available and one of us would go to the church and try the items on, whoever they fitted would be the recipient. It was the Cinderella's sister scenario, three of us would try a pair of shoes on and try to convince Mum that they fit correctly even though our toes were squashed into the front. I knew Mum was embarrassed by this and hated going, but she had no choice as there was absolutely no money to be had.

We'd walked into Lawson's, and the first thing that hit me was a series of paintings of the countryside. I'd never seen anything so beautiful in my life. I stood and stared at them in absolute awe. Taking in every detail, wondering how anyone could capture the beauty so realistically. I literally could not take my eyes off them. The images of the leafless sycamore trees and the dusty pink sunset fading into a golden horizon. A winding path lightly dusted with the first snow of the winter stuck with me as if a veil had been lifted from my eyes. My Mum tried to get my attention, but I was gone. We had to leave the store at closing time, and despite me trying to get Mum to hold on for just another minute so that I could look into the windows, the mechanical metal shutters closed ensuring I'd see nothing else that night.

As I read the first chapter of The Mayor of Casterbridge, the images I'd witnessed the previous day came into my head, and I could picture Michael Henchard, his young wife and their baby walking into the dusty distance, the book had real warmth about it and made me feel very cosy, despite the hardships they were going through. No book had ever had this effect on me, it was magical. A slice of warm buttered toast and a big mug of steaming hot, sugary tea made my life complete. The thought that my mates might find out what I was reading registered with me but only fleetingly. I could just imagine their taunts about me being a poof or a queer and to be honest, it didn't bother me, I think that was my first ever step into a world of culture and the appreciation of art.

The guy from Lawson's who collected the money from Mum on the never never was a decent enough guy. His collection day was Friday afternoon, sometimes when cash was too tight or non-existent, the older kids would be out like a mob of meerkats, taking surveillance positions all over the Court as there were several ways into (and out of) the place. We'd spot him parking his car in East Claremont Street to try to catch us out. And we'd head back to the house warning everyone that he was on his way making sure that the curtains were shut, the small kids were kept in the back room with a hand or two over their mouths to ensure silence for a few minutes. The guy must have known we were in as we never went anywhere. There would be three rapid knocks with about a minute between them, this would be followed by another two rapid knocks. The letterbox would then be raised, and a beady eye would scan as much of the internal estate as it could muster for any sign of life; sound or movement. Five to six minutes later and the sentinels upstairs would shout that he was back in his car. Thankfully when he'd gone Mum breathed a sigh of relief at another week's clemency. Another seven days to find the money from somewhere.

What a tough life of pressure she had, and not one of us kids appreciated that. I've no idea what kind of credit limit Mum was given, but our needs ensured that it was going to take decades to repay, kids grow, and need clothes and shoes and furniture. It was a blessing that Lawson's didn't sell food.

Supersonic

JOHN, MYSELF AND THE rest of our band, The Audette Syndrome, would meet at The Regent Bar up at Abbeyhill on a Tuesday night. We'd moved from the caves at Niddry Street to a more charming spot. The caves were incredibly eerie, and there was something mysterious about them that somehow helped with the mood of the music. The downside was that they were an old cave system under the bridge's network. They had dampness and fungus that Gollum would be delighted with. If I remember rightly, Chris and Malcolm never liked to be the first into the practice rooms as there were definitely some spooky noises. Anyway, the new digs were much better and had a better, more distinguished history. The old derelict Regent Cinema. It was opened in March 1928, and it closed on 2nd May 1970 with its final film being 'Carry On Again Doctor,' it was used as an occasional Fringe theatre and also a live rock concert venue for a while, but this proved to be unsuccessful, and the building was standing derelict in 1984. It was subsequently demolished.

One of the other bands we used to gig with, Burlesque, had moved there and offered us space at the place, it was great, you could play as loud as you wanted with no interference from anyone. The digs were pretty cheap, and it had this magnificent, ethereal atmosphere. One of my old school mates, Stevie Ross, had started the band Burlesque. I didn't even know he was into music as we'd never mentioned it during school at all. Stevie had also been a founder member of the punk band, The Exploited. We hadn't seen each other since leaving school, yet here we were sharing a practice room.

It was a great time to be experimenting musically. The Audette

Syndrome was a more relaxed Electro-pop band where most of the songs were about finding love, lack of love, lost love or prisons in Istanbul. I wrote most of the material but not all of it. Much of what I wrote was put down on paper in the wee small hours, one, two or three in the morning. There was a lot of deep thinking done then and even looking back now, I'm surprised at how good the lyrics are. I must have been more aware of words that I thought I was. I would then use the lyrics, go up to my bedroom and plug my headphones into my Korg - Multi-Preset synthesiser and try to make it all work. I loved that time of my life. There was so much going on that I wanted to cram as much as I could into this energetic and inspirational period. I'd also started college and running. Despite this confidence, I had absolutely no self-worth, I'd come home from nights out, mostly on my own, walk along Princes Street, and head back home to Claremont Court, sad and dejected. I wanted to find the perfect woman to share with me all the excitement of what was going on in my head. I remember one night, I got pretty drunk, but not so bad that I didn't know what was going on. I met this lovely young woman, and we snogged for a bit then headed down to her flat on Leith Walk. She was getting tired, so we sat on the steps of a chippy for a few minutes. We discussed our work, I was on the way to becoming a pop star. She told me she was a vet nurse.

For one beautiful minute, I hoped and craved that she had a German accent. The thought of her giving her lovely breasts to a lot of babies filled me with hope. Surely she'd have no problem whipping them out for me? Unfortunately, as she drolled on, her accent was more Muirhouse than Munich. I was caught in my thoughts when I heard her say something; 'You remind me of someone famous,' she said.

I trawled through a list, Clint Eastwood, Tom Cruise, Harrison Ford. To no avail.

'No, he's not a film star, he's a TV star'.

I couldn't think of anyone.

'Got it' she said.

I sat there ready to bask in the adulation.

'Supersonic Sid,' she said.

'Who the hell is Supersonic Sid?'

'The skinny one from Little and Large.'

'What, that wee runt is called Supersonic? I haven't heard that one. You actually think I look like that skinny little twerp?' I said. Horrified.

'Yeah, a bit, if you put glasses on and were a bit balder you could be his brother'.

I was devastated. My confidence was low enough, but this was a real kick in the nads. I'd now have even less chance of finding a decent bird if they all thought I looked like a speccy little twat.

I walked away from her.

'Where are you going she said'.

'Well if I look like Supersonic Sid we can't go out together'.

'Why not?' She said, looking confused.

'Because you look like Eddie Large the fat one and it's not the kind of double act I want to be part of,' I said.

'You cheeky bastard' She shouted and threw her shoe at me, missed by a mile.

I walked down McDonald Road feeling a wee bit better about myself after that. But not much. I looked at my watch, it was that time of day when it's both late and early. The realisation that it was another fruitless night made me feel incredibly tired, as I trudged down that long street, it started to rain, heavier and heavier, soaking me in my tee-shirt and blue suede shoes. When I got to the front door, I swore that this would be the last time I went out as every time I came home I felt like the fisherman who returned with nothing but an empty net and a lot of fish laughing and pointing at him from the big blue sea.

I was getting a lot of song-writing done, mostly sad stuff, angst at not being able to get a burd and all the time hoping that by the time true love came along I'd know how to appreciate it.

The band used to sit in a couple of pubs before and after practice. When we were in the haunted caves of Niddry Street, we'd meet up in Bannerman's Bar, trying to get the heat back into our frozen, mould-smelling bodies. The buzz was brilliant, especially if there was a gig coming up. Then when we moved to the haunted Regent Cinema we'd meet in the Regent Bar, again the atmosphere was brilliant, always really conducive to our creative thinking.

Every now and then, Brian Searle, one of the guys we'd grown up with would pop his head around the pub door, ignore all of us and speak only to John.

He'd stand there with an imaginary guitar and start playing imaginary chords he'd say something like.

'Am, E, C, D, F, G, Am'

This had been going on for a few years, John was meant to guess what song Brian was playing on his invisible guitar.

'Yesterday, the Beatles,' John would say

'Nope, that's F, Em7, A7, Dm, Dm/C try again sucker'.

'All right now - Free?'

'Nope. Stairway to heaven,' and with that, he'd walk back out of the pub and go to wherever he was going.

It was the weirdest thing. Brian was a lovely guy, but some of the things he did were mental. On the other hand, his wee brother Norrie was at the opposite end of the brain spectrum. I reckoned that what had happened was that when Brian was born, a good portion of his grey matter was left behind somehow and Norrie picked this up on his way out of the birth canal giving him the super-intelligence he now possessed. The bonds between all of the friends and aspects of my life were pretty close, music, running, football, BB's, work. There were always links between everything. It felt like such a good solid base to have, and I enjoyed dipping in and out of the different aspects when it suited me. Norrie and I grew pretty close but mostly to do with the fact that we were the defenders in our football team, he was right back, a tough wee guy who never shirked a tackle no matter what size the opposition was. I, on the other hand, tried to avoid tough tackles as I always got injured, my legs were about up to Norrie's chin, and I had to use my wits and speed rather than toughness to win tackles. We did a great job though, very few people scored against us when Norrie and I were playing together.

I hadn't seen Norrie for many years, decades in fact. It was only recently that I got an email from him out of the blue. He was now living in Uganda. We managed to meet up in central Edinburgh with a few of the old 46 BB ex-members. I remembered the first time Norrie and I were old enough to go to the pub at BB camp in Lilliesleaf, a wee village in the Scottish Borders. Norrie had got absolutely steamboats. He could hardly stand never mind walk the half-mile through the village and over the football field and river, then up the hill to camp. No chance. Harry and I had only had a few beers and were keeping a check on Norrie as he stumbled his way in the right direction. It was hilarious. He took forever, but it was very amusing.

'You know we'll have no chance of getting him over the fence at the river' Harry said to me.

'Why not?' I said

'He weighs a ton. He's solid'.

Harry and Norrie had grown up within a hundred yards of each other.

'I tried to lift him up to his window a few weeks ago because he'd forgotten his keys. There was no chance, I could hardly lift one of his legs'.

'Shit, what will we do then I said. He can't sleep in the field'.

'Or can he?' Harry said. 'I have an idea'.

We went over to the sports pavilion in the football field and dug out a bit of rope.

'If we tie his leg to the rope and attach the other end to the goal post, he'll not be able to go anywhere'.

'Brilliant idea' I said.

A while later Norrie appeared in the distance at the football filed gate, as soon as he'd crossed the little stream he collapsed onto his knees. He began to crawl towards the river.

Harry and I walked over to him, and he had not even the slightest clue that we were there. He was out of it.

We waited until he got pretty close to the goalpost and then we sprung into action. I grabbed his ankle and Harry tied the rope. Norrie's face was a picture, it was as if he couldn't see us and some sort of invisible being was assaulting him. We creased ourselves laughing. Eventually, we got the rope secured to his ankle and to the post. Norrie started to crawl again, and the rope tether was forcing him to crawl in a circular motion. It was absolutely hilarious. We could hardly stand for laughing.

'Think he's secure enough?' I said.

'Yeah, I think so, he's going nowhere fast' Harry said.

We left Norrie like a wee sheep crawling about the filed and headed off to camp.

The next morning there was a bit of a commotion in camp.

'Has anyone seen Norman Searle,' Haggie, the BB Captain was shouting.

Harry and I looked at each other and said nothing, as we didn't want to get Norrie in trouble as getting legless at camp, was a big no-no.

We sprinted down to the field, and there was Norrie, wrapped around the goalpost. Still unconscious. As we approached him, we could see that one of his shoes was missing and his foot had swollen pretty badly.

'Shit, I didn't expect that to happen,' I said.

Harry bent down and undid the knot which had, by this time completely blocked any blood from getting to Norrie's foot. It was blue.

'Shit' Harry said. He rubbed the foot to get the circulation going, and as he was doing this, Norrie woke up.

'What the fuck's going on here then?' He said. Immediately throwing up purple Pernod and blackcurrant vomit.

'It's OK pal' Harry said.

'You must have got yourself caught on a rope last night'.

He looked at me and right there we'd made a silent agreement that was precisely what had happened should anyone ask.

We got him up on his feet and managed to get him over the river and back to camp. He kept complaining about his dead foot. Both of us realised then what a stupid thing we'd done. Thankfully Norrie was fine later on, no damage done except that he'd lost his wallet and car keys.

Kisses For Me 1976

MY VIRGINITY WAS STILL well intact at this point, I tried
to pre-load my karma account by doing good deeds; praying
every night for good things to happen to people, trying to
be kind to strangers and animals, promising God I'd become
a missionary in a foreign land if he could arrange a shag
for me and I still hadn't seen any sign of payback. I figured
that if karma did exist and I did all of this good stuff, surely
some female in this big, bold world would be interested in
rewarding me with a wee shot in her bed, making me her
undercover lover. I was terrified of the thought but intrigued
and keen to know what it was going to feel like. I was going
out more, to discos and pubs, admittedly I thought, that stood
me in good stead to at least meet a potential girlfriend. I mean
I didn't think I was plug but then again knew I wasn't exactly
a catch. I was quick on the one-liners and reasonably good
company, but as soon as I got the opportunity to be alone with
a girl, I reverted into a shy wee boy who kept his hands firmly
in his pockets. One Friday night at Tiffany's Disco, just a few
days after I'd been to my first concert to see Ultravox perform
live there I was at the bar with Alex when my wee sister Susan
walked in with a load of pals from her work, Crawford's
Bakery. I'd seen a lot of them when I'd popped down to pick
up some out-of-date black bun and shortbread when she
worked in Elbe Street down in Leith. None of them looked
that attractive but to be honest, they were all wearing white
overalls, and hairnets and the only person I'd ever known that
could be turned on by this kind of attire was Jimmy's uncle,
Guppy.
As I stood at the bar, my jaw must have dropped about six
inches as I saw these workmates transformed into beautiful,
sexy young sirens. Susan waved at me as they headed over to

the table they'd booked that night. I caught the tallest one of
her group look over at me then whisper something to Susan.
Susan looked over to me and gave me a thumbs up.

As the night went on, I kept looking over at this vision in
a floral summer dress. Her brown hair was long and styled
like a catalogue model, she had long eyelashes and lips that
I wanted to be involved with. She looked stunning. After a
beer or two more, I managed to get Susan aside to get some
information.

'Yeah, Crystal has just won the Scottish leg of Miss Crawford's'
she said.

'She really likes you, Jim'.

She rubbed my arm and said I was 'in there'.

Quite where I was 'in' I wasn't sure, as I'd never been 'in'
anything other than awkward situations as far as females were
concerned. I Remembered 'bagging off' with Jackie Davidson
at a party we had in our house. I think it was the only party
we ever had that included girls in the place.

I remember it was a party to celebrate and watch the final
of the Eurovision Song Contest. We were all dancing to
the songs (I admit I snogged Jackie while dancing to the
Brotherhood of Man's 'Kisses for me'). I'd grown up with
Jackie, and she was always really sporty. She could run almost
as fast as me, and she could swing a rounders bat like a boy.
I don't think I'd ever really fancied her until that night when
I noticed she had grown some boobs, it might have just been
a stuffed bra, but it did the trick. After that night we never
really took it anywhere, it must have only been a brief bit of
'hormonal dovetailing' on both our parts.

It was about that time when singer Tina Charles had her
one-hit-wonder out 'I Love to Love (but my baby just loves
to dance)'. That song had me so confused as an angst-filled
teenager. There she was, wee Tina. Standing at the side of the
dance-floor gagging on the boaby and her boyfriend was like,

'Nah, sorry doll, ah ken ye love the boaby an that but ah just luv tae dance, ah'm just gonnae stand over here an dance'.
I often thought about ringing her up to let her know I was free, but I didn't have a phone, or more for that matter, her phone number. Ach well.

Towards the end of the night at Tiffany's, Susan came over to our table where Alex was snogging some blonde lass.
'Well Crystal wants to go on a date with you' she said.
'Now?' I said, hoping to start this thing right away.
'No, we're off to a house party, but she's given me this'.
She handed me a bit of paper with a phone number with two kisses and a few words.

'Call me Monday after seven'.

I looked over to her, and she bowed her head, smiling.
Something stirred in my nether regions.

I couldn't wait until Monday evening.
I fought the urge to call her on Sunday but decided I may jeopardise everything if I did and decided to leave it until the morrow. The hours dragged by and eventually, the hour arrived. I got to the phone box at Powderhall, just up from Redbraes Bakery.
Shit. There was somebody in it, and what made it worse was that they were smoking and talking smoke into the receiver.
I looked at my watch and contemplated running to the next phone box which was at Rodney Street a good half-mile away.
I reckoned I could run it in four or five minutes with my jeans and shoes on but then thought if I have to phone to meet up with her tonight, I'd be all sweaty and desperate looking. In the end, I decided to hold out and wait for smoky lover boy to finish. It wasn't too bad, six or seven minutes. He opened the

door, stubbed his fag end on the floor and walked out. It was stinking. I waved the heavy door open and shut a dozen times to get rid of the smoke-filled booth. I then wiped the receiver with my sleeve, it came away with a horrible brown stain. But this was the only way we had to communicate with each other, so I had to get on with it despite the acrid stink.

I was as nervous as I'd ever been. I rang three times, pulling out at the last number on the previous two until I'd decided how I was going to play it.
Cool. I hoped.

I could hear it ring at the other end, and ring again, and again. 'Shit' I thought, maybe she's sobered up and realised I'm not as attractive as I appeared to be in the dimness of the Friday night light. As I was fretting...
'Hello?'
'My heart thumped.
BANG!
Almost knocked me off my stride.
'Crystal?' I said It's Jim'
I didn't want to give her a chance to knock me back right away.
'Hi, Jim. How are you?' She said. I imagined and hoped she was smiling from ear to ear. She sounded lovely, adorable, sweet voice. I then thought. What the hell is she doing working in a bloody bakery?
'I'm great' I said.
'How are you?'
'All the better for hearing from you' she said.
I can tell you without a doubt, there was SEX in her voice. Something below the phone cable was showing an immediate interest. I'd never had a girl speak to me and get the wee felly excited, especially over the phone. I was now VERY

interested.

'Would you like to meet up for a drink or something' I said. Keen to get close to her and hopefully get this virginal monkey off my back.

'I'm not sure about a drink, but *'something'* sounds good' She said.

Jeezus, I think my red Y-fronts with white piping got their first rip in them at that moment. I loved those pants. They suited me right down to the ground, which was where I hoped they'd be soon. I've no idea where they came from, perhaps Uncle Richard's magical black bin bag of other people's discarded clothing that he'd deliver to the house every six months or so. I'd been wearing them for a good year or two now, washing them intermittently. They fitted so snugly around my teenage tackle that we became literally inseparable.

'When?' I blurted.

'How about Friday?'

'Tiffany's?'

'No, let's go somewhere a bit more private. How about coming to my house, there'll be nobody in?'

I was getting close to the old chicken soup on the red pants by this time but managed to contain myself.

'Sounds perfect' I said.

I think the pitch of my voice raised an octave or two.

'What time?'

'Seven?'

'Will I bring anything.'

'Only yourself, I'm not greedy' She said.

That week flew past like a Benny Hill chase. Nothing mattered to me except getting to her door. I told the guys at Job Creation about it and was given some incredible advice on how to handle women's tits. I'd no idea why they said 'women's tits' were there other tits I was unaware of? Pigs tits?

Cat's tits? How to bring women to orgasm, how to perform cunnilingus, everything I never wanted to know. It all meant nothing to me. I was only intent on trying to get my hand up her blouse and get a 'flour-free' feel. First base was Everest for me. Anything else could wait. In fact, anything else scared the living shit out of me. I'd only recently developed enough pubes to cover the small groin area so that I'd at least, pass as male should some woman ever get her hand down there, the thought of letting a fully grown woman explore me excited me but more to the point, the notion that I'd remove my red pants and let her see what was there filled me with dread. Rejection was not something I handled well. I could picture the scene:

The statuesque blonde stands statue-still for a minute. She then pulls the little floral dress over her head in a single practised move (as if she would be wearing the same dress as last Friday in her house), to reveal the body of an Amazonian Princess, big bulging, pert eager breasts and a body that has been cut from one of Leonardo da Vinci's forbidden Sex Statues. Fully laden with suspenders, bright red lipstick and so in charge of the situation that it's not true.

She walks over to me, I'm cowering in the corner with my White Granddad shirt and maroon tank top complete with my enamelled Orchestral Manoeuvres in the Dark badge, desperately trying to remove the Naytex jeans that Mum's just bought me from a market stall in Great Junction Street. They're too tight to get over the blue pods that John threw in the bin last week, which I retrieved. I'm struggling frantically, can't wait to get these damned clothes off.

I watch her walk towards me in serious, considered, metronomic strides. Looking straight at me, licking her glorious glossy lips with her silken tongue. As she approaches me, a slow, syrupy stain appears on the front of my red pants. I look down in horror not sure what kind of liquid it is. She stops, looks at me. There's not enough liquid to indicate I'd pissed myself. The stain spreads only a little bit now. I realise I've orgasmed for the first time in front of a real woman.

She creases her brow angrily, looks at me, shakes her head and points to the door.

I turned up at a lovely house on the side of Arthur's Seat. Again, I'd hung about, checking and double-checking the address just to make sure I was at the right house. Eventually, I looked in the window and saw that there was a coffee table with some drinks and snacks on it. I knocked gently on the door. Nothing.

I then knocked a little harder. I heard someone rushing down the stairs. My heart was banging like a drum, and my whole body was shaking in anticipation and dread at this point. I had bought her a bunch of flowers from the garage at Meadowbank which were now in danger of being shaken to stalks.

I heard the inner door being unlocked, then the front door. A woman with a heavy Aran sweater opened the door, she had long wiry hair and no makeup, and more to the point she had a fag in her hand.

'Jim?' She said.

The shaking stopped. I thought there had been some kind of horrendous mistake made. This was definitely NOT the girl I had seen last week. This was a very ordinary not in the least attractive girl. Where had my Amazonian beauty gone? I really did think there was a mistake, did she have a sister?

'Come in' she said.

'Make yourself at home. I'll just finish this', she said nodding down to the fag (held 'army style' between thumb and forefinger).

I sat on the couch, not taking my jacket off. This was not how I envisaged the night. I'd thought I'd walk away in the morning floating on air and at last, able to converse with my pals and the guys at work about how great it was to be able to touch women without being arrested. I was now faced with 'how the hell do I get out of this joint without having to kiss this imposter.'

We small-talked the evening away eating some dinner she'd made, but despite my attempts to either find the spark that was there on Friday or the real Crystal (perhaps locked in a cupboard somewhere), there was nothing at all.

I agreed to go out with her another time, but it all petered out to nothing. I didn't want to let her down, so we met quite a few times, and I always dreaded the night's kiss as she did smoke quite a bit. One night she asked me to call her, and when I did, she told me it was over. I was weirdly distraught at this news, and I cried a bit. I think it was my rejection gland kicking in, making sure I still knew that it was in full working order.

I got over it pretty soon, and by now, I was used to meeting girls, mainly by having a few drinks and letting my humour cover the embarrassment. It must have been a few years later when I got talking to this punk woman from the East Coast, her name was Norma, she was a bit chunkier than the normal girls I'd make a beeline for, but there was something I liked about her. She had a sense of humour and liked pints of cider and blackcurrant rather than the usual wine or Malibu. We got a bit tipsy and snogged after dancing in one of the discos in the caves down the back streets of Edinburgh's old town. We agreed to meet, and the following week she turned up at our house just after tea. She was wearing a big leather studded jacket with the words 'Anarchy in the UK' written on the back in scrawled red paint. She worked in a woollen mill down in Leith and had come straight from work. Mum had made some mince and tatties, and I'd scoffed mine before she got to the house. As she came in, Mum spotted her heading upstairs with me. She shouted up,

'Does the lassie want some mince n tatties, Jimmy?'

I was a bit red-faced.

'Yeah that sounds good' she shouted back down.

We sat in the room, on the bed, I got up to put some records on while she sat with dinner on her lap, scooping it up with the spoon that mum had provided, it should really have been a knife and fork for guests, but I let it go.

'What kind of music do you like?' I said, hoping she'd be into OMD, Ultravox, Human League, Japan, Squeeze and all that other great 80's stuff.

'I like Paul Young'.

'Good' I said. 'So do I'.

I liked his album No Parlez, it had a load of great songs on it. But I was still hanging onto that ever-growing millstone around my drooping neck - I was still a virgin, almost twenty-four years old. That is to say, I think I was still a virgin. I'd been to bed with, no that's really pushing it. I'd been to a school bench with a girl in the borders one drunken night a few years ago but honestly, have no idea if I did it right. The coupling was never quite hooked up and synchronised like it should have been, I thought about the black and white photocopied drawings of 'coupling' I'd seen is sex education at school, and I felt I was only around sixty per cent there. If you compared it to the coupling of a submarine refuelling vessel, I'd definitely have lost some able seamen. But as far as everyone I spoke to was concerned, I'd nailed it that night.

'Screaming she was, couldn't get enough'.

And I wasn't lying. She was screaming because she couldn't get any.

Anyway, I'm talking about this because as Norma was finishing her last spoonful of mince n tatties, she said.

'I like SEX'.

She licked the spoon slowly and repeated her words.

Jeezuz man, I was like Frank Spencer. Shocked that she should come right out with it.

'Betty, where are you?' I thought to myself.

She could see my discomfort.

'Do you like SEX?' She said.

'Erm, I ehh'...

'I mean on the album. The track, it's called SEX,' she said.

'Ah, oh yeah, it's a bit strange' I said.

I knew fine well she was only saying this to heat things up, I could see she was actually hoping to nail this fine young specimen tonight, in my own bed.

'Come over here,' she said, putting the plate on top of the record player and tapping the side of the bed next to her.

I walked over and next thing I knew I was on my back on my bed with this quite heavy punk rocker on top of me. She smothered me with red lipstick and started to pull my kit off.

'Jeezuz,' I said, and jumped up, pulling my white granddad shirt and tank top back down, tucking them into my jeans. Frank Spencer had returned.

'What's wrong' she said, laughing at me.

Within thirty seconds I'd realised that I'd invited the Edinburgh Woollen Mill's resident nymphomaniac into my room without protection and I don't mean the rubber kind, although she probably wanted that. I imagined that with the weight of her massive boobs, she could easily pummel me through the floor and into the kitchen below via the bed should she get the chance.

'Come on, come over here, don't be shy' she said patting the bed again.

I had now become the hunted by an expert huntress. She wanted this innocent young prey, and it was cornered, no matriarch or siblings to defend it. She had the cross-hairs of her lust pointed at a direct kill and started to undress,

revealing her WOMD (womanhood of mass destruction).
This virginal monkey on my back was as dead as a Dodo as far
as she was concerned
'Don't do that' I said.
She ignored me and pulled her Dennis the Menace jumper off
over her head, throwing it onto the floor, revealing a massive
pair of breasts in a black bra.
'Christ, if she ever has a bairn, the wee thing ain't gonnae go
hungry, in fact she could have sextuplets and there'd still be
plenty on coo juice to go around' I thought.
I could feel the wee felly trying to get in on the act but shut
him down immediately by thinking about Nora Batty and
Maggie Thatcher having a naked wrestle or something to that
effect. It worked.
Undeterred, she continued and had now moved from the bed
towards the door, blocking my only escape route.
My heart was pounding like a baby gazelle facing a pride of
lions in the African savannah.
'Help' I thought. I want to lose my virginity but not this way.
I wanted to decide who and when to lose it to, not have it
stolen like a half-finished jar of pickled eggs from a chip shop
counter when the chipmeister wasn't looking.
I didn't want to shout on my mum as it would be the most
embarrassing thing I'd ever done and there were a few
candidates lined up for that title I can tell you.
She was about to undo the strap at the back and let loose
those giant mammary glands when to my absolute relief,
Mum knocked at the door.
'Jimmy, do you or the lassie want the last of the mince and
tatties? It's just that there's a wee bit left,' she said.
'Aye, that would be great mum' I said, diving for the door
knocking her out of the way and knocking her bra off in the
process. I so wanted to touch those beauties but somehow
knew deep down that if I did I'd regret it, I still got a good

eyeful though as I left the room.

When I returned a few minutes later, she'd put her kit back on and was heading out of the room. As she reached the top of the stairs, I stood there with two tiny plates of mince and tatties.

'Don't you want this before you go?' I said. Like a real sappy dipstick.

'Fuckin pussy,' she said and stomped away. She stopped and looked back at me. She was sneering.

'You'd rather have a fuckin plate o mince 'n' tatties than a good shag?' She shook her head and laughed at me as she headed downstairs and out of the front door. Before she closed it behind her, she came back in, headed to the living room, popped her head around the door.

'Thanks for the mince and tatties Mrs Divine' it was lovely.

'Yer welcome hen,' she said.

I was standing on the stairs waiting for her to leave. She stood for a second.

'Fuckin virgin,' she said.

The door banged shut, I stood there, on the stairs in my stocking soles and finished both small plates of mince n tatties. I went into the living room.

'She seemed nice,' Mum said, still hoping that one day, some woman or man. Anybody. Would take me away from the house and get me, her 'special laddie' out of there before I was thirty, forty, or fifty.

'No she was a bit......... Forward' I said, trying to think of the appropriate word that would not be too offensive to Mum.

'Oh, OK,' she said.

We left it at that.

That was a close call. Losing my virginity was something that

I was now intent on doing but in the right way. This sex thing could be a dangerous arena, if I were going to survive, I'd have to learn what the game was all about. That was now twice in pretty quick succession that the opportunity literally stood in front of me, and I was too scared to grasp the situation or anything else for that matter.

Recurring Dreams

OVER THE YEARS, PROBABLY ever since I was around twelve or thirteen, I've had recurring dreams about where I would take my last breath. A bizarre thing for a kid to dream about but they happened every couple of months.

There were three places;
1. Outside the Oyster Bar down at the shore in Leith.
2. At the steps of St Mary's Cathedral.
3. At the top of Leith Walk near the Playhouse Theatre.

I'd dream that I was floating around the general area and would suddenly be hauled down to one of these three spots by some invisible force. There I would be, all alone and in a completely silent situation. The next thing I knew is that some dark stuff, clouds or mist, something like that would begin to form around me, and I'd have to run away. Like many dreams, this proved impossible, my feet were moving, but I was going nowhere. In seconds the black fog would surround me, and I'd be floating somewhere on my journey to the next life. I knew the route I had to follow in the sky: head north, towards the forth bridges and keep going, moving higher and higher until I had been enveloped by a white cloud. From there I'd find myself heading to the Highlands and would continue until I fell into such a deep, dark sleep and into unconsciousness. I still have similar dreams, but for some reason, they've shifted from Edinburgh to somewhere in Spain. I find that I'm out shopping with Trish in an underground supermarket when all of a sudden there's this commotion and again I'm heading north over towards the forth bridges and up north. I've no idea what it all means.

The Flat

THE FLAT WE'D BOUGHT was on a quiet side street in Leith, only about a ten-minute walk from Claremont Court. 34 Dickson Street, just off Leith Walk and along Albert Street. It was a real, pleasant place, and the first time we walked in to see it, we both had the feeling that it would be for us. There was a big, bright window in the living room and the ceiling was so high that I couldn't get near it even if I jumped up. It was owned by a couple who were looking to move out of town quickly, and so after a wee rummage around the place, our hearts were set on it. This was incredibly exciting for us both as the thought of freedom for the first time dawned.

After we'd bought the flat Trish was not allowed to stay over until that bloody ring was on her finger. I was annoyed at this, but we had agreed with her mum, and a deal was a deal. We were able though, to spend time getting stuff for the place like a bed, carpets, furniture and all the standard stuff that first time buyers require. It felt great. Planning a future, intending to find out who we were as a couple as most of our time was spent with other people or at other people's places. Before any of that was concluded, I had my stag weekend to look forward to. I was so nervous about this, I'd heard all of the stories about what happens to the stag. My brother John was arranging it so I knew that he'd be looking to ensure that no real damage occurred to me. But I knew 'something' would happen. Trish was staying in the flat that night as she'd banned me from staying there as we'd just got a new cream carpet and the last thing she wanted was for me to come home steaming and throw up all over it. Kirk had asked his mum Jo if Tom and I could stay at theirs after the stag night and she was always a real sport.

'Sure, you can all come home and throw up on my carpets,

they're washable,' she said.

So that was it. I only had the event itself to get over and done with. Tom, John and Kirk had arranged for the stag party to take place in a relatively upmarket pub called Jules, just next to Calton Hill. They'd threatened to get me drunk and stake me out face-down in front of the big monument. As Calton Hill was one of the main meeting places for Gay men in those days, I was worried. But I also knew John would only let it go so far, and that's what worried me most. I wasn't sure how far was too far, and it would unquestionably be at my expense. I trusted him enough to go ahead with the party. As it turned out they'd arranged a stripper for me. I'd downed about four Southern Comforts within half an hour as I wanted to be oblivious as quickly as possible. I'd never had a Southern Comfort in my life, but for some reason, I thought that drink would do the trick.

The stripper music started to play on the music system, and I braced myself. I'd seen a few strippers in my time, and most of them were decades past their prime, rougher than the hangover you'd need to get, to make them look half decent but as it turned out I had nothing to worry about. In fact, I was really pleased to see what I was seeing. This petite little black girl appeared through some clouds of dry ice, she was gorgeous. I could not believe my luck. As she started to undress, the wolf whistles went up. She then got me stripped to my underpants, thankfully I'd put decent ones on. She got me to lie down and then sat on top of me and produced a can of spray cream. I love cream and half-naked girls, I had to work really hard to ensure that my pleasure wasn't obvious. The whole thing was delicious. I could see the jealousy in everyone's eyes. She really went to town on me without actuals consummating the event. I was half hoping, after all, I wasn't married yet? The whole thing could only have lasted ten or fifteen minutes. When you expect something loathsome is

going to happen and it turns out like this, life really does feel great. She headed off to a round of applause and a few tips while we got on with the task in hand, getting drunk. The only things I remember from that night, apart from the stripper were Kirk and I on our knees being sick in Jules toilets.
'As we knelt there waiting for the next bout of bile to arrive all I could say was 'This is crap isn't it Kirk?'
He was about to acknowledge but threw up instead. Very soon after that, it was time to head to Kirk's house at Gilmerton, a good three or four miles from Jules. Five of us got into a taxi, and as soon as he'd moved off, I jumped out and was sick all over the road. They drove off, leaving me on my hands and knees, the bastards were waving to me as they headed up the North bridge. I was too out of it to be annoyed and did what I always did when I had a long walk ahead of me. I buttoned my thin jacket up, got my head down and ploughed onto Gilmerton, one unsteady step at a time. I've no idea how long it took me to walk there, but by the time I arrived, I felt a bit better, although absolutely shattered. I knocked on the door, and Jo answered.

'Come in Jim, I can't believe those sods left you on your own. She gave me a hug and said, come and be sick on my carpets, you're sleeping with Tom tonight. I was not bothered about anything but getting my head on a pillow. Tom was lying next to the wall under the covers, and Kirk was on the opposite side of the room in another bed. As I lay there, Tom was saying things like:' Greasy sausages, fried bread, streaky bacon,' his aim was to get me to throw up again, it worked, I sprung out of bed and headed to the bathroom where I threw up in the bath, Tom had also made Kirk sick again, and eventually, even he joined us. All three of us throwing up in the bathroom. Jo stood there, shaking her head and laughing at us.

The wedding took place on the 29th April 1988 in St Nicholas Church in Dalkeith. I was so impressed with the fact that the back part of the building had been ransacked and burned down by Oliver Cromwell. I can't remember too much about the ceremony, but Trish looked terrific. I really had no idea how I'd managed to get such a beautiful young woman to agree to this. Between you and I, I got that damn monkey off my back with a little help from this young redhead well before we walked down the aisle.

There was no question. This was the happiest I'd ever been. We both enjoyed our jobs, our training was going well and to make it even better, Trish was in the UK and Scotland elite athletic squads. My athletic career was not hitting the same heights as hers. I just couldn't figure out why I was running the same kind of times over 800m, no matter how hard I tried, I was not improving. I was working all sorts of hours, and I reckon with retrospect that was the thing that held me back. Marr Associates hours were crazy at times, although every other ad agency was precisely the same. Working 20 hours a day was not as unusual as you may think. I loved the buzz of burning the late-night oil when it was a fascinating client we were pitching for. It's incredible how creative you can become as the deadline creeps nearer and nearer. It would always be a last gasp sprint to the finish line, and always, about an hour or two before Colin Marr was off to present the work, we'd be scrambling to print and mount the work on boards. There was a real energy about the place, we became one of the most successful ad agencies in the UK even though we were only a tiny outfit compared with some of the big players in Scotland and London.

The Advertising scene had a real rivalry and competitive edge to it, and I think this is what helped the UK produce the best ads in the world. We had a ton of them, and I was so chuffed

Thunder At One AM

to eventually win many awards for my creativity.

Trish had moved from the Royal Bank of Scotland to Standard Life, a completely different role, but she was really enjoying the job.

We were still training six days a week. It was a tough time physically as we'd leave for work at 8am and not return to the house until at least twelve hours later. We always took our training gear to work as, in the past, we'd attempted to go home for half an hour before going to Meadowbank. This was not a good idea. As soon as we sat down on our lovely cosy sofa with a cup of tea and a biscuit after a hard day's work, the couch developed a velcro-like grip on the backside. The effort of getting up and getting our training kit on, then heading out on a cold, dark, miserable night to put ourselves through a tortuous training session seemed like stupidity. It happened a few times, but after one too many times we agreed on the training kit to work rule. I'd say those were the best days of our lives but only from the point of view that we were both doing what we wanted and being pretty successful at it. The aim for Trish was always to be part of a Commonwealth or Olympic team, and there is no doubt she had all the necessary qualifications, but like all athletes, she needed the break. We were both training really hard and were always competitive with each other. We stayed on the top floor of the flat in Dixon street. Sometimes we'd race up the stairs, race down the stairs it was crazy but bonded us very closely. One time I suggested to Trish that I reckoned I could do a thousand squats, a simple act of bending your knees down to a sitting position and standing up straight again. She thought she could do a thousand and one.

We started, you were allowed to hold onto the back of a chair just to ensure you didn't hurt your back. After three or four hundred, I was really feeling it. We were both sweating buckets but determined to go on. On and on we went eventually losing count it was now down to the last one standing. I'm not sure how it ended, but what I do remember is both of us wakening up in the morning and hardly being able to move. We just lay there pissing ourselves laughing at our stupidity. Getting down four flights of stairs for work was utterly exhausting. We had to tell porkies to our coach for the next couple of days as he would not have been pleased if he'd known the truth.

Most of the other residents in the stair were pensioners, all stuck in their ways. Every second Monday before work we'd get a knock on the door.

'Right Mr and Mrs Divine, it's your turn to wash the stair.' Some old lady who had nothing better to do would always hassle us even though we told her we'd do it when we had time. There were a few minor niggles with them, but after a while, we began to understand that this was all they had, routine. Quite sad really, we felt sorry for them. The only other non-pensioners were a couple of very overweight youngsters who lived directly below us. They were kind enough, but we took issue with them when we found out they left their two black Labrador dogs in the house the whole day, five days a week. The poor things were as heavy as their owners and spent the day howling for freedom.

We stayed in the flat for a couple of years but eventually had to get out of there and spread our wings. I'd only ever lived in the City and moving to somewhere bigger was very expensive unless you moved out of town.

Trish was brought up in Dalkeith, a small town about ten miles south of Edinburgh. I'd been there a couple of times to run cross-country races, as there were miles and miles of beautiful countryside to play with. When I'd first started going out with her and realised she lived in Dalkeith, I was rubbing my hands together. Not only was she a beautiful young woman, but it seemed she was from money. The reason

I thought this was that the only times I'd been to Dalkeith were for the cross -country races which were all held in the Eskbank area of the town. The houses here were magnificent edifices that reeked of good breeding, etiquette and loot, lots of it. I'll state quite clearly now that this is not the reason I fell for her. Thank god. As it turned out she was from the other end of Dalkeith, Shadepark no less. An adorable little group of council houses but a world away from where I hoped.

Ach well, my record with posh girls was not good anyway.

When I eventually got to meet her family, I was pretty nervous. She had a minuscule family circle compared to mine, but then again, so do the majority of humanity.

They were all fabulous. Her Nana's side of the family was known as the Dalkeith Mafia, not in the aggressive, bullying sense but the way they knew absolutely everyone and everything that was going on. My first introduction to them was the previous Christmas, I was nervous, I think it was the first time I'd met the parents and grandparents of any girlfriend. Tricia's Nana, Nancy, spoke about me as if I wasn't there.

'Doesn't he look like Seb Coe'.

'If only I could run like him?' I said, trying to break the ice.

'He runs the same event though,' Tricia's mum said.

'I wish I ran the same times'.

'Go on, sit down and tell us about yourself' Nancy said.

And on and on I went. Thankfully, they were all heading out to a Christmas party, so I didn't go on too long.

Trish and I were alone for the first time in her house. It felt extraordinary. Her dad was a TV engineer which meant he got to bring all the latest in TV technology home to test. They had a huge colour TV in a wooden cabinet; also two VHS Video recorders and the best part was, they were all hooked up to their Hi-Fi system. Trish stuck on a music video, and this was where we found out we had completely different musical tastes.

'AC/DC?' I said. 'What's that all about?'

'What's wrong with them?' She said. 'They were the first band I went to see live when I was twelve'.

'Nah, I'm just not into heavy metal,' I said.

She laughed at me.

'They're not heavy metal ya numpty, they're heavy rock'.

'There's no difference between them, Motorhead, Bon Jovi and all those other long-haired guitar bashers,' I said.

'I suppose you prefer some kind of new romantic stuff,' she said, indicating that she felt it was poncey.

'Actually, I prefer what we call electro-pop, OMD, Ultravox, Kraftwerk, Spandau Ballet etc.' I said. Feeling pretty superior. 'In fact, the first live gig I went to was Ultravox, the Vienna Tour, at Tiffany's, it was incredible'.

'We'll see, but if you ever come into the house wearing eye-liner and frilly shirts my dad will march you right out of Dalkeith.'

We spent the night drinking white wine and soda and dancing to the music, including AC/DC. I reckon from that moment we were a couple. It felt great.

I hoped that we could create the same kind of home that Trish had lived in all of her life. There was a real sense of solidity, warmth and happiness about it.

The first time we stayed the night with Tricia's mum and dad, just after we were married, was hilarious. Trish and I were lying in her old single bed about to fall asleep when the bed in her mum and dad's room started squeaking slowly, rhythmically.

'Oh my god!' Trish said, 'Do they think we can't hear through the thin walls?'

The squeaking got louder and louder, Trish covered her head

and ears with her pillow. 'How embarrassing' she said. 'And at their age! I'll never be able to face them in the morning'.
'If we do it in time with them, they'll never know we're doing it' I said jokingly. The squeaking went on for a few minutes more and eventually tailed away to a halt.
I could feel the heat coming from her face, it was hilarious.

The next morning I went downstairs for breakfast. Eric and Sandra were busying themselves with making a full Scottish, tea and toast for us all.
'Fancy a cuppa?' Eric said.
'Yeah, sure'.
'Did you sleep ok?' Sandra asked.
'Yeah brilliantly, the beds' a bit smaller than we're used to but cosy enough'. I said. Making sure I didn't give away the fact that I'd slept in it many times before when they were out of the house.
After a bit of small talk and shooting the breeze Trish slunk into the kitchen. All quiet and not sure where to look.
'Morning' said her mum and dad.
'Morning'. She replied sheepishly.
'Looks like your face is pretty red' Eric said.
Her face got even redder at this point.
'It's warm'. She lied.
'Are you sure?' Sandra said.
'Yeah, positive'.
'Are you sure? You didn't hear any noises from our bedroom last night, did you?' Sandra said, laughing.
'What are you two up to' Trish said, eyeing them suspiciously.
The two of them burst out laughing and pointing at her.
Sandra said. 'Your dad was bouncing on the end of the bed, and with each bounce, he was saying;

Just-
Watch-
Her-
Face-
In-
The-
Morning-
When-
She-
Comes-
Down-
To-
Breakfast-
It'll-
Be-
Absolutely-
Beetroot-
And-
She-
Won't-
Know-
Where-
To-
Look.

'You little shits'. Trish shouted at them, putting her hands to her face.
'You knew I'd react this way, I can't believe you'd do that to your own daughter'. She started laughing, her very red face sinking slowly into her hands. It was brilliant.

IRISH JIG

A MONTH OR TWO after moving into the flat, I decided that I should learn to drive. I looked around the different driving schools and instructors, got some ideas from pals who'd passed, and after comparing prices, I decided on the driving school called L - Ability. As I walked around the corner to Easter Road stadium, where I was meeting my new driving instructor. I'd wanted to meet there as the parking around in town was horrendous, I couldn't be bothered with trying to nervously navigate my way out of that congested city centre amongst the triple and quadruple parked cars.

As I walked past the Hibs shop, I spotted the car immediately. The driving school was called L - Ability and had a big red L in front of it, some wag had scribbled an 'i' after the L. it read LiABILTY.

It was pretty funny, but the fact that the instructor had left it there and not bothered to wash it off jarred a bit.

As I got to the car, I could see a wee guy inside fixing his hair in the mirror, smoothing it down, licking his palms and clapping his mop, like a cat after a good feed.

I opened the door and caught him unawares.

'You must be Jim,' he said.

'Yeah, spot on' I said, shaking his slightly damp hand.

I sat in the passenger seat, and he looked at me.

'Are you having a giraffe?' He said

'What do you mean?'

'Well you're obviously not the brightest tool in the picnic basket, you're the one that's learning to drive,' he unclipped his seatbelt and got out of the car, walked around to my side.

Jeez, I thought, this is a great start. I had half a mind to head off back home with his pissy attitude.

I decided to carry on as I'd never sat in front of a steering wheel before and I really had to learn to drive.

'Right mister' he said, clapping his hands a couple of times. 'La adventoor begineth'.

I had no idea what he was on about.

He gave me the basics of what I had to do to get the car started. It seemed like a lot to remember. After a bit of time, I turned the key, pressed the accelerator with my foot (I'd learned well so far), and we moved.

He went on about how good a driver he was and all of the different jobs he'd done over the years. It sounded like complete bullshit to me, but you have to give people a chance. 'Yeah I drove one of the cars at the Iranian hostage thingy in London, I was also in Rome when president Regan was shot.

'Were you a bodyguard,' I said, trying to take the piss and concentrate at the same time, the guy was about five foot two and wider than the river forth.

'Kind of' He lied.

'Back in the day I was a bit of a force, used to help out the SAS, a couple of jobs with the SEALS and shit like that.'

'Really? Was that up at the Zoo?'

'Fuuuuck offf,' he shouted, Gen up. I was cool, back in the day.' By this time I was convinced the boy was a crackpot, I'd only been in the car fifteen or twenty minutes, and already I was getting all his pent up pish talk. I'd also spotted he was wearing a wig from the second I got into the car, but I couldn't take the time to take a good look at it without being obvious. We drove for a good forty minutes and to be fair to the boy, he was pretty good at instructing me. I began to feel confident and even got up to thirty miles an hour at one point.

At the start of the lesson I was giving him one chance, but by the time I'd finished, he seemed OK.

We agreed to a dozen lessons and shook on it.

Weeks went by, and I was becoming a pretty decent driver, I could do most things expected of me, but after all of these weeks, I had never done an emergency stop. It was plain to me that if he asked me to stick the anchors on hard, his syrup would go flying into the windscreen. I desperately wanted this to happen, the devil in me pictured the scenario many times, and I creased with laughter when I thought of it.

By now, I was competent in every aspect of driving except for that one area. I pointed it out to him many times until one day he said the words.

'Emergency stops today'.

'Eh, are you sure?' I said.

'What changed your mind? Get some double-sided tape for the syrup?' I said, chuckling under my breath.

'What was that?' He said.

'Is this a double-sided tape?' I said, pointing to one of his Val Doonican cassettes.

'Of course it's a fuckin' double-sided tape, what planet have you been hiding under?'

'Sorry, just asking.' I said. Glad that I'd got away with it.

'So what were you saying/' I said.

'Well, to be honest, I never really thought you were ready for that emergency braking stage, but after last week I was convinced you had it nailed.

I sat there and thought to myself.

Emergency stops are one of the most obvious things on the planet We'd have to be on a road where I could get a bit of speed up, there could be no obstructions just in case I really did have to brake if somebody or something ran out. I'd also see the instructor's head spinning around like he was watching Wimbledon, making sure there was no danger, and finally he was going to hit the dashboard with his clipboard. I'd also figured that this guy would have to put his hands on the top of his napper to stop the syrup flying off.

'Right big man' he said, you are going to do three emergency stops today. You will not realise what's happening then suddenly I'll say STOP, STOP, and you'll hit the anchors like Mike Tyson.

'Cool' I said.

Then realised I'd no idea what he was on about.

'Mike Tyson?'

'Yeah' hit those anchors hard, bang, bang. Iron Mike'.

'Like this,' I said just touching my foot onto the brakes.

SCREECH!

His hand went straight onto the toupee.

'No! Fuck. What did I say? Wait until I say STOP and hit the dash'.

'OK, calm down' I said, 'Cool the beans.'

We drove around Restalrig, Lochend, Portobello and eventually onto the big wide road at Joppa.

'Right increase your speed' he said, looking around him in all directions he looked like his head was on a swivel joint.

'When I tap the dashboard with my clipboard I'll say STOP, STOP Is that clear?'

'Clear as Sellotape' I said.

He gave me a quick side-look. I wasn't sure if he'd made the glue-wig connection.

I got up to thirty-five, saw he was looking all around like a wingless pigeon in a cattery. He put his hand onto the top of his head and smacked the clipboard onto the dashboard.

'STOP, STOP.' He shouted.

Inside, I was in fits. It was the most obvious test I'd had in my life. We did this three times, but I was determined to catch him out on the last one just to prove to myself that this really was a syrup and not just an awful haircut. As we drove along to Portobello and towards home, I decided to put in an unscheduled emergency stop. I stomped my foot onto the brake, heard the tyres screech under me and felt the seatbelt tighten around my chest.

'What the Fuck?' He said as his clipboard and ginger wig went flying onto the dashboard hitting the windscreen.

'What the fuck did you do that for?'

'Sorry, I thought you said stop' I lied, pissing myself laughing.

'Right, oot the fucking car' He said. 'You did that deliberately'.

'Can I be honest?' I said.

Before he had a chance to say anything, I continued.

'That wee flap of hair at the back of your head that sticks out like a bit of cardboard was really niggling me, and I wanted to flip it with my finger to be sure that it was an Irish, but I was never going to do that so I thought I'd try it in a more subtle way. Surely you can see my point, I've nothing against bald guys, and I understand why you wear it. One of my mates told me that if you were a salesman in the '70s and you suffered from Male Pattern Baldness, you were booted out of your job. I have every sympath....'

'FUCK OFF.' He screamed. 'Oot'.

'But it's miles to the house,' I complained.

'Tough, if you're such a fucking smart arse, you'll be able to figure a way hame. You should've thought of that before being such a dick'.

I unclipped my seatbelt and handed him the wig which had slipped over to my side of the dashboard. I stepped out of the driver's side of the car and waited while he walked around to my side, covering his shiny chrome dome with the dead guinea pig. I was kind of hoping that the cold air would cool him down a bit and he'd come to his senses, give me another chance.

I just could not look at him as I was desperately trying to stifle a whole load of girly laughter that was building up inside me. As soon as he'd patted his wig down and driven off, I erupted. I lay on the ground in front of Kwik Fit at Portobello, unable to move. I felt incredibly guilty, but the endorphins from the laughter cancelled the guilt out.

I've no idea how long I sat there laughing, but not much later I heard a car rev up behind me, looked around and saw that it was Bobby, driving too fast for a driving instructor in a 30mph zone.

He slowed down a bit as he approached me, the window was already wound down. I was thinking he'd changed his mind and was going to take me back to the house.

Wrong.

'I was only fucking seventeen in the 70's ya cheeky wee bastard,' he shouted, without stopping.

The clipboard flew out of the window and almost hit me, thankfully I managed to avoid it.

As I walked home, I realised I'd have to find another driving instructor who could teach me emergency stops.

The smile never left my face all the way home.

Humans are so funny I said to myself as I laughed a bit more.

A month or two later Tom and I were attending a marketing conference in some hall in George Street, I think it was the Assembly Rooms. We'd been training that day and also worked a nine to five. When we got into the hall after taking a glass of fizz, we sat down. It was roasting in that hall where I could feel my eyelids grow heavy. This was not a good sign. The boring conference hadn't even started yet, and I was almost zonking.

Tom nudged me and whispered.

'Look at that guy in the front row'.

He was nodding off, his head was nodding forward than jerking up fast, he was just catching himself from hitting his head onto his knees, it was hilarious, we were pissing ourselves under our breath, as this was a serious conference.

I sharpened up a bit, and as my focus grew better, I saw it was my ex-driving instructor.

Thunder At One AM

'Shit Tom' I said
'What is it.'
'That's Irish down there'.
'Your driving instructor?' He said.
'Yeah, jeezus if he doesn't watch himself his wig will come flying off the amount of neck-breaking he's doing'.
'How funny would that be?' He said, and again we both pissed ourselves laughing.

BLACKPOOL

I HAD JUST SPENT the last eight days working on three separate pitches for new business with my work. We averaged about four hours of sleep during those long, hard days and spent those four hours on the agency sofa doing shifts. It's now Friday evening, and word has got around that we've lost all three. I feel lower than a depressed snail's bottom lip.

In the world of advertising and design, the way that most agencies get business is to be invited onto a pitch list with other agencies. A brief is then given to the agency by the potential client, and after all the work has been created and planned and visualised, the potential client invites the agencies to present the work. The agency with the best all-around answer, according to them, wins the business and the losers get sod all.

All that shitting effort and lost time for what. I'm now knackered, grumpy and have no energy left. I want to crawl into bed and sleep for a week.

I leave the office to meet Trish in the centre of Edinburgh just outside her work. It's early September, and the rain is coming down in sheets. I've only seen her fleetingly during the past eight days. Tell her that it has all been in vain she gives me a hug.

'How did your promotion interview go'? I ask'.

'As expected' she says.

'John Newcombe got the job,' we half expected this as he can brown-nose to any specific Pantone colour and in the RBS it's a distinct shade of blue brown-nosing that helps you climb the corporate ladder. We both sigh, shrug our shoulders and head back to our lovely wee miner's cottage in Newtongrange. As we head down Leith Walk and onto Portobello, to pick up some fish and chips from the Rainbow cafe in Musselburgh and a bottle of wine from the lovely little wine shop down there, we're so tired that there is no conversation between us.

'How do you fancy getting away for the weekend?' Trish says to me out of the blue.

'Away, where?' I say.

'I don't know? Blackpool?'

'Blackpool?' I reply quizzically.

We've just picked up our first ever car after I'd passed my test three weeks previously. I found a brilliant driving instructor called Arch after the wig boy débâcle.

'I'm not sure I'm in any state or have the confidence to drive to Blackpool' I say.

'And apart from that I don't really fancy the M1 or whatever you call it, seems a bit scary'.

'You've never been scared of anything in your life' she says 'Why would a road scare you?'

'It's not the road I'm scared of, it's the idiots that use them'.

'Just drive carefully, and I'll navigate,' she says reassuringly.

After thinking about it for a minute or two, I say 'OK, let's go'. In my mind, I picture this gorgeous sunshine, beaches, fish and chips, rolling, refreshing seascapes and lots of laughing. It's a done deal.

I really fancy the idea now. Driving further than I've ever driven before down to England. What an adventure.

We go to the supermarket to pick up provisions for the trip; a big bag of fruit pastilles a bag of chocolate limes and a packet of Refreshers. These will help to keep me awake with their fizz. We get back to the house, Trish cooks the fish, and we devour it with some small potatoes. She then gets some clothes and stuff together for the trip and stuffs them into a sports bag. Just as we're heading out of the door, the phone rings. It's Gordon, my little brother.

'What are you up to tonight, would you mind if I come around to the house' he says.

'Well to be honest Gordon, Trish and I are just heading for Blackpool for the weekend, sorry pal'.

He sounds so disappointed, he can't get a job and has been on the dole for the past ten months. I feel sorry for him.

My mum comes on for a quick chat, and she's bored rigid, this is compacted by the fact that the telly has still not been repaired after the cat pee'd down the back of it three weeks ago. Gordon, Mum and Tigger are the only ones left in the five-bedroomed council house in Claremont Court that in its heyday boasted twelve Divines and a varying number of cats. Nowadays the three of them float around inside it like human screen savers.

I come off the phone and feel really guilty that we are about to go and enjoy ourselves while Gordon and Mum will be sitting there in abject misery. Trish can see that I'm concerned.

'Why don't you invite your Mum and Gordon down with us. We've got enough money in our savings to pay for a hotel for us all for a few nights, and there's plenty of cheap and cheerful places to eat, come on, it'll be a great laugh.'

I'm delighted and give her a big cheesy grin and a hug. I really appreciate that she understands how I feel and that she's prepared to give up some of our money. I hug her again and then get straight on the phone to Gordon.

'Blackpool?, Wow, Yes' he says

'That'll be brilliant, I've never been to Blackpool, and I don't think mum's been out of Scotland since she was twelve'. Having said that, there was a horrible trip that I took down to Great Yarmouth after Mum had rented a caravan. I'd rather forget about that holiday.

We turn up at Claremont Court at five-thirty or thereabouts. Mum and Gordon are really excited and stand there with a small plastic bag each, which contains their clothes and toiletries.

'What about Tigger' I say.
'Catherine's going to come in every day to feed him after her work.' Mum says.
Two minutes later we're on our way. We've not had time to make a plan or decide which roads to take, book a hotel or B&B but we're confident that we'll get something really nice – after all money talks.

After driving through the pouring rain with the windscreen wipers on the 'Crazy Mental Speed' setting, for about three or four hours, we finally get into Blackpool. It is still pissing down and getting darker as the hour's pass. By this time my eyelids weigh an absolute ton, and I have to keep crunching down handfuls of refreshers and cola to keep me awake, let my brain know that there is still a job to be done here.
We've gone into a few friendly hotels, but there are no rooms to be had. We continue, stopping at any hotel that looks like it will have the facilities we want. After an hour we're soaked and still have nowhere to stay. We've reached the level of lowest standard B&Bs and are becoming more and more frustrated as the night grows shorter. After driving around all the streets in the vicinity, we spot some people getting into a car with their suitcases. It looks like they're leaving the B&B. Quickly I pull the car up to the side of the building, and Trish and Gordon run in.
A minute or two later they both come out with the thumbs up. I am so relieved. At last, we can get on with our weekend, put our stuff into the room, have a quick wash, get a pint and go out for a well-deserved slap-up meal.
I park the car a wee bit better, and Gordon and I take in our baggage. We get to the reception area, and Trish is looking slightly concerned.
'I thought you said you had room for the four of us' she says to the little bald man in the blue tartan shirt, red bow-tie and

tank top.

'We av' he says in his broad Scouser's accent.

'Well I don't see the problem' says Trish.

'We only av two rooms, and oanless you are two coaples loav, we do av a problem'.

'I don't get it' says Trish.

'Both rooms only av a doable bed in them' he explains.

'Is the older lady the yoanger gentleman's moather?'

'Yes,' she says.

'Doas that mean that you and the gentleman with the sports bags are a coaple' he says.

'Yes,' Trish says exasperated.

'The gentleman with the sports bags is my husband, and the older woman is my mother-in-law, and the younger gentleman is my brother-in-law.

What accommodation do you have for us?'

'Well' says the man, 'I soajest that you two ladies sheh room woan oandred and the two gentlemen sheh room woan oandred and woan as it 'az the biggest bed'.

Room one hundred and one? I think to myself, who is this guy kidding if he thinks we'll believe this shithole has a hundred rooms. Twat.

We know we have no option and agree to this shitty, pissing me off arrangement.

'We'll look around and get a better place tomorrow' I say, ever the optimist. I've had enough for now and just want to get settled. We agree to meet downstairs at the 'Pool Over' bar after freshening up. The guy thinks he has a sense of humour, you'll have a sense of a punch in the puss if you carry on like that, I think to myself.

Gordon and I get to 'our' room, and as he steps through the door, he starts laughing. There in glorious Technicolor is a king-size George and Zippy, Rainbow bed-cover. It's meant to be a double bed but is in actual fact only big enough for one

and a half people. I jump onto it and find that my legs are far too long. The king size duvet cover is far too big and is there to hide the bed's inadequacies. We both throw our bags into the bottom of the shoogly wardrobe and head downstairs.
On our way down to the bar, we pop in to see what Trish and mum's room is like. At least the guy was honest, our bed was substantially bigger than theirs.
Mum and Trish have never really spent that much time together as we've only been married a few years. I know that after this weekend they will be a lot closer, we had no idea how much.

We go out for something to eat, and although it's still raining heavily, we all feel that we can relax a wee bit tonight and look forward to getting a really nice place in the morning.
In all honesty, we're all too knackered to appreciate anything and go through the motions of being on holiday. The evening passes without too much happening, and after all of the trials and tribulations beforehand, all we want is to settle down and sleep this shitty evening into history.

The next morning I awaken early, pull back the curtain and am met by another dreary skyline. I brush my teeth noisily to waken Gordon it works, he gets up, and we head down to breakfast.
As we sit down to breakfast which includes the chewiest cornflakes I've ever tasted – (I actually search on the box to see if Wrigleys or Hubba Bubba have somehow been involved in the production process). My curiosity is addressed when I notice that the sell-by date has passed just over a year ago. I point this out to Gordon, and he ends himself. He's still laughing when the guy comes through with our 'full English breakfast' When he looks at it he laughs so much that he has to make an excuse and leave the table. The portions are

pathetic. Those rashers are so small they must have come from a Percy Pig.

After breakfast, we go out to find a new place to stay, I am still chewing on the occasional ancient cornflake which one by one are dislodging themselves from the gaps in my teeth. We look around the whole area for hours and hours in the pouring rain and can't find one single vacancy. I feel so flat, the thought of going back to that horrible wee place just makes me more depressed. By four in the afternoon, we've given up hope of finding anywhere else to stay and contemplate our position. Should we drive back to Edinburgh and get a Chinese and a video, we could be home by seven o'clock. It really does seem tempting. Mum has just had two hip replacements, and she's still suffering a bit from all the sitting on the journey down. As always she tries to hide her pain, but I can see she needs more rest before we head back. The decision's made for us.

We entertain ourselves for as long as we can, none of us wants to go back to that hell hole and put it out of our minds for as long as possible. We go to the shows where Gordon wins a wee rubber duck on the 'Drop the Claw' machine having spent a good few quid doing so when the actual duck was worth fifty pence. This is the life I say to myself somewhat sarcastically and raise my eyebrows quickly in self-acknowledgement. We spend another night eating drab food and drinking, trying to lose ourselves but only finding more depressed versions. When we get back to the hotel, the wee guy invites us into his 'Pool Over' bar and offers us a free drink as long as we listen to him playing some Daniel O'Donnell on his Bontempi organ. At first, it seems not too bad a deal but halfway through the first song we down our Malibu's and head out. Pronto.

By the time Sunday morning comes, Trish and mum look

Thunder At One AM

utterly broken. The central strut of the bed they are sharing has been snapped many times before, the two of them are forced into the middle of the 'V' shaped bed. Trish realises that when there is any movement, they will automatically roll into the middle of the bed. Try as she might, she cannot avoid falling and bumping against mum's new hips. Every time she hits mum, there's a cry of pain which mum tries to cover up. This really puts Trish on edge. She is so conscious of hurting mum that she spends most of the night clinging to the side of the bed to stop herself from rolling into the middle. The next day her arms are hurting from the exertion. (Think Sylvester Stallone in Cliffhanger).

By comparison, Gordon and I spend a relatively comfortable night or two. We'd shared a room a few years ago and are well used to each other's company.

As we meet up with the girl's we're demob happy, it's the last day.

We get outside it's now a glorious Autumn day. The sun is shining, the golden leaves are blowing along like a ticker-tape parade congratulating us on passing our endurance test.

We get our bill. The wee guy is not speaking to us now after being snubbed. Not a bad thing, I think. We put our belongings into the car and have a last wander along the promenade. It's incredible how different the place feels with the heat and the right light conditions. There is a touch of us being demob happy I suppose, knowing that we will be spending the coming night in the comfort of our own beds. As we walk along enjoying the freedom and the warm autumnal sunshine, Gordon spots a man with a huge metal gyrosphere.

'This is the same kind of machine that NASA astronauts use during the selection period,' he tells us.

'The idea is,' he continues.

'Is that the person is secured inside the machine and after

a gentle push from the operator the subject has to find the balancing point and return himself to the classic da Vinci 'Renaissance Man' starting position. This is difficult as the Gyro has three separate axes'.

'Where did you hear that bullshit?' I say to him.

'I saw these things years ago in the States, always wanted to try one out as I think my balance is pretty good, reckon it would only take me a few minutes to stop the thing' he says.

'It's four pounds fifty a go' I say and I quickly dig out the money for him to go on.

I REALLY want to see this. The operator doesn't look like he has gained his qualifications through NASA, or even heard of them for that matter. The only NASA he'll be familiar with is the Numpitie's Association for Substance Abuse.

He's wearing a ripped old hooded sweatshirt with Dirty Sanchez in red letters, and his trainers are torn to buggery. He's smoking something that looks like an extra fat roll-up, and he's got a strange grin on his face. Roll up, roll up he says, pointing to his cigarette, smirking.

Gordon goes over to him and asks for an experience. He explains to the guy that he's seen these things on TV and has always wanted a shot.

'An experience? The guy says.

'I'll give you an experience alright'.

The guy is not the least bit interested and just stands there holding his hand out, I drop the cash into it, and he opens the metal door, sucking on the doobie like it's an oxygen supply. Gordon steps eagerly inside, giving us a thumbs-up as the guy straps his wrists to the top section, then straps his feet onto the bottom part. Gordon is smiling. He's really excited and wants to show everyone how good his balance is. There's a small crowd gathering now. Gordon's growing in confidence. Just before he shuts the gate, the guy reaches into a little green nylon bag at the side of the Gyro and pulls out what looks like a black canvas bag. He steps into the cage and proceeds to stick it over Gordon's head kidnapper style, it looks like he's done this many times.

'What are you doing'? protests a muffled Gordon.

The guy completely ignores him and deals quite easily with Gordon's futile struggle. I can hear muted swearing from Gordon. He's trying desperately to shake off the hood but to no avail.

By this time I'm creasing myself laughing. Mum and Trish are looking concerned, but I can hardly move, the tears are running down my face. The guy turns to the assembled crowd and says.

'Is everybody ready to see how green the human face can turn'. He laughs, a real evil laugh and begins to dramatically spin the machine as fast and hard as he can. He's making a lot of extraneous movements with his hands and arms to add drama to the unfolding spectacle. He spins one axis horizontally, one vertically and the third diagonally. Gordon is shouting at the top of his muffled voice. Thankfully being Scottish and knowing Gordon's voice so well I can make out every word.

'I'll fuckin' kill you. Stop this right now ya jakey bastard,' he's forgotten or doesn't care that mum's here. The guy just keeps spinning and spinning and spinning. The crowd are loving it, after about ten, maybe twenty or thirty spins my laughter has subsided, and I begin to feel sorry for him.

'You can stop now' I say to the guy. He doesn't even hear me. I have no idea what he is smoking, but whatever it is it obviously makes his ears stop working.

'You can stop there' I say, much louder this time. Still no reaction. I grab him by the arm, and he looks around at me, I can see the fury in his eyes. This guy has real problems, and he wants to take them out on poor Gordon. Eventually, he kind of comes to his senses and lets the machine stop of its own accord. It takes a good few minutes to decelerate, and as it is slowing down, I reach over and help it to brake to a standstill. It stops, and the guy reaches in and unties Gordon's hands and legs before taking off the hood. There is sickness all over the inside of it. Gordon is whiter than a sheet in a soap powder commercial. I remember seeing Mr Spock sweating heavily in an episode of Star Trek, where Jim Kirk had given him a beating in a 'fight to the death' for a maiden, scene. Gordon's complexion is precisely the same. Waxy. Although Spock's skin might have just been shitty make-up from the Star Trek make-up guys.

He wobbles down from the machine and heads straight for the doped up boy. He tries to punch him, but because of his disorientation, misses him completely and falls onto the ground. The few dozen people who are being entertained laugh and point at him. Gordon hates being ridiculed by anyone and to be ridiculed in such a public way makes him even madder. He lunges for the guy again and misses Completely. The guy looks at me, astounded, and holds both his arms out – 'What's his problemo man' he says.

He is genuinely shocked that Gordon is trying to kill him. The guy looks like he's just returned from a bad trip to planet Wack Ball and finds himself 'beamed' into this confrontational position.

'What the fuck is he doing' he says to me in earnest, pointing a finger to his head and making the looney toons motion. Gordon attacks for the third time and still fails to hit his target.

'Listen buddy' says the guy, 'I'll give you fifty pence off if you didn't enjoy it'.

'You're getting nothing ya bastard' said Gordon. I had no idea what he meant. He's obviously forgotten that the trip's been paid for by me. He staggers over to the side of the promenade and throws up over the Ride a Donkey sign, walks back toward the car with mum and Trish. I shouldn't say it out loud but I really, honestly enjoyed that. We get into the car and going home has never felt so sweet.

'Mind if I keep the window down?' Gordon says.

Nitten

AFTER LIVING IN OUR flat in Edinburgh, for a couple of years, we felt things were getting a bit cramped in the one bedroomed, top floor flat. We decided to look elsewhere, somewhere where we could get a bigger bang for our buck. There was no way we'd get anything decent in the centre of town, but we looked at a few places that offered a wee bit more space and another bedroom. Some of the flats we looked at were eye-openers. One of the first ones was advertised as a two-bedroomed flat. The guy had not even bothered tidying up. We looked around and had to hold our tongues. The main bedroom was average size, but the 'guest room' was a thing to behold. 'It's a bit tight' the guy said.
There was basically a mattress with a sheet thrown over it, but the thing was, the mattress was wall to wall. There was no room to walk around it.
'A bit tight?' I said. 'I've never seen a wall to wall mattress before,' he took the hump, and we made our excuses and headed out. The other outstanding one was just next to Meadowbank. Very handy for training. It looked like a lovely, clean stair. The dad opened the door, and he was charming, he introduced us to his wife, teenage son and daughter. 'Right, let's begin the tour,' he said.
'Tour?' Are you kidding? There were only two rooms, one which was the parent's bedroom, the other was a tiny room with bunk-beds. 'Trish and I looked at each other quizzically'. Both thinking how does this work, these kids were way too old to share a room never mind bunk-beds. The tour continued. Trish whispered to me 'Where's the kitchen?' I asked the guy.
'Ah, I thought you might ask about that' He said.
'Follow me'.

We went back into the hall, and he opened up a cupboard. There sat the smallest cooker I'd ever seen, There was a shelf above it on which were placed tins of food and packets of cereal.

'A bit on the small side' I said.

'You'll get used to it,' he said.

'It took us a while, but now it's second nature'.

Again we acted all polite, pretended we'd consider it and legged it out of there. 'What the hell? How the hell?' Trish was asking half questions.

'Weird' I Said. 'Just weird'.

After much looking around in town, we opened our horizons and started to look outside of Edinburgh and into Midlothian, where Trish had grown up. Her dad was born in Newtongrange, an old mining village. There was a big petition to save the village from being flattened. The powers that be had decided the village had passed its sell-by and had decided to knock it down despite the impressive history it had. Thankfully after a programme on the BBC about 'The village that wouldn't die,' they reconsidered, and the rest is history. We finally settled on an old miners cottage in Newtongrange. I must admit that when I first saw it, I was not too impressed. The guy that owned the house looked so lazy, he had his dirty dungarees only half done up, one of the straps was hanging from him as if he'd just been for a shit, he smelled like it as well. The place looked incredibly tired, and with kids running around, I just did not feel the love for this place. However, Trish convinced me otherwise. We were basically getting a three bedroomed house with front and back garden and an attic space that could be made into a room. For the money they were asking for it, it was a steal.

Roll with it

WE HAD JUST PACKED the last of the boxes into the cupboard in our room at Tricia's Nana's house. We would be staying here until our new home was ready in about six weeks. We'd sold our flat in Easter Road and bought a cottage out in the sticks, Newtongrange to be specific, or 'Nitten by the Bing' as the locals called it, in an attempt at humour, it was meant to add glamour like 'Barcelona-By-the-sea, or Windermere-By-The-Lakes,' (a 'bing' was a pit heap, built of accumulated spoil, the overburden or other waste rock removed during coal and ore mining).

'Staying with your Nana's going to be a long haul,' I said to Trish.
'I really am not looking forward to it'.
'The time'll fly by, in no time we'll be settled in the new place'.
'It's all right for you' I said, 'you'll be away while I'm bustin' a gut with the removals n stuff'.
Trish was heading for Antarctica for the last three and a half of those six weeks while I'd be in this house with her Nana, chewing the fat.
Standard Life had an annual programme that allowed two of its employees to go on a three to four week trip to Antarctica and other exciting countries. It was part of a charity scheme that helped a worthy cause. As you can imagine, hundreds of people applied for the weeks of paid leave and the experience of a lifetime to boot. After many interviews and tests, Trish and a guy called Derek Ireland were chosen.
In the meantime, I was left in the halfway house.
Don't get me wrong Tricia's Nana was a lovely woman, and she loved all kinds of sport so we'd sit and chat about that most of the time. She also had our tea ready for us when we came in

from training every night.

I guess though what was really hard, is the fact that we had to walk around on eggshells. After you've had your own place for four years and your personal freedom, it's challenging to reel yourself back into someone else's constraints. I finally accept that it's kind of her to let us stay and it will not really be for long.

The day before Trish was due to leave for Antarctica, her Nana was up to high doh.

'What if the plane crashes? What if a polar bear gets you? What if you crash into an iceberg? What if those Russians take you hostage?' On and on and on she went. I left the room and got on with packing the two large red and black explorer bags. Trish came through, eventually

'She's calmed down a bit now' she said. ' I had to explain to her that you don't get Polar Bears in Antarctica, only penguins.

'I don't know how you can stand it?' I said.

'All that negativity and fear, she's trying to get you to abandon your plans for her selfish reasons?'

'Maybe?' She replied, 'she's hardly ever been out of Dalkeith for the past forty years, and I think she just worries about me going to the other side of the world, when she watched that programme about the Drake Passage being one of the most treacherous places on earth she actually had her head in her hands.'

'Well let's face it' I said, 'This is exactly why you're going there, get rid of all of that fear that she has built up in you over the years. Scared of her own shadow she is. Imagine being that age and still hiding in a cupboard when thunder and lightning strike.'

'I know she wants me to give up, but there's no way I'm pulling out now' she said.

'What time is the flight to London?' I said.

'I have to be at Heathrow for 10.30, so that'll mean getting to Edinburgh airport for 5ish, did you manage to get those bags shut?' 'Yeah, no problem' I replied.

'I put in a little something, but you're not allowed to open it up until you're standing on an iceberg in Antarctica, promise you won't open it until then?'

'Yeah, I promise' she said.

I looked at the clock at the side of the bed.

'That's just after eleven now, we better get to our kip you only have about four hours till you get up,' she looked at me as if she'd just got a fright.

'Shit, I didn't realise it was so late, I'm starting to get butterflies'. She went through to the living room to say night to her Nana.

We had never once had any intimacy in the three weeks we'd been there as Trish was mortified that her Nana would hear us, our headboard was against the same wall as her Nana's headboard different rooms though and the bed squeaked like a little grassing bastard.

'We can do it as much as we want when we get our new house,' she had said a few times, just to pacify me. I was hornier than Kid Creole's brass section. We were training bloody hard for the Scottish Championships, this meant training sometimes twice a day. When you have so many chemicals pumping around your young body, everything takes turns to be king, and at this time, it was my libido. We got ready for bed, and she cuddled up against me, I could tell she was terrified, not of my desire but the fear of the unknown, I knew it was something she had to do, it would change her life - no question. I didn't say anything to comfort her as I knew it would get her thinking that there may be a chance something could go wrong, and this would lead to no sleep.

Thunder At One AM

Early the next morning, I drove her to Edinburgh Airport, where she met up with the guy who would be her expedition leader. All I knew was that he was ex-SAS and that his name was Mick Ward-Brimstone. He shook a firm hand, took the bags from me and said to Trish.

'Better get going doll. See you in London around a month Jim' I gave her a quick snog then they were off.

A FEW DAYS LATER

'...Hi honey, how are you?' She said over the weak Internet phone connection.

'Yeah, good I said, I take it the plane didn't crash, or the polar bears didn't get you?' I could hear her laughing.

'No although you wouldn't believe some of the stuff that's happened and this is only the second day!'

'I'm sure I'll hear about it soon enough' I said. We chatted for the next five minutes as she had limited time, she was using the Internet facility at the Chilean Antarctic base as the Russian line was down. There was a great deal of camaraderie and cooperation in the South Pole, I guess they all felt they were in this hostile environment together. She was spending two weeks at the Russian Antarctic base after moving on from Punta Arenas, Patagonia and Buenos Aires. After that, it was back to Buenos Aries and then home. 15 flights in 14 days would cure her fear of flying – I was in no doubt about that. That still meant that I wouldn't see her for at least another two weeks.

With Trish being away so long, I threw myself into my job. I loved my work so much, I thought I was in heaven. I couldn't believe that I was actually getting paid for doing this. Here I was working in one of the countries top agencies mixing it with the best creative talent available. I couldn't wait to get to work every day. I even had my own set of keys to my own office.

My best mate Tom was working beside me, Tom and I were in the same athletics team. On our first trip away competing in the British League in London, we hit it off straight away. Tom was a fantastic athlete and had the goods to get to the top of his tree the 3000m Steeplechase, he eventually went on to finish sixth in the Barcelona Olympic final, only 8 seconds outside the Bronze medal and that was after hardly training in the months just before with an injury. He was awesome, and without a doubt, one of the best athletes that Scotland has ever produced.

Our first real job together was an advertising campaign for one of our Hi-Fi clients. We were working on the campaign, which highlighted one thing and compared it to another. A previous ad was an illustration of a stick of chalk compared with a block of cheese. On this occasion, we were comparing a real woman dressed in suspenders and sexy knickers to an inflatable doll. Tom and I thought about where we could get a doll to draw the initial concepts. 'I'm sure someone gave Lawrie an inflatable doll for his twenty-first' Tom said. We phoned Lawrie (one of the athletics teams' hammer throwers). 'Yeah that's right' he said, I did get an inflatable doll, but I don't know where it is'.

'Can you look for it?' Said Tom.

'Sure' said Lawrie, 'I don't know where it is, but I'm sure it's in mint condition, In fact, I'm sure it's still in its box. Give me an hour I'll look for it and if I find it I'll get it round to you. Are you guys still in George Street?'

'Yeah' said Tom.

'Can you do it urgently as we need to have the concepts now'.

'OK,' said Lawrie, 'I'll get onto it straight away'.

That afternoon a courier turned up at the office with a delivery for us.

'Great' I said, we can crack it this afternoon'.

We went for our usual run, George Street, down through Princess Street, down by Abbeyhill then Meadowbank and a loop around Arthur's Seat and then back to the office.

There was never anywhere in the office for us to warm up, so we used the toilet. It must have been annoying for the guys from other companies who shared an office with us. We did a good half hour warm-up and chatted through it. Some guys would be desperate for a shit or piss and just go for it, but others would wait. There was one really shy guy. He'd go into the cubicle and sit down. Waiting desperately for us to leave so that he could jettison last night's supper. Many times we'd make out that we were leaving by saying things like, 'let's go then? 'Pretend to shut the door and just stand there waiting for him to drop his bombs. Then we'd piss ourselves laughing. We did this to him quite a lot. It was incredibly childish but great fun.

When we got back to the office, Tom handed out the packed lunches. His Mum Agnes had offered to make me the same lunch as Tom as making sandwiches for two was more cost-effective than preparing them for one. I paid here a fiver a week or something like that, and they were always spot on. After we'd finished them, I opened Lawrie's package and reeled back.

'What in hell's name is this?' I said. There was a black inflatable doll, which had sellotape running all the way through her middle. It was as if someone very heavy (like a hammer thrower for example) had used the doll so much that she'd split in two.

'Shit' Tom said, 'we've no time to use anything else, the illustrator needs those preliminary drawings this afternoon. The deadline for the ad is next week'.

'We'll have to use it,' I said. I put the package under my desk, and we went to the kitchen to make a coffee. On our return I went into my office and pulled the doll from under the desk, Tom headed to the Repromaster in the darkroom to make some prints for the ad.

The rest of the office was tranquil as most of the staff were out celebrating some award that we'd picked up recently. After a sip or two, I picked up Lawrie's package and gingerly lifted it onto my desk.

'Well here goes' I thought, and put my lips to the valve. I began to blow the doll up to do a preliminary illustration. As I was halfway through blowing her up two men walked past my door and looked in, they were apparently taken aback.

'BT' said one of the men.

'Where do you want your new points?' I immediately threw the doll onto the floor hoping that they hadn't seen me blowing, it would have taken too long to explain and I knew they would never have believed me anyway. I told them to go through to the reception area, and I'd be there in a minute. I went through to show them where the new phone lines were to be installed. I could see that they were trying to hide their laughter. There was no question that they would go and tell people the story later on. I couldn't really care at that moment as I had to get the drawing done and get it off to the illustrator. I went back to my office, blew the doll up, did the drawing and eventually all was well. The ad appeared in the Penthouse a week or so later, and our complimentary copies were very well received.

A quiet Sunday morning. A week before I was due to fly down to London to meet Trish from the Buenos Aires flight at Heathrow. I was still like a dog in heat, and there was no way that the 'hermits hallelujah' would do the trick. I had thought about this for ages and decided to bring Lawrie's inflatable doll back to Tricia's Nana's from the office.

On the previous Friday evening, I'd found it, hanging over the coat rack in the camera room. It was half inflated and had a nurses uniform on. I managed to strip her, and as I was deflating her, Carol came through, really quietly, as if sneaking up on me.

'What are you up to Mr Divine?' She said in her secretarial voice. 'I have to get this room cleaned as Colin is giving some clients a tour on Monday, and this is the last thing he'd want them to see' I said bluffing. She laughed.

'I thought you had a date for the weekend.' I laughed with her and raised my brows when she left. After she'd gone, I put the doll, complete with nurse's uniform, under a pile of boxes and took them through to my office. I was desperate that no one would see me and hurriedly slipped her into my briefcase, which I'd emptied earlier. I put a sweaty t-shirt on top to deter anyone who wandered too close.

Back at Tricia's Nana's I cleaned the doll thoroughly using soap and boiling water, the last thing I wanted to do was catch some kind of STD from an inflatable, jeez, imagine the shame of it?

I could just imagine the clinic nurse asking some awkward questions;

What was the name of your last partner?

'She was Swedish' I'd say.

'Her name please'.

'Bloa'

'Surname please'.

'Updohl'.

'Bloa Updoll? Do you think I've never heard that one sonny?'

I did not want that scenario, so I went to town on the plastic entry points. I put some disinfectant on her pubic hair and scrubbed it with the potato scrubbing brush, just to be sure. I then rewashed her with some pre-war carbolic soap that looked like it had lain on the bunker since Spitfires were the new kids in town. I could hear Tricia's Nana hanging around outside the bathroom as I was doing this and although she was curious about what I was up to, I was confident I could bluff it. She wandered off eventually, and I sneaked the doll into the big cupboard, storing her for the right time. I really hoped I'd wake up, and the urge that had to be purged would have diminished, but it didn't.

All I could think about was sex. Everywhere I looked, it was all I could see. Even in the morning when Tricia's Nana went to feed the birds when she said she'd spotted a couple of great Tits I was jiggling beneath my jammies. Man, this was torture.

The following Sunday morning 9.30 on the dot I heard the front door click shut as she wandered off to the shops for the paper and some rolls.

'Now's my chance.' I thought. I pulled the doll from the cupboard. It had more wrinkles than Tricia's Nana, I had to blow extra hard to get rid of the wrinkles. After blowing my lungs out, the wrinkles would still not go away, and the last thing I wanted to do was to shag a wrinkly inflatable doll that had the complexion of a pensioner. I had to go and find a bicycle pump as even my strong, healthy lungs couldn't get rid of the creases. After a long time pumping, I had finally managed it. Her skin was taut and glowed like a nubile young Hawaiian, (with a sellotape hula skirt). I knew I had around an hour as Tricia's Nana wandered very slowly to the shops and back again. I ripped open the condom and threw the packet onto the floor. I looked at the doll, and it just wasn't doing it for me, its face looked pathetic and comical. What the fuck was I up to, how far do you have to fall before you'll contemplate this shite?

As I was in the throes of putting the Johnny on, my arse decided it needed to hit the toilet. Immediately. I shat like I' had shares in Andrex, I must have eaten something dodgy but couldn't remember offhand what it was. Jeez, my guts were hurting after that. I must have only been in there no more than five, maybe seven minutes. I wiped myself down, threw the Johnny down the toilet pan. I'd come to my senses, God knows, with the size of big Lawrie, the poor doll's toilet parts would probably be too flappy for me. I opened the bog door and was sure I could smell bacon. I then jumped as I heard a noise from downstairs. Tricia's Nana must have got back a lot quicker than usual.

SHIT, SHIT, SHIT! That fuckin doll was lying on the bed dressed in a nurse's uniform. I ran back into the room, pulled the valve from the doll and sat on top of it to get rid of the air, it wasn't coming out fast enough. I grabbed the midriff and ripped the sellotape off. The doll split in half and deflated instantly. I hid it under the pillow, covered myself with the candlewick cover and was about to pretend I was asleep as I heard footsteps on the stairs. I reached without looking, to turn off the light on the little wooden bedside table. As I reached out, I knocked unexpectedly against something.

I looked up. A fresh cup of coffee wobbled and managed to stay upright. Two bacon rolls lay there, steam rising from them adding to the condensation on the windows.

I sighed heavily, this was really going to take some explanation.

The Paintball

TOM AND I WERE still having a brilliant time at Marr Associates. The work was great, our training was going really well, and we were loving life. We'd won so many awards over the years that it became a real hassle, as we were responsible for hanging them up around the large office and Colin, our boss liked straight lines. Sometimes it could take a whole day to get these bloody things lined up and so straight that you could draw a line over the top of them all. It was very frustrating especially as the walls were so old and wonky. One day we were told that we'd be leaving our office in George Street and heading down to a brand new office in Leith. This was perfect for me as I'd grown up down there and knew the area well.

It would take a while to sort out the removal and sort out all the new furniture and everything that goes with a new move. After a good three weeks or so we'd got to a point where we were ready to go. The landlord insisted that the place was put back to the state in which we found it at least ten years ago. This meant the decorators would have to come in and paint the whole place magnolia. Which they did. We'd almost completed the move to Leith by this time, but there were bits and pieces of equipment that still had to be moved. Tom and I were responsible for sorting them out. We headed back up to the office in George Street to finalise the move.

When we got into the office, it was empty. The whole place was just this vast magnolia space, wall to wall carpet and nothing else. Tom and I love football, and when I challenged him to a game, he was right up for it. We had no ball so got a couple of rolls of masking tape, peeled them off the roll and fashioned them into a ball. We got down to our shorts and started to boot this ball all over the place. It was a close game, as always and I probably won by the odd goal or two. We got so carried away. It was brilliant, felt like being a kid all over again. We shook hands, put our kit back on, by this time we were sweating buckets.

'Shit,' Tom said.

'What?' I replied, doing my shirt up.

Tom began to piss himself laughing, holding his hand over his mouth.

'What are you up to?' I said.

'Look?' He said. Pointing to the walls.

'Fuck.'

There must have been at least a thousand grey marks on those walls. Every time the masking tape ball hit the wall, it marked it.

'Shit Tom, what are we going to do?'

Tom's dad, Martin, was a painter and decorator, the best I'd ever seen, he was so meticulous. In fact, he offered to decorate our flat free of charge as long as we got the paper off the walls and got it back to the plaster. It seemed easy enough until I started. There must have been a century's worth of paper and varnish on those damned walls. I gave up after three or four weeks, spending the evening with a scraper only to get a square inch of paper off. I had a ton of blisters and had got so bloody frustrated that I began to gouge the damned thing into the wall to get that horrible stuff off.

Tom looked around the room, he was also a great painter and decorator. 'It should wipe off easily and dry in if we rub it with a damp cloth. He sounded so confident.

We got a couple of damp cloths and spent the next couple of hours going around the walls wiping them. As soon as we applied the wet rag, the marks disappeared.

'Brilliant Tom,' I said. Feeling immensely relieved as I was the senior partner and responsible for the mess, at least in the bosses eyes. This was going well. After a while, I went back to the first wall to see how it had dried in. It had dried in a different colour, there were now a thousand even darker marks than before.

'Tom?' I said, desperately.

'What?' He said, taking his time to carry on wiping.

'It's not working. In fact, it's made it worse.

'It just needs a bit of heat.' He said.

We went around the office putting all of the heaters on full blast and waited an hour or so.

Still no difference.

'Fuck' Colin's going to go mental' I said.

'There's always one more option' Tom said.

'What's that?' I said.

'Nobody knows we're here. We could just leg it and see what the consequences are'.

'You know something?' I said.

'That's a great idea'.

We removed all signs that we'd been in the office and headed out quietly leaving no trace.

The following day in our new offices in Leith, I was in Colin's room speaking to him about a job when Liz, his PA came in.

'I've managed to get those bloody decorators on the phone at last,' she said.

'They said they know nothing about the marks, but you know what bloody decorators are like'.

'Thanks, Liz. Excuse me, Jim, can we pick this up later, I've got to sort out some cowboy decorators very quickly'.

I nodded and left.

I guess the decorators would have been utterly stumped when they saw all of those marks on the walls. A real mystery.

Tom and I told nobody.

There was another similar incident a few years later. By this time, Tom had left Marr and had become a full-time athlete, running all over the world. We still trained together occasionally when he was home. One day we were out for a run from his house up to Corstorphine Hill, a steep climb up with a series of pathways through a nice bit of woodland. It was summer and perfect for running. The plan was to go for a three or four mile run through the woods and home to his place. I was delighted that I could run at his training pace, which was still fast. Tom led the way as this was his route. As we jinked and wound our way through the twisting pathways, I was no more than a step behind him. Up and downhill and dale. It felt incredible. Until.

Tom jumped over a tree root right in front of me. He shouted for me to look out for it, but as I was so close to him, I missed his call. My foot caught the thing square on, and I went flying, arse over tit down the hill. I landed smack, bang on another big tree root, right on my chest. I swear to god, I thought I'd cracked my chest wide open. I lay there rolling around in agony, trying desperately to get air back into my lungs. Tom knelt down beside me, trying to help.

'You're only winded' he said. 'Give it a couple of minutes, and we'll try to get you up'.

He was right, but I still felt as if I'd broken every bone in my chest. I've no idea how long it took, but we eventually got back to his mum's house. She ran a bath for me, and I lay there for hours trying to breathe correctly, Tom popped his head in every now and again to make sure I was still alive. Anyway, I digress again.

George Mathison, one of my training pals and another top Scottish Steeplechaser, had asked Tom and me if we could come around to his house to paint a mural for his son Ross. 'Sure', I said what kind of things does he like?'

'He loves Noddy and Big Ears' George said. 'I'll pay you for it'.
'Well, let's see how it turns out, and we can take it from there'. I said.

Tom and I did a couple of small drawings and popped round to see George and his wife, Ann.

'Yeah those look fantastic' they both said.

'When can you do it?'

We'd never done a mural before and had no idea how long it was going to take.

'We can start it next week' I said.

'I'm waiting on my dad getting some special quick-drying paint,' Tom said. 'As soon as that arrives we can start'.

The following week Tom got the black tube of quick-drying paint. We headed round to Ann and George's place.

'Shit Tom' I said. 'We never even checked the room for size'. What a couple of muppets. It was bigger than we thought but even worse was the fact that the whole room was covered in wood-chip wallpaper. How the hell are you meant to get a straight line on that stuff'.

'We could strip it back to the plaster and paint on that' Tom suggested.

'No chance. You saw the mess I made of my flat, I'm not going through that again. Do you think we could get a semi-decent finish on this'? I said, hopefully.

'Possibly' he said.

We got the drawing of Noddy and Big Ears out and tried in vain to scale it up, it was useless, the room and the illustrations were the wrong proportions to each other.

'Tell you what,' I said.

'You draw Big ears and the bouncing-ball-folk over there, and I'll draw Noddy and his car over here, we'll think of something to make them join up at some point'.

We worked away and found there was no way we were getting paid for this, it was looking shit, but we'd committed so had to go for it. After a while, we had a rough pencil drawing covering the whole wall.

'That'll do for tonight I said. 'We can fill in the colours next time and then finish it off with big thick black lines using that special paint your dad got us'.

'Yeah, I guess the thicker the line, the less wobbly it'll look' he said. A night or two later, we turned up and filled all of the big bright colours in, it looked OK but needed the black lines to bring it together. We were pretty happy with it and began to think that there may actually be a wage at the end.

Tom had to go abroad for the next few weeks as it was the height of the season. When he returned, we headed back to Ann and George's to finish the job. Both of us got a small paint tin and a brush that would lay nice big, thick, black lines. It looked great. We were now sure that we were getting paid for our first professional mural.

After we'd washed the brushes and cleaned up, we went through to the living room to get Ann and George to inspect the work. They were delighted. George handed us an envelope each. I can't remember how much was in it, but we were well pleased. A day or two later, I got a call from George.

'Jim, how long will it take for that black paint to dry?'

'I'm not sure' I said. 'Tom said it was quick-drying paint, so I'm surprised it's still not set. I'll give him a call'.

'What?' He said incredulously. 'Still not dried. Is he sure.'

'Well, put it this way, every time wee Ross goes into his room, he comes out with black hands, and he's got black paint all over the furniture'.

'Shit,' he said. 'I'll ask my dad'.

'Did you mix in the fixer when you were making the paint up?' His dad said.

'Fixer?' What fixer?, Jim and I took it straight out of the tube and painted it right onto the walls'.

'You couple of Wally's,' in that case it'll probably take a good year to dry, in the right conditions.'

'What are we going to do?' I said.

'Well, for starters we'll have to give him his money back'.

'Yeah, I guess so,' I said. 'But what about the paint?'
George informed us that the paint was still wet a good six months after we'd applied it. They moved house shortly after that.

The pochard

EVERY MORNING FOR THE past two weeks I'd got into the office really early as I did every summer. I'd dump my bag at my desk, stick a couple of slices of bread into the toaster, knock the kettle on and wander over to the front window to look for Bob who I knew would be hiding behind the bushes on the opposite bank of the river with his binoculars.

The Water of Leith flows past our office, in fact, it had flowed past thousands of years before our building was even there and still had a nonchalance about it that I love.

About two hundred yards downstream, it frighteningly turns into the sea, yet it seems such a calm wee thing in front of me right now. It had seen so much: life, death, war, peace, recession, expansion, sadness, happiness, drought, flood, ducks, swans, moor-hens and Pochards.

The toaster magically popped and flung my bread heavenwards into toast, and the kettle cheerily whistled me into my working day. Things were brilliant on planet Marrs. Carol, Reg, Bob, Phill, Ally, Richard, Ian, Tony, Neil, Martin and Mark. Everyone was part of this fantastic experience. We were loving life, we loved our jobs. It was like going into a sitcom every day, nothing was too serious, we were creating great work, winning an incredible amount of awards and most of all we had the best fun doing it. It had been years since I'd laughed so much at work.

I buttered my toast and made a lovely hot, cup of sweet tea and wandered over to the window, Bob was still in the bushes. He was an ornithologist, like me, he loved birds. I opened the window as the condensation made it hard to see, leaned out and enjoyed my breakfast while watching Bob. He had a stern expression on his face, more concentration than severe, but he was definitely in the zone. I traced my eyes along the path in which his binos were pointing. Something was floating upstream from us. I wondered if it was another body. The cops had fished three people out of the river since we'd moved there from George Street. Seeing this really brought home to me how lucky I was; a beautiful wife, loving family, healthy lifestyle and a fantastic circle of friends but I also loved the sense of hope and excitement that I had, and still have to this day.

After a moment or two getting my visual range sorted out, I could see that it was a bird he was stalking. A red-headed duck by the look of it from this distance. I couldn't see what all the fuss was about, but Bob was into ornithology in a big way and had even gone to Alaska on a three-week tour to see if he could catch sight of a rare migrating goose.

I walked over to my desk and turned my computer on. The familiar Apple encore blasted from the speakers and my day had begun.

A while later the Engine Room door opened (we called our part of the business the Engine Room as we did most of the graft), Bob walked in, trousers soaking, his face covered in sweat.

'Morning Jim, how're things?' He said, as always.

'Morning Bob, things are good. I see you've been stalking that wee bird again.'

'Well, what you've got to understand is that it's not every day you get to see a POCHARD in Edinburgh, sorry, Leith'.

'A Pochard?' I said, wondering what the hell a Pochard was and why it was so worth looking at for two weeks.

'This bird has probably only been seen here ten times since the turn of the century and by probably only ten people, does that not make you feel special?'

'No, not really'.

I kind of got it, but that kind of thing was not really on any scale of importance to me.

Thunder At One AM

He shook his head, took off his jacket and headed to the kitchen.

I turned up the volume on my speakers and let the Blue Nile's 'Walk across the rooftops' blast out.

I've loved this album since the first time I'd heard it. Tom and I were at Kirk's house in Gilmerton after a run. As we were showering and drying ourselves, while Jo, Kirk's mum prepared our tea, Kirk stuck this record on. I was instantly mesmerised, as was Tom. Since then, I'd always stuck it on when I wanted to feel good.

Just before Marr had abandoned George Street due to the exorbitant rates and rent, The Blue Nile had paid us a visit as we were creating the artwork for their newest album 'Hats'. I'd listened to the new stuff for a couple of weeks and couldn't help thinking how inferior it was to the first album. I tried and tried to love the new material, but it never happened. The band had taken an eternity to create this follow up, and I know the music press eagerly awaited the results. When the group showed up at our office, Colin and I had already drawn up some ideas for the cover.

I was dreading the meeting as Colin said they'd want to know what I thought about the new stuff. The truth was I was indifferent to it. I was their biggest fan but felt I couldn't lie to their faces. I kept going back to the first album, in my eyes they'd peaked then, to me it was like they'd won Olympic Gold. You don't improve on that. All you can do is re-live the memory, it is unrepeatable when you reach a pinnacle like that.

As I walked into the board room to meet them, I was sheepish.

I remember Robert (Buchanan) asking me what I thought.

'Can I be honest?' I asked.

'Sure', he said.

'Ricky Lee Jones is one of your biggest fans, isn't she?

'I think so, why do you ask'.

'I love her, especially the B side of Chuck E's in Love' I said.

'A lot of people loved Chuck E, but when I played the B side 'On Saturday Afternoons in 1963' I loved it. It had so much emotion and meaning to me.'

(I'd first heard that song when I was looking after my big sister Karen's flat in Portobello, she didn't have many records, so I ended up playing all of the B Sides for a bit of variation and when I'd heard RLJ singing that song it really got to me. I'd recently lost a good friend, Dennis in a motorbike accident, he was the same age as me, and the memories of all the laughter and sadness we'd shared together, including the death of his big brother Billy at the age of six when we lived in Pilton came flooding back). I was jolted back by Paul Buchanan.

"And Hats?' He said.

'I'm a traditionalist, I love A Walk Across the Rooftops, and you don't come close to that on the new album, I'm really sorry to say' I said, and I was genuinely sorry. I'd hoped that they'd create something spectacular in the many years (some rumoured to be seven years) in the making of this album. But as it was, at least in my opinion, a waste of time.

'Well everybody's entitled to their opinion I guess' he said. I left the room, I'd met the band but felt like a lousy cheat and traitor. Richard Harris, who'd recently joined us as a copywriter was sitting on the couch doodling some cartoons, looked up as I left the room.' How was it?' He said in his broad Oswestry accent.

'Honestly, Richard,' I said.

"I was disappointed'.

'Shame, I really liked their last album' He said, and returned to his doodling.

Bob returned from the kitchen.

'Well, how did you feel when you saw the wee felly?' I said.

'You know something'? he said. 'I felt exuberant. I've tried to see one of those since I was a kid.'
'Good for you Bob' I said. 'Good for you,' I felt happy for him.

ALLY'S HAMMER

'I'M PRETTY SURE THIS fuckin' hammer's got a leak' said Ally. He was sitting at his desk with a half-eaten cheese and beetroot sandwich and had set aside a packet of strawberry Hubba Bubba bubble gum for afters.

'I've checked and checked it, but I can never find any sign of a leak' he said somewhat bemused, scratching his head and getting red beetroot juice over his bald spot.

He'd bought a two-foot fluorescent pink inflatable hammer from Great Junction Street Market almost three weeks previously, the purpose of the hammer was to hit Barry, the commercial artist on the head every time his concentration wandered from the task in hand. Barry was notorious for being easily distracted, and Ally had tried being subtle with him, but it never worked, so he opted for the inflatable persuasion route. Every time Ally hit Barry, Barry would threaten to crack from his cool laid back approach to life and once or twice grabbed the hammer from Ally and tried to rip it. It was made of stern stuff though.

Ally had taken up the post as production manager after the temporary production manager had packed in and gone to drive buses for Lothian Region rather than 'do this shitey job'. Reg, the man who was interviewing people for the job, had told me that he quite liked the experience that Ally had, but his one concern was that he looked like he was 'a drinker,' due to his unshaven appearance and lack of 'giving a fuck'. A few days later, Ally was appointed. As he got used to the company and his surroundings, he began to open up to the folk in the office, this was perhaps not his best ploy.

On day two he admitted that one of his biggest fantasies was to go to bed with wee Jimmy Krankie dressed up in suspenders and crotchless panties.

As the weeks and months went on, I began to realise that this guy had issues. Don't get me wrong, he was a great laugh, he was good at his job, and he was generous. I had the feeling that he was telling the truth when he told Gordon and me about the time he dressed up as a woman and spent an afternoon being the physio for a female football team.

Just before he bought the inflatable hammer, Ally, Gordon and I were walking along Great Junction Street chilling out during lunchtime. When we passed the pet shop 'Paws for thought' Ally started to laugh out loud. There in the window was a cagoule for a cat. It was bright red and had a little hood and four small blue and white striped elasticated cuffs. I contemplated getting one for our cat but thought about what the neighbours would think. I decided against it.

After several weeks of being hit by Ally's hammer, Barry took a flaky. Ally had just finished bashing him on the head for the third time that day when Barry grabbed the hammer from him, sellotaped a heavy stapler to it, opened the window and threw the hammer about a hundred feet over the road and into the water of Leith. His head was a dangerous shade of red. Ally shrugged his shoulders and went back to his desk.

'Was there a particular reason you did that?' Ally said.

'What do you think?' Barry said.

'Do you realise you've just chucked Colin's favourite stapler into the murky waters of Leith. I just borrowed it from his desk this morning'.

Barry's face went white. I knew Ally was only kidding, but there was no way he would tell Barry. He'd make him sweat until the end of the day.

Making Muzik

LIFE ON MARR'S WAS good after moving from costly offices in George Street down to a refurbished grain store on the shore at Leith. The transformation that's taken over this part of the city is unbelievable. When I was growing up the only reason you'd have ventured into Leith was for broken biscuits at the Crawford biscuit factory, or you were after some kind of paid-for entertainment.

The building we'd acquired was called Waterside House. We have two floors and a massive, sprawling expanse of office space. Colin has big plans to turn this into the best advertising office in Edinburgh and the whole of Scotland. Based on creativity and awards we're right up there with the best of them, and when this is complete, we'll look the part as well. It's handy for me as I only live up the road.

I know the area well, so all I need to do is find the best places to run and eat at lunchtime. My brother John had recently started at a computer factory, working on their networking systems. They had some incredible technology, including a system that allowed you to paint on screen. He let me know that if I could get him a hundred quid, he could get me a top of the range machine. I was hooked.

As soon as he brought it home, I was on it. I loved this new technology. I quickly learned the basics and took it into work one day to show the guys how you could type something into the machine and scale the words up or down, then print them out. Some kind of magic was involved. Since that day, Colin wanted a piece of this electronic action. Six months later and I've been tasked with getting our computers sorted out. I've been researching the best models and feel I'm ready to rock n roll. I've been in touch and met a local guy who can supply us with what we need at a reasonable price. His name's a bit weird though; Malky Muzik. After a lot of hassle with purchase orders and job numbers I eventually managed to order all of the bits and pieces last week, they should have arrived yesterday, but I give him an extra day just to make sure.

I walk the two hundred yards around the corner to a darkened shop in Bernard Street. It's just after twelve in the afternoon, there are no curtains in the windows, yet barely any light is able to penetrate the exterior or interior due to nicotine and dirt-stained glass. I peer through a small translucent space in the corner of the main window to see if there's anyone in. A small shaft of light falls numbly onto a red sofa, or at least it used to be red before the nicotine engulfed and tainted its colour. I spot a bit of movement in the corner of the shop, a flickering computer screen tells me that Malky has at long last, returned.

I go to the door; the half-closed sign says 'clopen,' I depress the small black metal handle and push, there is no give on the door. I push harder and almost fall into the shop as the piece of cardboard that is lodged in to hold it, flies out. The Victorian-style bell above the door rings and springs around like a demented bat on a stick, obliterating the utterly dirty silence that lies within.

I walk through the clutter of boxes and papers towards the brightly flashing corner, there is no expected greeting, the computer screens are whirring through some calculations at the speed of light, and there is a half-smoked cigarillo burning in the old glass Capstan branded ashtray. The smoke and the light from the computer screen create a subtle, relaxing effect on the walls. Usually, Malky would look up from his desk through his blue-tinted heavy black glasses, shake my hand and go to the kitchen to knock the kettle on.

I hear a loo flush in the toilet. Malky shuts the door behind him buttoning up his jeans and fixing his belt as he heads towards me, he's so busy trying to get the belt to pin into the tightest hole that he doesn't notice me. He is almost at the desk before he looks up and falls over.

'Fuck!' He shouts. 'Where did you come from?'

I point towards the door.

He quickly regains his composure and walks towards the kitchen. 'Coffee?' He shouts, as he finally gets the pin into the hole of his Black Sabbath belt.

'Yeah, coffee's fine, I say'.

'Nescafe or Mayan Blue?'

'Nescafe's fine,' I say. 'One sugar though and a dollop of Coo juice'.

I remove the plastic bag with my home-made sandwiches from inside my jacket pocket and put it on the desk.

I open the bag and take out one of the big doorstop sandwiches, the beetroot and cheese filling tries to escape from the bread, but I manage to shepherd it towards my mouth. Malky returns with two chipped cups of coffee.

'Sorry' he says, 'no milk today,' the shop was shut when I came in at three this morning.

I don't offer him one of my sandwiches because I know that he doesn't eat. His routine is a liquid lunch at three. Every day. And food on the way home, if he can be bothered. He's the unhealthiest person I know. That diet combined with his 30 cigarilloes a day habit is definitely going to end him. If nicotine were nutrition, he'd be the healthiest guy I know.

I take my jacket off and hang it on the back of his chair. Continue tucking into my sandwiches and don't say another word until I've finished both of them. I wipe my mouth with the sleeve of my jumper, and a red, greasy, crumby residue ends up there. I rub it to see if I can blend it with the dark

Thunder At One AM

blue material but to no avail. I have a sip of coffee, but by this time the coffee has become lukewarm, and I wince as the sweetness jars with the greasy after taste of the cheese and beetroot. There is too much sugar in the drink. I put it down and automatically wipe my mouth with the same sleeve.

I shake my head as I look down at the mess of the sleeve and the big black marks on the front of the jumper. I sigh deeply. This gets Malky's attention.

He puts down the soldering iron that he has just been dabbling with and lifts the last tiny burning ember from the ashtray.

'What's up?' He says. As he blows smoke from most of the holes in his head.

He looks closely at my jumper.

'What happened there?' He says pointing to the big black marks that sweep over the yellow golfer that dominates my Nick Faldo jumper, almost touching the jumper with the cigarillo butt.

'Careful' I say. Pushing his hand away,

'It's bad enough without you burning a hole there'.

'Well, what happened?'

'It's not my jumper' I reply. 'It's Tricia's'.

'She's gonnae be pissed' he says laughing.

'Tell me about it' I reply glumly.

'Well?' He says.

'OK, if you really want to know, I was in the boardroom this morning preparing the video and TV for a presentation to some potential clients.

As I was putting the videotape into the player, I pulled the machine out a bit, and the power cable fell out and down the back of Colin's new curved, Pear Wood units,' *(his newly decorated board room was a beautiful black and brown creation and was neatly toned down with some hand-crafted, specially curved, pearwood tables and units. The boss had paid*

a bloody fortune for this stuff and was rightly chuffed.)
I continued.

'There was very little room at the back of the units probably just enough for me to squeeze along the back and with the agility I still possessed, and I reckoned I would manage to get the cable back into the machine. As I got underway, It was much tighter than I thought. I tried for a while to manoeuvre my hand into the right shape to insert the small cable into the very tight socket. The room was sweltering as the heating had been put on early to warm the room up for the clients. I had maybe been there for about ten minutes and was sweating buckets. My wrist was getting cramp as I tried and failed many times to get the bloody thing in. It was too tight, I needed leverage, every time I pushed, the unit slipped forward.'
Malky laughed, interrupting me.
'Sorry Jim' he said.
'Please continue'.
I took a deep breath and carried on.
'I was getting frustrated, hot and bothered by my lack of progress, and I knew the clients would be arriving soon. I shouted a few times to no-one in particular. I lay there absolutely knackered, hidden from sight behind the video and TV cabinet. I took a few minutes to get my breath back and was overjoyed when eventually I managed to push the power cable so close to the socket that the TV powered up. The wire was only balancing against the socket, but it was enough for now. I stretched out my arms to begin the get out of there. Just as I moved, the office door opened.

'Come in gentlemen' said Liz the receptionist, 'make yourselves comfortable, I'll fetch some coffee'.
'Fuck' I thought to myself as I lay there hidden, I could hear

my breathing getting heavier, suddenly aware that I could not afford to move. I lay there out of sight. What should I do? Stay hidden? I was meant to be in this meeting, and the ads I had been working on were downstairs lying on my desk.

By this time I was lying on the ground with my arms above my head like an outstretched goalkeeper as I had to freeze like a statue when they came in. I was now getting cramp in my shoulders. I thought through many different scenarios and wondered if I could come up with some quick excuse and maybe a funny line that would get me into play again.

A deep voice whispered ' I wonder if he thinks we're going pay for this décor with our fees?'

'It looks like it cost a fair penny', A younger voice replied.

'There's no way we're going to be giving them our account if he..' Whispered the older man.

He cut his sentence short as Liz reappeared with the café lattes and amaretto biscuits.

'There you go gentlemen, Colin will be with you in a minute or two. Feel free to browse through our award-winning portfolio if you like' she handed them a big book and stepped elegantly out of the room.

'The Leith Agency's ideas were much better than these', the older man said.

By this time I was in a right state. There was no coming out now. I was going to be stuck there for a good two hours while Colin prattled on about the benefits of spending more money than your competitors, and more to the point I was going to miss the meeting.

After a while, Colin appeared and eventually got round to showing them the advertising show-reels on the video. I could hear him playing with the controls on the front of the system. After a few minutes, the power cut out. I could hear him fiddling with the remote control trying to get the thing working again. I looked, and the tentative grip of the power cord had given in, it now lay on my head. Colin was obviously very embarrassed, I could hear him press every button and knew fine well that he had no chance as the power had gone. After a few minutes of silence, he shouted.

'Liz'

There was no answer.

'Excuse me gentlemen' he said. I heard the room door opening and his footsteps stamping angrily on the wooden floor towards Liz' room.

The two clients, let me rephrase that, the two never-ever-going-to –be clients. Started up again.

'This is bullshit' said the younger, 'Can we go soon?'

'Let's wait until we've seen the video then we'll make our excuses'.

Colin came back in, and I could hear Liz's footsteps going twice as fast as Colin's in her attempt to keep up.

'Sorry about that' he said, sounding out of breath.

'Liz'll get it sorted'.

I heard Liz fiddling with the remote control,

'Jim was supposed to be setting this up this morning'.

She said to no-one in particular. I then heard the dreaded words.

'It must be the power cable, it's always falling out',

Colin laughed confidently while Liz's footsteps got closer to where I was lying. She opened the cabinet and pulled the unit out from the wall, the bloody thing was on wheels all of this time, and I never had a clue. She jumped back involuntary as she saw me lying there,

'What is it', said Colin, concerned.

I immediately mimed the SHHH sound to her, I would have put my finger to my lips, but couldn't as they were above my head and stuck fast with cramp. Thankfully the clients couldn't see me from where they were sitting.

'It's only a spider' she said as she quickly put the power cable snugly into the socket. The TV immediately boomed loudly enough to cover my cry as she returned the unit back too tightly against the wall crushing me even more.

I lay there for over two hours in total, and a minute or two after the client had gone, she came back into the room and pulled out the unit. She stood there with her hands on her hips as I slowly curled up, crawled out from behind the unit and rolled about the floor in agony as I stretched my aching muscles. I was just lying there, making some funny sounds. 'Torture' I said.

'What was all that about?' She said, demanding an explanation.

'You'll never believe me' I said, as I stood up and painfully stretched my arms and legs.

It was then that I looked down and saw that I had managed to get black paint from the pillars at the back of the units all over my wife's brand new Nick Faldo golf jumper. I touched one of the pillars with my fingers and shook my head as they were covered in wet black paint. 'How come this is still wet?' I said to her.

'The painters came in last night and touched it up for the meeting today' she said, laughing at me.

I pulled the jumper over my head and lay it on the pear-wood table. 'Will this come off in a wash?' I said rather worried.

'No way' she said, 'looks like its there for good, is it new?'

'Brand new' I said. 'Only the second time it's been worn....and it's Tricia's. She only bought it last week.

'Well sunshine looks like you're in deep shit' she said and walked away.

By this point, Malky was creasing himself, almost falling off his chair with laughter.

'That's some story' he said after he'd recovered his composure, jolting me back to the reason I was in his shop.

'Yeah, I know, I said, I'll have to hide the bloody thing at the bottom of the washing basket and keep putting it at the bottom until eventually I can get rid of it'.

He got up from his chair, 'So I guess you're wondering if your new computer stuff's here?' He said walking towards a pile of brown boxes covered in DHL tape in another corner. He lifted a few small boxes away and revealed a pile of five big boxes. Pointing to them individually he said '20 inch monitor, 3 Megabyte hard drive, state-of-the-art Syquest back up machine complete with 44megabyte tape, IBM 420 CPU and finally a top-of-the-range Xerox A3 laser printer, how's that?'

'Wow.' I said.

I was delighted, I had waited almost three years for this level of system, I had introduced computers into our company by buying my own and, through time, convincing Colin to spend money on a decent setup. Finally, here it was.

'Brilliant' I said. 'When can I take it?'

'Take it now if you want', he said. 'I'll give you a hand round with it, and I can set it up for you'.

We made a path through the messy shop to ensure that we didn't trip over anything and began to haul the heavy boxes to the front door. We managed to get them all round to the office and upstairs without much hassle, I was sweating again.

After we'd ripped off the packaging and were setting the system up he dropped the bombshell.

'I'll be away from this afternoon and will not be back for a couple of months. Decided to go back home to Kansas to see my parents and catch up with some old mates and stuff, it's been a while'.

'What if there are any problems with the system?' I said in an extremely panicky tone.

'No problemo' he Said. 'First I'll set it up, and we'll test it out to make sure that it's working properly, my plane doesn't leave till ten tonight, we've got bags of time, huh? It'll be a cinch buddy'.

He crawled, pulled, pushed, shook and banged the system into some kind of order, but by eight o'clock, there was still no life from the printer.

'I've tried everything' he said, 'Must be a faulty motherboard'.

I was really pissed of at this point, I'd missed a golf outing with some friends and more worryingly this printer and supplier, which were both my choice, were letting me down badly. I had promised Colin that we would be able to print our own stuff tomorrow.

'I have to go in a few minutes, ' Malky said. Plane to catch and all that.'

My fists were rolled up into tight, angry balls, and I could feel the tension in my jaws.

'What about the printer?' I whined.

'Tell you what', he said.

'Maybe it just overheated, we've had it on standby for a full day. We'll switch it off and let it cool down,' when you come in tomorrow morning, it should be A-OK, no problemo'.

'What if it isn't' I said with a definite tone of anger.

'It will be, I guarantee it'.

'What if it isn't all right?' I said more angrily.

'No problemo times two' he said less convincingly.

'I have someone on standby. He's taking over the shop while I'm away'.

'Is he any good though?' I said.

'He's brilliant, I was fortunate to get him'.

'How do I get a hold of him?' I said.

'Here' he replied and scribbled down a number on the back of the laser printer manual. 'His name's John'.

He looked at his watch, said 'I've got to fly now, literally. Remember when you come in tomorrow morning, switch the machines on in sequence, printer first, then the biggest to smallest machines, should be a breeze, it'll work like clockwork, sound as a pound, guaranteed'.

He put his jacket over his shoulder, shook my hand and ran downstairs – that was the last I ever saw of the bastard.

For three weeks after Malky left, I phoned the number he'd given me and went around to the shop every single day, sometimes two or three times a day. It was always closed, not a peep or sign of any life. The bloody printer was still not working. I could get it to print out a test page, but that was all, it did not want to communicate with the computer. Colin was mad at me, he let me repeatedly know that I had spent a lot of 'his money' on a bit of equipment that was holding everything up. I really felt the pressure.

One day I got the shock of my life when I went round to the shop and saw that there was a light on. I looked in the dirty window and saw that there was someone in Malky's corner. I went to the door, but it was locked. I rang the bell, banged on the door, but there was no response from whoever was in. I went back to the window, took a key from my pocket and pinged the window, this got a reaction. The guy ran and hid behind the sofa, the black plastic floor lamp next to it then went out. There was silence. It was evident that he was hiding until I went away. I shouted through the letterbox.

'Are you John?'

Nothing. Not a peep.

I was furious. I went back to the office and doodled on a pad. Much later that afternoon, I decided to go around to the shop again, just for the hell of it. I got to the door, and there was a guy in a cheap grey flannel suit, that was a size too big for him, locking up.

He looked really weedy, he was smoking a fat roll-up.

'Are you John?' I said.

'Who's asking?' He said, looking around suspiciously. He had a long drawn face which was very pale, and he hadn't shaved for a few days.

'Me' I said, 'Malky Muzik said that he was being covered by somebody called John while he was in the States'.

'Ahh?' He said, I know what you're talking about, He locked the padlock, took the cigarette from his mouth and shook my hand.

'You must be Jim?' He said.

'That's right' I replied.

'Jim with the printer problem?'

'Yes, the printer problem that needs to be fixed now' I said.

'Sorry pal, I have to be off just now. Can you come back next Thursday?'

'Next Thursday? ' I said, I can't wait till then, 'I need the printer working now. My boss is going absolutely radio rental at me'.

'No can do' he said.

'Tell me where your office is, and I'll come round next Thursday, I guarantee that I'll get it working,' he put the keys into his trouser pocket, a few pounds worth of loose change rattled.

'That's my bus' he said, pointing to the number 35 that was coming round the corner.

'Catch you next week,' with that, he was off. He ran across the road got on the bus, and I realised that I hadn't told him where the office was.

'Shit', I'd have to make up another excuse to Colin.

A week or two passed before I got a hold of John again. Eventually, he got around to getting back to me and came up to the office on a Thursday, and managed to fix the printer. It worked a treat.

'Thanks John' I said as I printed out reams and reams of backlogged stuff.

'Anything else I can do for you fella?' He used the word 'fella' all the time, even if he was talking to a female. He had a thick accent, not sure where exactly it was from but it was definitely borders, probably near Kelso.

Bob, our art-working guy, had an Apple Mac, but as the printer was fitted up to the PC, he couldn't use it.

'Is there any way that both Bob and I can use the same printer?' I said. Maybe hook both my PC and his Mac together and then both to the printer?'

'I'll have to get my Big Mac guy to have a squint at it' he said. 'He can get in through the back door of most things'.

As he was leaving, he said 'See you.' Before he could finish, I said 'next Thursday,' he gave me the thumbs up and disappeared around the door.

He turned up at precisely two o'clock on the Thursday. He had this big red-headed guy With him, sleeves rolled up on his light denim shirt. He had a cigarette behind each ear and tattoos all over his big red hairy arms.

'Where Are the randy bastards?' He shouted at a volume that was unheard of in our room.

John comes over to me and shakes my hand. 'This is Big Red' he says. I go to shake his hand, but he tells me to lay my hand flat.

He looks at his hand, then mine, puts out a big hand slaps it down onto mine pretty hard. It was like getting the belt at school.

'Jeezus!' I say and look at John, who kind of laughs.

Red hasn't taken his eyes off me since the slap.

'Where're the randy little bastards then?' He repeats. I look at him without a clue as to what he's talking about.

'He means the two computers that have to link up' John says.

Big Red takes the orange leather bag from his shoulder and lays it on the table. He pulls out a cardboard box, opens it and pulls out a small metal box with three sockets and a black plastic switch on the front.

'Meet the matchmaker' he says, laughing, rubbing his hands together.

The toilet in the far side of the office flushes and Bob comes out wiping his hands with a paper towel. He stops dead, looks bewildered by the appearance of these two random guys then looks insulted as Big Red is fiddling at the back of his Mac. Bob's Mac is Sacrosanct, even I am not allowed to go near it.

'What the fuck are you doing with my machine?' Bob says as he rushes over.

'I'm doing what I came here to do.' Said Red.

'Getting these fuckers to hump each other'.

'I don't want you touching my machine. Hands off.'

'Whatever you say chief' says Red, holding his hands up, mocking him.

'Bob, I, thought you wanted to print and get these machines to work together?' I said.

'I do' he said, 'but I want professionals to do it. What the fuck's this?' He held up Red's little metal box mocking it.

"Can't we get Tom Madden in, you know how good he is at sorting these things out?'

'Sorry Bob, Tom's now working for a company in Linlithgow, I've been in touch, and he said he can't commit to anything right now.

Red grabbed the box from Bob. 'This is the latest in Mac to PC technology' he said.

'Fuuuuck awwwwf.' Said Bob. 'It's a fucking switcher socket, you've got no chance of linking anything up with that. Where's the software and the drivers and the SCSI port?'

'It doesn't need software' said Red, I now realised Red was way out of his depth. John, at this time, was just sitting at a desk making a roll-up. Bob and Red started to have a go at each other. I was amazed at Bob, having the guts to stand up to someone a lot bigger and bulkier than him. But when there was any threat to his Mac, he would defend it to the hilt. John got up and handed Red the bag. 'Let's go' he said. Red's eyes were bright red, the same as his face and hair, he was ready to go for Bob, thankfully John pacified him.

Over the next few weeks, John came back to the office, on his own and fixed all of the bugs and teething problems that I'd been having. He got all of the account managers Macs working and linking up to each other, he even set up Email so that for the first time in Marr history we could contact each other via the computer, it was magic.

The account handlers were more interested in playing the new international flags quiz game that had come as part of the entertainment package with the Mac. Ian Dommett and Tony Leatherbarrow were the worst. Tony was on edge the most as his computer screen was visible when anyone came through the door. These guys would be playing this game for hours, pretending they were doing agency work, as soon as Colin came into their office the entire account team would quickly grab their mice and put on screen-savers so that Colin wouldn't see what they were doing.

We never got the Mac to PC thing resolved. Turned out even Apple and Microsoft were struggling to do this. One time John did not appear. This was strange as I'd been expecting him that Thursday to put in a new back up drive, to date he had always turned up on time.

I got into the office on the following Monday and heard a lot of chattering going on between the five girls in the office. As I came into sight, they went quiet.

'Morning Jim' said Lorna.

'Morning' I said hesitantly, wondering what was going on.

'Did you see the Sunday papers yesterday?' Said Irene.

'No' I said.

'Go into the boardroom' she said.

I threw my bag onto the wooden floor, walked to the boardroom and pushed against the frosted glass doors. I could see that there were several newspapers opened up on specific pages, they were spread all across Colin's pear-wood table. I took my jacket off as I walked towards them, wondering if I had won another award or if one of my ads had done something.

I leaned onto the table and looked at the biggest headline. It was the News of The World main front-page story.

'BRUTAL MURDERERS RUN COMPUTER SHOP
ON DAY RELEASE.'

There right on the cover was a picture of John outside his shop in Bernard Street, he was talking to someone who had his face pixelated out. It was ME! I'd been round so often they must have thought I was involved in the scam, the caption even had me as his 'accomplice,' there was a smaller picture of the guy he had murdered and a cut-out of the weapon he had used.

Things fell straight into place, Thursday afternoons, Big Red, John's ill-fitting out-of-date clothes, his constant shiftiness.' Shit.' I thought. I immediately thought about the consequences. Did we pay for something that he would now, never deliver? Did he steal anything when he was on his own in the office? What would I do for maintenance? All of these questions were going through my head when Bob came into the room. He looked at the papers and turned ashen.

'Fuck me' he said. 'If I'd known that two weeks ago, I may have acted a bit differently'.

'May, have Bob?' I said, raising an eyebrow.

.....Every now and then Trish would ask me if I'd seen her

golf jumper. 'Yeah I think it's in the wash I'd say', I was not technically lying as it really was at the bottom of the laundry basket, every time it nearly got to see the light of day I'd bury it underneath the towels and bedclothes again. After a month or two of doing this I eventually took the step and binned it, would've been easier to go and buy her a new jumper but choosing the easy route never seems to be an option for me.

The Blairs move in

THE HOUSE NEXT DOOR to us lay empty for a while. The village of Newtongrange was just beginning to come up in the world after receiving a stay of execution from the local council. The houses were good solid brick and stone, built with craftsmanship and belief that a home should last at least three centuries, and by the time we'd bought ours, it was on its way to passing the first. More and more houses in our street were coming up for sale as sadly, the older population were dying off and the homes that had been rented since they were built were now being sold, and at a high price. Our old neighbour Nancy's house went up for sale around four months after she'd passed away and as soon as the viewing dates were set an enormous influx of people visited. Many of them wanted to have a look inside our house to see what you could do with the space. We'd had time to decorate it but nothing more as we had no money to add anything on.

As the deadline to put an offer in came to a head, more people were visiting. One day a couple got out of their car and Trish spotted them.

'Oh my god, that looks like Elaine and Blairy,' she said.

'Who?'

'They were at school with me'.

'And?'

'Elaine was really nice, very brainy but he was a bit of a case'.

"A headcase?' I said as if there could be any other kind in that context.

'He was a punk at school and an outstanding boxer.'

The last thing I wanted living next door to us was a mental case who could fight, I'd had enough of them growing up.

'Do you think we should try to put them off?' I said.

'He looks really different now, he used to have permed blonde hair, but now he's completely bald'.

Elaine spotted us at the window and waved, we went out to meet them. It was apparent that Stevie had changed, he was now a guy with a wife and two kids and seemed pretty sound to me and after discovering that he was a dab hand at all of the trades; joinery, plumbing, roofing, building and so on and if he wasn't able to do something, he knew a man who could. I was in no doubt as to who I wanted our new neighbours to be as my DIY skills were embarrassing. I'd tried to do some DIY in the flat and always ended up making a complete arse of the whole thing, eventually having to get a skilled person in to repair the mess I'd made. It always ended up with Trish and I getting into a row and costing about three times as much, taking twice as long as it would've done and me admitting that I should have thought about it a bit more before ripping something or other out of the wall and wondering how the bits all fitted together.

Thankfully Stevie and Elaine got the house. This was going to be the start of a big adventure for all of us. I laughed when I figured out the kid's names as it meant there was Andrew, Ross, Stevie and Elaine - ironically they spelt the word that best summed me up as a DIYer.

I'd set a date for the launch of 21Nine Advertising & Design, and with Stevie there to build my new attic studio, all I had to do was purchase some equipment and get out there and get some clients in the door.

My first job was an offer from my athletics coach John Lees. He owned a cater-hire company that had been going since 1880 and provided a brilliant service providing all of the equipment for the Royal Garden Parties in Edinburgh. It was a pretty lavish opportunity and I was glad to take it on. It went without a hitch, and they were delighted with the end result. I got paid, and there it was, my first job done and dusted. As the weeks and months went on, I got more and more opportunities, and before long, I needed someone to look after my accounts. Trish offered to do this for a pittance, and I jumped at the chance for her to sort out the side of the business that I hated. It worked a treat. Although one morning I was up and in the attic working away when I heard the ladders creak. Trish was heading up in her pyjamas.

'Where are you going?' I said.

'I'm' coming up to work, where did you think I was going?'

'You're not coming up here until you get dressed' I said.

'Get lost' She said.

'No seriously' I said, this is a place of business and if you come up here with your PJ's and a cup of tea and toast it'll just be an extension of the house, and I don't want that to happen'.

She looked at me as if I was a moron, but I was serious. She reversed and headed back down in the huff.

'You can do your own accounts then,' she said and stormed off.

Every time I stepped into the attic, I took on the persona of a designer and businessman, it worked for me.

Trish arrived, dressed properly, about an hour later.

'Is this OK Sir?' She said with a large dollop of the most excellent sarcasm.

'That'll do nicely' I said. 'See how easy it is?'

I saw her sticking the Vicky's up as I turned my back.

Work came in very slowly at first, but I joined a couple of networking groups and got out there, meeting people, showing them the quality and range of work I could do. I eventually became chairman of one of the groups, and my first bit of organising for them was typical Jim Divine.

This organisation had groups all around the world, many in the UK and quite a few in Scotland. One day I got a call from a guy called from another group based in Yorkshire.

'Hi is that Jim Divine?'

'Yes, who's asking?' I said hesitantly.

'Hi Jim, my name's Peter Rabbit' he said.

I arched my eyebrows, '

Here we go I thought, another crank caller. I decided to go along with it, hoping I'd manage not to ask how Mrs Tiggy-Winkle was.

'Hi Peter, how are you?'

'I'm fine sir, fine. I've been given your name by Mr Falk who, as you, no doubt know, is your leader in Scotland East District, and he informs me that you guys will be the perfect group for us to visit.'

We got talking, and it seemed that his group travelled all over the world visiting different groups. I hope my thoughts of 'Sad bastards' didn't come over as that's exactly what I thought as he described the places they'd been to Australia, France, Spain, Holland. For bloody networking meetings!

'But not Scotland yet?' He said.

He sounded like Nigel Farage and had a pompousness about him that grated with me. What did he think he'd see up here. Six guys and two women with small businesses gathered at the Scottish Mining Museum on Tuesday mornings at six-thirty and did our bits of the protocol (we never stuck to the mandated scripts). The organisers of our group, the heid yins at the top who were the only ones making money from this organisation had been on at us for a while to up our numbers as we'd been under-performing. I was not interested in doing this as I'd been trying to up the numbers for ages and nothing made people come along especially as you had to pay around £25 to attend and then put in lots of wee shifts during the week where you'd try to get referrals for your guys. It was hard, pointless work a lot of the time and by the time I'd realised this I still had six months left on my membership which you had to pay a year in advance. You may be asking why I committed to this in the first place, but in the first year it really worked for me, now it was bloody hard, unrewarding work. Although the guys in our small group were brilliant and we still keep in touch to this day.

Anyway, back to this Beatrix Potter's boy Peter.

I agreed that he could come and visit us on the first Tuesday meeting in January, our first of the year.

He was ecstatic.

'Right Jim' he said

'I'll get right onto the guys and tell them the great news can't wait to see you all.'

Right. I said to myself, all I have to do now is get some organisation done, then it struck me, how many were there of them?

I called him back up.

'Hi Peter, Jim Divine again, how many of you are coming up?'

'I think only half of the group will be able to make it that early in the year'.

Thank god for that I thought, as I knew we could only handle another eight or ten people.

'So that'll make it around twenty-seven of us'.

I'm sure he heard the shit hit my boxers all those miles away.

'Yeah that should be fine' I bluffed, thinking about this now impossible task.

By this time my office was actually in the Mining Museum. I'd developed their branding and marketing for the last few years, and they offered me a deal to take a couple of newly refurbished rooms in the museum. They were brilliant, a massive departure from my attic and they allowed me to welcome clients rather than have them climb the Ramsay ladders. In one case, a new client, a young woman said she was nervous about climbing up as she was sure I would look up her skirt as she climbed the stairs!

'What the fuck' I thought.

She wasn't a client long. Way too weird even for me.
Most of my clients were happy for me to look up their skirts.
I'd been along to the museum cafe to let them know that
the first meeting in January would be a cracker with around
thirty-six people having breakfast. They were delighted as
they made around seven quid a head.

The morning came after a good Christmas and New Year.
I got to the office really early, like 4 am early. I wanted to make
sure everything went to plan. I got in, put the kettle on and
had brought a couple of slices of bread to have a bit of toast.
I put the Macs on, and the big Hum sound eased me into the
new year, it sounded perfect. I popped over to the fridge on
which the toaster sat and stuck in the two white slices, put the
teabag in the cup and headed downstairs to the loo.

As I sat there thinking about the coming day the most
almighty siren went off, I jumped up and not even taking
time to wipe my arse I pulled my breeks up and ran out. The
whole museum was on full alert. What the hell was going
on. I am not the panicking kind of guy, but at this moment I
was struck still. Lights were flashing in every corner and the
most terrible din. I ran upstairs to my office, and the place
was full of smoke. The toast had got stuck in one of the bits
of the grill and was burning away. I got hold of a dish-towel
and waved it frantically at the offending smoke alarm which
lay directly above the toaster. SHIT! I'd never noticed it was
even there. The towel-waving made no difference, the bells
were still going off, and to my horror, I looked out of the
window and could see that I'd set the alarms off in the actual
museum across the road as well. I ran downstairs looking for
some kind of stop button, but there was nothing. Next thing I
knew there were more sirens, this time it was the Fire Brigade.
Three big trucks all blaring, zooming towards me wakening
up the neighbourhood.

'Shiiiiit, I shouted. I was aware that a false alarm could cost

Thunder At One AM

me hundreds of pounds and that was the last thing I needed right now. I tried to think of a way out of it. Should I turn the lights off and hide. Should I pretend to be unconscious and act a bit?

There was no need. The next thing I knew the phone in my office rang.

'Is Jim there?'

'Yeah, Jim here' I said.

'It's John Wheeler, Chief Fire Officer.

'Just letting you know that all of the key-holders to the museum have been awakened and are on their way over. Can you join us?'

'How did you know I was here'.

"There was a light on in your office and Fergus the Museum Director informed us it was your office'.

'Ah, OK, I'll be right over, I said.

Shit! Well, that was that, I was in deep shit, all of the key-holders lived a bit away except the main man Fergus. Bloody typical of my luck, I cursed myself.

I walked over with the offending bits of black bread in my hand, just to prove that my excuse had at least some kind of evidential material. Fergus was raging. I could almost see the steam coming out of his ears, but he said nothing. The glare I got did the work there. One by one, the key-holders turned up and chatted to the Fire Chief and Fergus. Fingers were pointed in my direction, heads shook in my direction, and I stood there feeling exactly the same as I had years ago when mum and dad had admonished me for taking the kids new toys to bits with a screwdriver on Christmas day.

After a whole lot of hoo-ha and bluster, being taken aside by the Fire Chief and told basically not to be such a naughty boy in future, they all left. Fergus gave me one last glare as he got into his big warm car.

I toddled back over to my office still with the toast, I intended to scrape off the black bits and put a bit of butter on it.

I made a point of moving that bloody toaster well away from the smoke alarm. By the time I'd settled down again, I had realised it was nearly six o'clock. These guys had taken a bus up from Yorkshire and had all checked into a hotel overnight. The thought of them doing this visiting thing still rankled as I could not see the point in it. They'd be here in less than half an hour, so I got on with getting on with it.

I walked back over to the main museum where we'd be having the meeting and breakfast. I thought Melanie, who was the catering manager would be here by now. I'd seen her earlier as she was one of the key-holders who'd been rudely torn from her dreamlike state by my stupidity.

I waited ten minutes, there was still no sign of her. A couple of guys from our group turned up, and I regaled the story about the toast. They laughed, looked at their watches and put hands in pockets.

Another ten minutes. No sign of any doors being opened let alone breakfasts being cooked or even ovens put on. My calculations of all the different things that had to happen at least ten minutes ago in order for things to work out, were assembling into a mass of jumbled numbers: 27 of them, 8 of us, 35 cooked breakfasts, 35x1 minute introductions, 35 x 35 business cards being handed around but the most crucial number jumped into my head. Jane's phone number. I'd forgotten that She'd given it to me a few weeks ago when I told her about this. I dialled quickly. No answer. I was seriously hoping she was on her way down in the car so couldn't answer. It rang and rang and rang. I assumed that she'd been so pissed off at having to get up early that she decided to catch up on the sleep that I had denied her. As the minutes ticked by, the chances of that door being opened and the oven being fired up was drifting like a hot air balloon on a tether of thread. As soon as I heard the roar of a diesel bus engine coming into the car park, the thread snapped, and I was faced with something I'd never experienced before. A blank brain. I had absolutely no idea how I was going to tell these twenty-seven people how on earth I'd managed to muck up a meeting. How to explain to them that the money they'd just spent on an overnight stay and transportation was wasted. I got a couple of our guys to try to come up with a story that could explain why there was going to be no meeting. In the end, as they trooped off the bus, I met Peter, shook his hand, noticed that his badge said Peter Rabbat, felt a wee bit embarrassed as I'd been taking the piss out of him about how he'd hop off the bus or leave a trail of chocolate raisins behind him.

I explained that Jane had taken ill and had to be rushed to the hospital only twenty minutes ago. He swallowed, hook line and sinker. My acting abilities even surprised me. I was faking a bit of shaking, pretending how upset and confused I was by this unexpected situation. I apologised for causing them all of this hassle and was actually given a round of applause (the group leaders liked us to do that) for my honesty. I addressed everyone and said that the only thing I could think of was for us all to head to Tesco. Which was only up the road. They got back into the bus while we led the way in two cars. After a hassle trying to get the bus parked all thirty-five of us trooped into the supermarket and headed for the small coffee shop. To my horror, even though it was a 24/7 Tesco, there was a sign at the coffee shop informing us that they didn't open until seven-thirty, a good hour away. I think my face was as red as its ever been in my life. As the back of the line was trooping in, we were heading back out.

'I have an idea' Iain said.

Iain Thomson was one of our guys who'd lived in the area for decades.

'There's a van that sells hot rolls, and he's usually parked up by the garage at the back of Newtongrange, I'm sure he starts at six-thirty. I was right onto this whipping out my pad.

'Right we'll take orders for who wants what' I said.

It took forever, but by seven-thirty, everyone had a bacon roll and a coffee or tea. I was going to suggest we had our meeting in the park, but it started to rain.

Peter instructed them all to get back on the bus, and that was the last I saw or heard from them. Well, not quite.

I found out a year or so later that my name had been black-listed by our founding fathers and when trying to join a new group after ours had folded, I was informed that I was not suitable for their organisation. I had a laugh at that.

I'd had enough of that bullshit anyway. At one point they sent along a 'Fixer' as we were not performing at a level they wanted us to. We were slacking and were now the only group in Scotland who hadn't increased numbers for over a year.

'Yeah that's because it's a shite idea and rip-off ya bunch o fannies' said Ian, our resident photographer and Victor Meldrew doppelgänger.

I had been going to other networking events which had a wider spread of businesses and didn't require you to promise your first born and an annual fee that was enough to fund a small country.

These meetings were definitely paying off, I was now meeting the main protagonists of businesses, the decision-makers, the heads of marketing and advertising. It had taken a while, but now my circle was growing, and I was getting the chance to work for good companies.

As my experience at running a small business grew, so did my vocabulary and mannerisms, I was able to dress well, talk like I knew what I was talking about and I learned to listen to people waffling on about themselves. I also learned when to say nothing and when to speak. Invaluable lessons that Trish had taught me over the years.

One of the clients I managed to pick up was a group who owned leisure parks and marinas around Scotland. They were big. The owner Sharon had grown up in some outstanding properties including castles and mansions, she had boats and houses all over the world, and I was thankful that the Jim Divine she was meeting once a month was not the old version. That would have lasted a minute or two max before she called 'Security.'

By this time I'd been making a decent living and needed help. Gordon, my youngest brother was out of a job, and as we'd worked together at Marr for a while I knew what he was capable of, and I was able to give him some work.

Things were great, and 21nine was going in the right direction.

I'd met Sharon quite a few times by now, and one day she asked if I could come through to one of her marinas in the West of Scotland to discuss a new brochure. I drove through on a cold winter morning, it was lovely though, as that side of the country can look glorious in all conditions. A bright blue sky and a cold frosty air helped make the freshness zing.

We met around lunchtime in the restaurant at the marina and Sharon had just ordered fish and chips.

'Would you like something to eat Jim?'

'Yeah sure Sharon, I'll have the same if that's OK thanks'.

There was the usual thing of too much cutlery on the table, knives for fish, knives for butter, forks for all kinds of things. Thankfully my training as a waiter at the George Hotel way back came flooding to my rescue. You basically work your way from the outside in. We were engrossed in talking about the new look and feel for the brochure as we ate our lunch. I got into some deep thinking as I always do. I fidget a lot, and my hands move in all directions as I try to explain what I mean. I excused myself to the loo and did the business required. As I washed my hands, a spot of brightness from my forehead caught my attention. I looked closer into the mirror and was horrified to find a dollop of tartare sauce smack bang in the middle. Shit, how long have I been sitting there talking to this extremely high-powered businesswoman with a fucking forehead that looked like I was ready to go sunbathing.

I had no idea how to play this one and decided, in the end, to act as if nothing had happened. As I walked back to the table, I was sure I saw a laugh pass her lips at the missing blob. Anyway, thankfully nothing more was said. After that, we had a stroll around the marina looking at possibilities for a photo-shoot. All was well, I breathed a good long sigh of relief. As we said our goodbyes, I headed to the car. Trish and I had bought a blue Ford Escort a few months before winter and initially it had seemed like a good car, the only problem was that when it got below a specific temperature the locks froze and the only way in was to open the boot and clamber through into the front seat. As we'd been sitting in the restaurant for hours, the temperature did indeed drop to the required level to make me worry if I was going to get in the conventional way (front door) or the embarrassing way. Sharon was still hanging around, and we were small-talking, she was obviously seeing me off which in normal circumstances would be OK. I tried the electronic key, and there was a click, but no button on the door popped up to ease my worries. I tried again and again, hiding the key behind my back while doing this so that Sharon wouldn't see, or suspect anything. I was getting more of the cringe with every push of the button. Sharon was oblivious to the whole thing as the chances of this ever happening to her top-of-the-range Aston Martin DB9 were slightly less than mine.

'Oh Sharon,' I said.

'I think I've left my pad in the restaurant'.

'No worries, I'll nip in for it'.

'Thanks,' I said, knowing that I had around forty seconds to open that bloody boot, clamber over the stuff in the back seat and get my whole body into the driving seat and open the front door before she got back. I tell you if that were an Olympic sport I'd have won the gold medal, no problem.

I climbed in the back, faster than I'd moved in a long time. In my panicked state, I got my new shirt caught on the headrest of the back seat and was stuck. I saw the reception door open and pulled as hard as I could, ripping three buttons off the shirt, which at least, allowed me to slip into the driver's seat and compose myself. I did it with about two seconds to spare, thankfully someone must have shouted on her as she opened the door and she turned back giving me the time I needed.

I sat there pulling the shirt together like a curtain, trying to appear suave and sophisticated like the advertising executives she'd been dealing with in the past. As she approached me at my car window, I'd managed to zip my jacket up hiding all traces of the missing buttons.

'There was no pad there' she said

I dipped into the bag on the passenger seat and feigned surprise and lifted the pad out.

'Sorry Sharon, here it is, must have been here all the time, sorry.'

'No worries' she said, 'See you next month'.

'Will do, thanks again.'

As I turned the key, I prayed that the bloody car would start. It did, I breathed an extra big sigh of relief as I drove out of the car park, Sharon waved me off.

'How in hell's name do you get yourself into these fucking scenarios?' I said to myself out loud. I was furious that I could have lost a good bit of my income through another potential scene from the trials and tribulations of Mr Bean. It happened way too regularly, and I promised myself to sharpen up. I'm sure if she'd seen me clambering into the car through the boot doubled with the Tartare sauce incident I would have been listening to a message on the answering machine on my way home about 'Not being the right kind of agency for her. Using the wrong type of face cream and getting into your car through the Tradesman's entrance is not the look we want from our Creative Department.

She had no idea that it was only Gordon and me as her previous agency were about twenty folk and posh offices in the centre of Glasgow. Thank god the great work we did for her was up to scratch and she never took me up on the many offers to visit us.

There is another embarrassing episode with a client that comes to mind. I was helping a label company to design some packaging for a new nutritional drink that was coming out. I'd done a lot of work, and it took ages for them to square me up for the money they owed. One afternoon I was sitting in my boxer shorts watching the World Cup, Republic of Ireland V Saudi Arabia it was an excellent game. I was eating some tomato soup with a corned beef roll. I just happened to glance out of the window when I spotted the client walking down the street towards the house. Shit. I thought, I'd better get changed.

I grabbed the half-eaten roll and soup and ran out of the living room, aiming to get into some jeans and a polo shirt. Just as I was going out of the door, Robbie Keane scored a goal. I went to go back in to see it but was so uncoordinated that I smashed my nose on the side of the wall at the door. I dropped the roll, and the soup went all over the place. By this time, the client was almost at the door. I desperately needed the cheque, so could not let him disappear under any circumstances. I went through to the bathroom to look at the damage I'd done to my nose, I kid you not, it was like a burst

Thunder At One AM

tomato. Fuck! I said out loud, this looked serious, could even be a stitches job.

The doorbell rang. I put on the light at the mirror and very carefully and quickly put all the bits of the splattered nose in as close to the right order as I could. I pressed them together and ran to the kitchen. The doorbell rang again. I grabbed some ice cubes and wrapped them in a damp dish-towel. I pressed it firmly against my throbbing beak and went to the bedroom to put my clothes on, not easy with one hand. I got to the door just as he was heading out of the gate.
'Ralph?' I shouted in a nasal whine.
He turned around and looked at me.
'What in hell's name happened to you?' He said.
'You'd laugh if I told you'.
'Pray, do tell' he said.
'I thought I'd pop down and deliver that cheque personally'.
He handed me a small envelope.
'I explained to him what had happened. I was right. He pissed himself laughing, I could still see his shoulders shaking as he walked back to his car.
I opened the envelope, and it was a nice little amount. I went back to the bathroom and carefully peeled the dish-towel off, fearing what I might see.
I was gobsmacked. It looked like a plastic surgeon had repaired it. I went to have a look at the damage to the decor, it was a mess, the wall at the door had a chunk missing where my nose had thumped it, there was blood, butter, corned beef and soup all over the room door, thankfully it was only on the gloss and I'd be able to wipe it off quickly. Three bonuses in one day. You don't get many of those to the pound.

The Things you love

TRISH HAD ALWAYS BEEN a dog lover whereas I'd always loved cats. One day when I was in the office at Marr Associates, Bob came in, and we chatted before work started.
'You love cats, don't you Jim?' He said.
'Yeah. I do, why are you asking. It sounds suspicious,' I said.
'As you know, I live in a farm in East Linton, there's a cat who's just had a few kittens on the farm,' he said.
'There's no way the mother can look after them, would you fancy taking one of the kittens?'
'I'd have to ask Trish Bob,' I said.
'I'm not sure she's into cats, she's more of a dog person'.
'How about you both come down to the farm on Saturday, have a look at the wee fellow I have in mind for you, and we'll take it from there?'
'I'll ask Trish tonight' I said.
We headed down to East Linton on the Saturday morning. It was a nice drive as it's such a beautiful part of the world.
Bob met us at the gate to the barn the kittens lived in. '
He climbed a ladder up to a big wall in the middle of a barn.
The kittens had been born in a cavity wall in the barn.
'They've been brought up on squirrels' he said.
He pulled out a few bones from the cavity and also a few furry tails. He then reached back in and pulled something out which he concealed in his palm.
As he stepped from the ladder, he opened his hand in front of Trish and revealed this tiny little blue/grey kitten. I could see she was immediately smitten. It was the cutest wee thing we'd ever seen.
'Well?' Said Bob.
'We'll take him'.
'Are you sure?' Trish said.
'I saw your face, there's no way you can refuse now, surely?'

Four weeks later, we headed back down to the farm to pick him up. When we got him home, he was bonded to Trish. She was still reluctant.

'This is your idea, so this means this is your kitten,' she said. Within a week, Blue had her around his little claw. He was so adorable and cute. We loved him. He was the first thing we'd ever had together. We'd discussed having kids or not a few times, but we felt we would just wait and see what happened. As it turned out, we never got round to it. Blue was the closest we'd get to having a child, and we were happy with that. As he grew, and he really flourished. It turns out he was a cross-breed but mostly Russian Blue, a big, robust and healthy kind of cat. Some nights he'd sit on the tallboy in our bedroom, and when he wanted attention, he'd leap onto Tricia's chest in the middle of the night. Trish thought she was having a heart attack until she realised what was going on.

Blue had been with us for about six years when my youngest sister Catherine came to our house one day.

'One of my neighbours is treating his kitten really badly' she said.

'I'm planning on going into his house and taking the poor wee thing off him. If I do would you take it?'

Catherine was one of the most highly qualified female Tae Kwon Do experts in the UK, and I certainly wouldn't mess with her so I knew her neighbour would probably hand the kitten over.

'Yeah we can see how it gets on with Blue, and if it's OK we'll be happy to take it' I said. Trish agreed as she was now well into cats.

Catherine brought the kitten over the following week, and Blue was neither up nor down about the intruder.

They got on well together.

We were now a family of four, it felt perfect.

We had a routine. Blue would go out in the morning as we

were going to work, and Casper would stay in the house. She loved the warmth while Blue loved adventure.

In our village of Newtongrange, an old mining village there are a lot of old fashioned hobbies, one of the main ones being pigeon racing. The guys that lived in this world were called 'Doo Men' They were a law unto themselves, and their whole world revolved around the 'flying Rat' as they're called in Edinburgh.

These guys hated cats with a passion. Cats threatened their livestock, and some of their pigeons could be worth thousands if not hundreds of thousands of pounds. If a cat became too curious it could end up in a water barrel, no questions asked. They never saw cats as animals, they saw them as enemies.

My first experience of this was when I came home early from work one afternoon. I went into the back garden and Blue was standing there, staring at the side gate. He paid no attention when I called his name. I walked out into the garden and saw our neighbour Billy doing a kind of New Zealand Rugby team HAKA. He had his tongue out and was making all kind of signs to Blue. As soon as he saw me, he rushed back into his garden without a word. Weird.

Trish had been going down to London more and more with Standard Life, She'd worked for them for a good few years and was now having to travel quite a bit.

We always put Blue out at night as he hated being tied up in the house while Caper loved it.

One morning I went out to let Blue in. He usually was at the front or back door, today there was no sign of him anywhere. This was unusual but not unheard of. He could disappear for days at a time. I went back inside and had some breakfast. I shouted on him again, and still, there was no reply.

I decided to venture out to see if I could find him. I got as far as the back of the garden when I spotted him at the base of our fir trees. He was just lying there with his eyes open. I shouted on him, but there was no response. My heart ramped, something was wrong. I rushed over to him and picked him up. His head flopped to one side. He was dead. I lay on the ground next to him and cried out loud. My wee pal had been killed. I lay there for ages just crying my eyes out.

Trish was in London. I called her but only got her answer phone. Trish and I had run around the area where we lived, there were tons of woodland walks and pathways. I remembered one particular place that was so tranquil, I decided that I'd like Blue to be buried there. I lifted him up and took him into the house. We'd just bought him a wee cushion bed that he loved, it was behind the bedroom door. I gently laid him into it and curled his soft body around to fit the shape. I thought about leaving him there until Trish got home later that night. I wanted her to see the poor wee soul for one last time. I called her several times but got no answer. Eventually, I decided that I had to bury him in the woods.

I went into our hut and picked up a good, sturdy shovel. I picked him up in his little bed and put him into the car. I then drove to the woods. The spot I had in mind was much further away than I remembered. I struggled through the undergrowth with a very heavy Blue in one hand and a spade in the other. The tears I was shedding somehow helped me get him there. I put him down and started digging. A few people passed by and must have wondered what the hell I was up to. I'd dug a big hole and was about to place him into it when the phone rang.

It was Trish. All bubbly as usual.

'Sorry honey, I was in a meeting, I saw your call but couldn't get away. How are you?'

I had no idea what to say. As I was in the middle of the woods, the signal was breaking up. I picked Blue up and headed to a clearing.

I told Trish what had happened, and she broke down in tears, absolutely devastated. After a minute or so, she regained some composure.

'Don't bury him there, he'll be all alone in the woods,' she said. We were both crying. Inconsolable hurt.

'OK, I'll take him home,' I said.

As I walked back through the woods with a shovel and a dead cat in a basket, a guy out walking his dog passed me. He looked and ran the other way. It really must have seemed so weird.

I picked her up at the airport later that night.

As I said, we were in the throes of extending our house. By the time we got back, Stevie, next door had been into our garden and dug this beautiful hole on the garden he'd lined it with flowers and had some soft sand to throw on the wee man as we buried him. I was so grateful for that. Blue is now lying with us under our extension. A few years later, in the middle of the night, we heard a strange meowing sound. We'd no idea what it was. I went into the hall, and Casper, our other cat, was lying there in all kinds of agony. It was awful. We called the vet, and they said to bring her straight in. She was in getting operations and treatment for three or four days, but after a while, they had to turn off her life support. She had a tumour on her spine that had suddenly flared up and had caused the agony. We went into the vet to see her last few moments before she passed away. I'd spoken to Stevie that morning to update him as he and Elaine had always looked after the cats if we were on holiday. As we came home from the vets with Casper Stevie had dug a hole in the garden for her. It was such a sweet, thoughtful thing for him to do.

A month or two later, Stevie came into the house to tell us his mum was really ill and had not long to live. Eventually, she died. Stevie called me to tell me the news.

'Jeez, I'm really sorry to hear that I said. Are you OK?'

'Yeah, I'm fine, she'd been hanging on for a long time. It's a bit

of relief actually that she's not suffering anymore.'
Well Stevie' I said.
'If you think I'm going to dig a hole in your garden for your Mum you're sadly mistaken'.
I heard him laughing on the other end of the phone.

Kurtis with a K

KURTIS PUT THE PEN down neatly by the side of his university issue note pad (which he'd bought from the Harvard University gift shop on his last trip to Disneyland with his mother. He'd specifically taken the twenty-hour road-trip just to buy a single pad). He inspected the two words he'd carefully crafted over the past fifteen minutes and said them aloud.

'Dear Moader' he said in his thick Irish brogue. He waited a few minutes, paced to and fro over to the window overlooking Leith Docks, stopped to look at the pigeons that coo'd on the window sill and walked back over to the big red sofa that sat in the middle of his plush office. He picked the pen up, scored out the two words and replaced them.

'Dearest moader?' He said.

He looked upwards to the office ceiling as if trying to find inspiration. As he did this, he chewed on the plastic end of the pen that now resembled a little blue raisin. He winced as it wedged itself into the filling that he'd had repaired that morning. As the filling fell from his mouth, he spat out a bit of blood followed by the blue pen end, in a dribble of coloured saliva that slavered onto his desk. He felt a trickle from his front teeth and automatically wiped his mouth with his sleeve.

'Aargh! Foakin cheap pens' he said. His hands were covered in blue ink and blood, mixing together to form a really vibrant Papal purple. The top pocket of his cream suit had also taken on a bit of the ink and his attempt to wipe it with the napkin from his well-deserved (in his opinion) post-dentist cream and jam doughnut, only made matters worse. A bit of residual cream and sugar mixed with the ink and blood, forming a mini Helen Glassford abstract landscape on the ever so subtle cream canvas background of his suit.

'FOAK OFF' he shouted under his breath as he threw the pen top away. He ripped the sheet containing the two words from the pad, wrapped them with the pen and napkin and rolled them into a tight ball which he slammed viciously into the corner bin in his office. He immediately noticed that the expensive gold filling had disappeared. He got down onto his hands and knees and searched for it, getting purple hand-shaped stains onto the white Axminster carpet as he crawled around.

After a lot of blood, sweat and tears, he saw it in the corner and managed to tease it into his jacket pocket.

He stood up, undid the button on the back pocket of his trousers, took out a sheet of paper and unfolded it. It was a full A2 sheet of thin layout paper.

It was very crushed.

He smoothed the big sheet out onto his desk and took off his shoes. There were already a few shapes drawn onto the paper; the outline of a hand depicted in green crayon. The outline profile of a man's curly head drawn in red felt pen with a few grease marks where the hair had been forced onto the paper and a size nine shoe outline, drawn in blue crayon with the number nine in black biro. He took off his cream slip-on shoes and put one either end of the paper to weigh it down, unlocked his desk drawer and raked about under a pile of documents. Eventually, he pulled his hand out, clutching an indelible whiteboard pen. He removed the sock from his left foot and stood on the seat of his leather office chair and almost fell over as the castors moved under his immense weight. Realising the potential danger, he stepped down from the chair, went into the drawer again and pulled out a red stapler, wedged it underneath one of the castors. It stood solid. He shook the chair a few times to check the stability. He then climbed onto the chair again, this time a bit more carefully and stepped onto the desk. As he put his right foot down onto the paper, he slipped as the smoothness of the sock acted like ice against the shiny paper. He managed to stay on the table and balancing on his left foot lifted his right leg and removed his sock, throwing it away, where it ended up on the back of the chair. He smiled and congratulated himself on his accuracy before looking for a clear space on the paper. He then placed his left foot flat onto the clear area next to the blue shoe drawing. His tongue lolled at the side of his mouth as he stretched down to draw a rough outline of his other foot. The desk creaked as he did this and no sooner had he leaned over beyond the point of no return than one end of the desk collapsed as the legs gave way. Kurti's chin hit the glass desktop with a bang, as he slid dizzily towards the floor, he grasped for something to grip but only succeeded in pulling the architect lamp onto his head. There was an almighty crash as the whole thing settled onto the floor all of the desk's contents keeled over onto their side, the drawers opened and threw up all of their contents onto the already stained carpet. Kurtis, though dazed, was busy trying to hide everything from Liz. He knew she'd be through as soon as she heard the crash. It had happened twice before........

This is how Phill and I imagined Kurtis spent his days. Kurtis was our Head of Sales, that's a laugh. In the three years he'd been with us he made one deal which fell through after a long protracted fight with the potential client and our lawyers.
He'd always been a nice guy, but he was just not suited for work. Any work.

We got to the restaurant all feeling pretty good, I'd gotten over the baby oil gift, and the new MD looked a bit taller than I remembered him. The Christmas party was always a very dull affair, sticking a lot of creatives with a bunch of suits and telling them to go and have fun has never really worked, not just in our company but any. It was like trying to get MP's to party with their constituents. We'd been to many places in my fourteen plus years, and I cannot remember a single time I thought it was fun. Tonight we were getting on with getting it over with, in as civilised a manner as we could muster. That was until Phill Clark decided to see if he could flick stuff into Kurtis's Christmas hat. His first go was pretty accurate. He managed to flick a wine cork straight over the top of everyone and into the hat. It might be worth pointing out that Kurtis's hair was similar to Will Ferrell's in Elf. Thick, and curly, identical to his personality. Kurtis felt nothing. And so it continued. It was mainly Phill and I and every time we got a bullseye, we were pissing ourselves and high-fiving. Phill decided to go for the big one. Using a tablespoon that sat in the trifle, he, loaded it up and prepared to launch a big dollop of fresh whipped cream.

'No Phill', I giggled. 'You can't, that's taking it too far'.

He ignored me and let fly. His hand slipped, and the cream splattered straight into Norma B's face.

It's probably worth pointing out that Norma B was no shrinking violet. She called herself Nordic Norma.

She was a nice enough person, but boy did she look scary, short-cropped hair and a voice that would make a bouncer shit himself.

'ARRRGH. You stupid little bastard Clark,' she reached over and grabbed Phill's hair attempting to stoat it off the table. Thankfully Phill had a good helping of non-drying, wet-look gel in his hair that prevented her from gripping him, her hand kept slipping. She grabbed and grabbed and was only getting more frustrated. She got out of her chair and chased Phill around the table. We were in hysterics.

Phill got to the door and flew out of it as fast as he could run. It was a classic advertising moment.

I caught up with him in a pub later on.

'Well?' He said.

'Put it this way, you're not getting a Christmas card from her ever again'.

'Jeezus Christ,' he said. 'I don't think I've ever run so fast or been so scared in my life, she would have killed me and I'm not being over-dramatic' He said.

'I'm sure she'll have forgotten all about it when we go back after the holidays' I said.

'She was OK after she wiped the cream away, but the biggest laugh was that when we all left to go home, Kurtis pulled his hat off and a ton of stuff fell onto him; cream, corks, a balloon, a teaspoon, and other bits and pieces. He just stood there looking at the ceiling'.

'Fucking moron,' he said and started to piss himself laughing at the thought.

Phill was my copywriter and is a great friend. In Ad Agencies, you have creative teams, generally a copywriter (who writes the words, headlines and body copy) and an Art Director (who looks at how the thing should look). We'd been a team for a wee while and really liked working together. It was not like a regular job. You were given a brief by your account manager, and the deadline would determine how hard you worked on it. Usually, there were very tight deadlines, so we never had that much time to come up with the stuff. We always delivered, though. One October, things were pretty quiet around the office, we'd just lost a big account and were in the process of pitching for others. When we pitched for work, Colin would always leave it until the last few days before the deadline until he decided which route he was going to go with. This inevitably meant that we'd all be working for at least two to three days solid, no break, no nine to five, a straight seventy two hour shift with no time for sleep just the sneaked-in cat nap when you were in the nice, warm, cosy photography room.

As I was saying, October was quiet, we were really enjoying being paid for doing little.

'Do you ever play golf?' I said to Phill.

'Yeah sure, and I'm pretty good'.

'Really?

'Yip, I haven't played for a year or two, but that shouldn't matter too much,' he said.

'Fancy sneaking out and going for a game now?' I said.

'I left my clubs at mum and dad's,' he said.

'No worries, I've got an extra set in the attic, and if we go to Vogrie we'll be heading that way'.

'He immediately turned his computer off, and we headed to the door.

'Where are you two off to?' Reg said.

"Out to do some research, be back in a few hours'.

'See ya,' Phill said, and we headed.

It was a glorious Autumnal day, the sun was bright, the air was warm, and the leaves on the little nine-hole course were resplendent in their warm, shimmering tones. The perfect day for golf. Not a breath of wind.

I teed off on the first hole. A straightforward par three, right up the middle. Phill shoogled his club a couple of times. Then missed the ball completely. I pretended I didn't see it. I didn't want to embarrass him.

He swung again. Missed. This time a little swear.

The third time, he actually hit the ball, and it trundled off the tee and landed about four feet in front of us.

'Just start again' I said.

'You sure?'

'Of course, we're only out for a nice walk, no need to get all competitive'.

He picked the ball up, placed it on the tee and this time hit a beauty, right into the woods.

By the time he'd hit his thirteenth shot I had lost it, so had he. We were both lying on the ground, laughing.

Back in our office, we had so much floor space that we had an actual putting green. I'd brought in some spare golf balls and a couple of old putters. We'd spend thinking time putting for hours, it was incredibly therapeutic. The putters also came in handy for delivering messages.

On the odd occasion when Phill and Barry weren't talking, Phill would stick a post-it note on the end of a club and hold it over his computer to the opposite side where Barry sat. 'What are you writing?' I said one day, this had been going on for a few days. Phill would stick a note to the putter, hold it over his computer, Barry would take it off, crumple it up and throw it in the bin without looking at it.

When both of them were out, I took some of the notes out of the bin.

.....'TWAT'
FUCKWIT'
'SPECCY TWAT'
'Dick Splash'
'TIGHT WAD'

I shook my head.

Dnipro Kids

ONE DAY I WAS sitting at my desk in the office, eating lunch and reading through the online papers. It was a Monday, and I always liked to read the sport, especially if Hibs had beaten anybody decent at the weekend. We'd recently beaten Rangers three-nil at Ibrox with wee Ivan Sproule getting a hat-trick. Trish and I had been on holiday down to Torquay and had driven overnight to get there. When we'd arrived at the hotel, we were so shattered that we conked out for a good few hours and woke to the news that we'd hammered Rangers. It felt great. This past weekend we'd also beaten Dundee United and were on a great run, the only downside was losing four-nil to Hearts earlier in the season.

As I was reading, I spotted an article for a Hibs charity. It was called the Dnipro Kids Appeal. As I read the article, I got more and more interested. The basic story was that Hibs were drawn against a Ukrainian team called Dnipropetrovsk in the Uefa Cup. We played the first leg at Easter Road, and it ended nil-nil. On the return leg, we got gubbed five-one. Hibs took a big support over to Ukraine, and as there was not a lot to do before the match, a few of the guys had heard about an orphanage near to the football stadium, they had a whip-round and were able to raise a bit of money for the kids. As it turned out, the relationship grew and grew, and before too long, the Hibs fans were raising thousands of pounds a year for these orphans.

By the end of the article, I couldn't believe what was happening. Tears were streaming down my cheeks. What the hell is going on, I thought. I don't do tears unless my cat's die or I burst a football. I went online to find out more about this charity, and I was blown away, so much so that I called them up that day to see if there was anything I could do to help them.

I eventually got round to meeting up with the two guys who'd started the charity. Steve Carr and Mark Strachan, two of the most solid Hibs fans you could hope to meet. They were aided by some other Hibbies; Colin Dudgeon, Alix Murray, Graham Barclay and many more.

After a few hours chatting and getting to grips with what they wanted to achieve, I was able to help them. Their logo and marketing material had been produced by the committee, none of them had any graphic design or marketing experience. This was my area of expertise, and after a week or two, we had a brand new Dnipro Kids identity which was ready to propel the charity to a new level. I also joined the committee and eventually became the chairman. Trish joined, my brother John joined, and another few members of our family lent a hand as well. Steve Carr was the guy who'd put, (and still does put) in the most effort and time. He even learned to speak Ukrainian fluently, not bad for a Hibs supporting, alarm engineer. One day Steve asked me if I'd be interested in going with him to Dnipropetrovsk to deliver supplies and gifts. After talking it over with Trish, it was a done deal. I was so nervous. I thought I'd break down and bubble my way through the week with the poverty and plight of the orphans. A four-hour flight into Kiev followed by an eight-hour train ride in an antique train with no food or drink made for a memorable journey.

At the airport, we'd been told that a lot of the gifts we'd brought for the kids had been confiscated. We were furious, a lot of the kid's sponsors had spent time getting to know the kids through email and letters and had bought them presents as they knew this would be the only treat the kids would get. We tried to get hold of the person in charge of the airport but to no avail. We left feeling pretty downhearted and cheated,

but this was nothing compared to our train journey. We'd
pre-booked our seats well in advance, but when we got to
the station, we were told in no uncertain terms that if we did
not pay the 'Special Tax' our tickets would be taken from us
and we would not be permitted to travel. As you'd expect,
we had no option but to pay. Thankfully it wasn't too much.
Our first stop was Kiev. Steve had booked what seemed like
an Oompah Loompah's bedroom, the thing was tiny. Both of
us were to share this space but thank god it was only for one
night. I remember barely sleeping, wondering if anyone would
come through the unlocked door. We were rudely awakened
with the sounds of a lot of people shouting outside. I looked
out of the window, and as we'd arrived in the dark, I had no
idea where we were. Right in the middle of the main square in
the Capital city virtually right next to a statue of Lenin. There
was a fully-fledged market going on, and it wasn't even nine in
the morning.
Steve was already up and showered.
'Right Jim lad, let's get out and about for a bit of breakfast' he
said.
We walked a hundred yards or so, and as Steve had been here
so many times, and spoke the lingo, it made life a lot easier.
We ended up with some kind of beetroot muesli and coffee
despite their looks, were perfectly acceptable.
We headed back to the room after breakfast and got our
things together, now the journey had really begun.
We'd paid the 'Special tax' and were well settled into our seats.
There was a video playing on the ancient 'entertainment
system', but it was in Ukrainian. I'd no idea what they were
saying, but as it was an eight-hour journey and the video
looped after an hour, I eventually got the gist.
A good eight hours later, we arrived at our destination station,
Dnipropetrovsk. It was much bigger than I'd imagined and
much more decorative. We were met by Ira (Eera), and after

a few hugs and kisses we got onto the minibus she'd hired for us. Ira had been our Ukraine based help since the inception of the charity. She lived in the city with her two daughters Masha and Natalia. The three of them were the lynch-pin to making the whole thing work, especially the language barriers as trying to organise things from Scotland via English to Ukrainian and to try to get through the swathes of red tape would not have been possible.

We spent the next few days with them, and I was dreading visiting my first orphanage as I'd imagined I'd be blubbing like a wee lassie at the poverty of the kids.

We drove through the wide streets of the city, it looked as if there were six lanes on the road, but as there were no road markings, it made things very hairy. The vehicles on the street had mostly seen better days, I got the impression that they used these vehicles until they died (either people or vehicle, whoever croaked first), I had absolutely no idea how or if, there was a roads or vehicle department. At times I completely understood why there were so many orphans as well as the low life expectancy. These were mainly due to poverty which leads to overindulgence in alcohol and inevitably arguments and crime, the bitter, bitter cold of the winter (down to -30 most years) and the lack of proper nutrition.

As we approached the orphanage, I braced myself for the impact. I took a few deep breaths to steel myself against the horror that lay beyond those doors. It was an entirely different impact than I was expecting, the kids ran to me, and as I fell to the ground, they were all over me, laughing and shouting, it was the most amazing feeling of joy. I was hooked right there. As the day went on, I got to know a few of the kids, and I was blown away by their spirit, despite the life they were forced into. It was unfortunate, but I understood that they were entirely oblivious to the conditions. They were just kids, and they were brilliant. There was some kind of annual celebration on the day we were there. Something akin to our harvest festivals in the UK. The kids made a special crown for me made from some vines and flowers, I really was taken aback by them. The one thing that really got me was my inability to communicate verbally. Their language is so far removed from ours that there are very few words that make sense to either of us. I managed to remember a couple of words, but that was it. Steve was terrific, translating what they were saying and relaying it to me. After the celebrations, it was time to do what we'd come here for. We were going to assess the most urgent needs of the orphanage. We did a tour of the whole place, and as we walked from room to room, my heart and jaw dropped. It was horrendous. The shower consisted of two hoses attached to a cold tap, there was no modesty curtain. The three toilet pans which were shared by all had no seats, the bedroom was a long narrow room filled end to end with beds. Each of the kids had a numbered one, but the only storage they had was under their pillow.

After that, I was back to the stage where I had a lump in my throat. It was so sad. I thought about the so-called poverty and recession that was just happening in the UK and scoffed at the thought. What we had was a cutting-back on luxuries, there was no way it was recession or poverty, at least compared to this place. Even the most impoverished people back home had so much more than these guys. I swore with Steve that I'd do whatever I could to alleviate their suffering. I spent a great deal of time taking photos of the kids. The idea was to use the images to show what they were going through and from that, we'd be able to tug enough heartstrings to pull open purse strings. It worked a treat.

Within a few months, we'd arranged a show-piece dinner in the Sheraton in Edinburgh. Hibernian football club embraced us with open arms and their contribution to the cause has been nothing short of amazing and continues to be to this very day.

It must have been three or four years later when I returned to Dnipropetrovsk. This time the only members of the committee who could make it was me and my brother John. We were due to go out for a week and had never spent that long together since we were sharing a room in the early eighties. We had a ton of stuff to take out with us, mainly gifts for the kids from well-wishers in Edinburgh. Our main aim was to help establish a baby centre in the middle of Dnipropetrovsk. Over the months, we'd spent time looking around the city for an apartment to house Natalia who was to look after this new part of our charity. She was going to be responsible for looking after young women who'd got pregnant through the disinformation spewed by the religious sects in the city. They preached that using condoms would spread aids and sexual disease. Although this is obviously untrue, the young women believed it and never used any form of protection meaning that there was a hell of a lot of unwanted pregnancies in the city and worst of all, there was very little to no government support. We'd decided to open a baby centre where these young girls could come to and get some basics; nappies, baby food and talk with someone who cared. In extreme circumstances, we'd offer the girls a place to shelter for a few nights as the temperatures regularly get to -30 in winter. On our arrival, John met Natalia and Ira for the first time. These were our Dnipro employees who kept the whole operation ticking over.

We arrived pretty late on Friday night and headed right to the apartment that we'd leased for a year. The idea was that we'd sleep here to save the cost of a hotel. We grabbed a pizza and a beer before heading there. As soon as we hit the hay, we disappeared into sleep.

The next morning we awoke early. There was so much to do in a short space of time. John is really good at organising whereas I'm as good as a cat on catnip.

We headed to IKEA or the Ukrainian equivalent and picked up the furniture and fittings we'd need. We then went to some kind of cash and carry where we bought the nappies, baby food and all other supplies. John was shocked at the state of the place. It was so run down. We in the UK were, but it looked like these guys had been there for the past fifty years. The contrast between the area where the orphanage was based and the newly developed million-dollar flats, could not be more significant. There was only a distance of hundreds of metres between them, but to the people with the money, the orphanage was invisible.

We spent most of the day getting the baby centre fixed up. I say we, but in all honesty, as well as organisation John was also good at DIY. Building the furniture that we'd just bought. I felt as useful as an indicator on a submarine.

We eventually got everything completed. The place looked brilliant. Natalia and Ira were ecstatic. They now had a place that they could operate from and make a big, big difference to young girls lives. It felt great.

'OK,' Ira said. 'Now that we've completed that we have to go and see Vasily at the TB sanatorium. The TB sanatorium looked after a hundred kids. They were shipped here from all parts of Ukraine, and they were here because their parents had no money and no other place to send them, this was the last chance saloon. Tuberculosis was rife at this time and is still on the increase.

Vasily was so glad to see us, we were the only people who helped his institution, he received a fraction of money from the government but what we gave them was their primary income for the year. It was ridiculous and incredible at the same time.

When we got there, he'd laid out a whole spread for us. I'd been there the year before with Steve (Carr) and Robert (Brown). Vasily had plied us with 100 per cent proof Russian vodka and a whole spread of treats such as smoked salmon, pork and black bread. All I remember was downing three or four straight vodkas and sinking into some kind of dream where I was aware of what was happening to my floating body but had absolutely no control over it. I think Robert and I were about to pagger each other. He was a sixty-five-year-old professor of languages at Stirling University. He'd had slightly more than me to drink and was away with it.

'I'll get one of my Russian KGB pals to fucking shoot you Divine' he said.

'Don't ever take the piss out of me again'.

It was true. I'd slagged him earlier in the day thinking it was a bit of banter.

I now looked at him with different eyes. Did he really know the Russian Mafia?'

'Fuck off' was all I could muster in my drunken state. I think he attempted to punch me but missed completely. Steve walked along with us, just laughing, he was well used to the vodka.

As John and I looked at the spread that Vasily had laid out for us, I swore to myself that I'd stay away from that dangerous vodka. As we sat there, Vasily gave his usual speech about being so honoured to accept the gifts from these people thousands of miles away who cared so much for his kids when people in the city did not give a toss whether they lived or died. It was emotional and incredibly touching. I felt the lump in my throat again as I had when I first got involved with these kids.

Vasily poured John and me significant measures of the vodka in specialised shot glasses.

'Here's to Scotland' he said in his best English. Both he and John downed them in a oner. I pretended to but emptied mine into the plant pot which I'd deliberately positioned myself next to for the occasion. Much praise and appreciation was going on and well-deserved if I say so. Two, three, four glasses were raised and sunk, more toasting. The girls were not allowed vodka, in such occasions in Ukraine, it is customary for the female kind to partake in fizzy liquid, generally champagne or prosecco. In the meantime, I could see the plant wilting as I poured in my fourth glass. I sipped at a glass of sweet red wine which was given as a side-drink. We chatted, and it really was brilliant to hear Vasily go on about how much our efforts had changed the landscape of the TB sanatorium. He could not believe that people in Scotland were giving money to kids that were a million miles away. It was an incredible, humbling feeling. As we were yapping in broken English/Ukrainian, Vasily piped up.

'Ver ees Jon?'

I looked around, it was a small room, but I'd never even noticed him going out.

'How long has he been away? ' I said.

'Tventee meenoot' Vasily said.

'Really?' I said.

'Yes, he's been away for a long time' Ira said.

I became instantly concerned.

'I'll go and look for him' I said.

I walked all through the dark, depressing sanatorium, it was like something from a Charles Dickens novel. Metal cages and locked doors everywhere. As I walked through the long corridors, I spotted a shape lying on the linoleum floor in the distance. I ran along, and sure enough, there he was. Lying on his back oblivious.

'What happened he said. Where am I'.

'It's OK' I said. Trying to comfort him but also feeling guilty that I hadn't warned him how lethal this stuff was.

'Did I get to the toilet?' He said.

I looked down at his crotch area, and there was a big wet patch. He'd pissed himself. John is not like me. He's very proud and respectful. He was about to say something when Vasily and his friend came into view. They had a torch as the lights were knackered.

John put his hand up to his eyes to shield the light.

Vasily and his pal marched along with military-style. They said nothing. They merely grabbed John and dragged him to a nearby toilet.

'Help. Jim? Help' he said.

I stood there. I reckoned these guys had seen this all before and knew what they were doing. Vasily's pal sat John on the toilet seat and started to slap him forcefully around the face. John tried to put his hands up to protect himself, but Vasily held them firm. The guy kept on slapping.

'Help me, Jim, I can't see anything,' John pleaded.

Again, I stood there reckoning they knew best.

They forced him to drink a big dollop of salt, immediately he threw up.

'Help Jim' he said as he slid into oblivion and unconsciousness.

At that moment, Ira and Natalia appeared.

'They said something to Vasily in Ukrainian.

The next thing I knew is that we were hauling John into the back of the minibus. He was out of it. He lay across the back seats almost dead to my mind.

We got back to the apartment, and somehow, the three of us hauled him up to the seventeenth floor or whatever it was. I got him undressed to his pants, and we put him to bed. Natalia and Ira said their farewells and headed off. I looked at my watch. It was twenty past five on a Saturday afternoon, and by the look of things John was going to be out of it for at least a good ten hours. What could I do? I was on my own on a lovely Saturday evening in a city that was alive.

I had an idea. This whole Dnipro connection had come about purely because of football. If Hibs had not been drawn against them in the Europa League cup match, this scenario or the help to the orphanages would never have happened. I then had, what I thought, was a brainwave. I went into my room, rummaged in my bag through my kit and pulled out my Hibs strip. I put the whole outfit on, checked that John was still snoring soundly and headed out of the door into the city centre.

I headed to the plush shopping mall, I'd been there earlier in the day and was surprised at how modern it was.

I walked around, conscious of curious glances in my direction. A middle-aged man wearing a full football kit on a Saturday evening. The Ukrainians are incredible. Their dress sense is immaculate. They have real pride in how they look. I once asked Natalia why it was so important to them.

'When you have nothing' she said. 'It does not mean that you are nothing. We always try to look our best and believe that we are worth something. Does that make sense?'

It did. It made complete sense to me.

The effort they took to dress up, and the pride they had in their best clothing was something to behold. I've never been a dressing up kind of guy, but I got exactly what she meant. The girls looked absolutely stunning, and the blokes looked not bad.

As I strolled around the shopping mall, I spotted a sports shop. I walked in and looked through the selection of footballs they had on sale. I picked up a couple and kicked them about to see how they felt. I finally decided on a fluorescent yellow one. It felt just perfect, right weight, the right level of inflatability. I bought it, I think it was around fifteen quid. Expensive for this place. I got out of the shop and started to do keepie-uppies with the ball. I then started running through the marbled hallways dribbling against invisible opposition, probably shouting that I was playing for Scotland against England.

'Yes, Divine goes past Beckham, dummies the Neville brothers, nutmeg's Wayne Rooney and hits a wonder goal into the net, David Seaman did not even see it. I booted the ball off a couple of empty shops. Next thing I knew there was a bit of shouting. I'd no idea where it was coming from. Did I have something to do with the escalation of voices? I caught a reflection in one of the windows. A security guard was running after me, he had his gun pulled out of its holster. I stopped dead in my tracks. Another security guard appeared from the opposite end of the mall again, he had his gun out. I was stumped. Was this for real? They were shouting something, but I had not a clue as to what they were saying. I spotted a third opening to the centre, picked up my ball and ran towards it. They followed me, but I was out of there as fast as my legs could carry me. I was still pretty fast. I ran for maybe seven or eight minutes, as fast as I could. The last thing I wanted was to be locked up in some Ukrainian jail. I was way too pretty for that lark. After the distance had lapsed, I took the time to look behind me. They'd given up. I thanked the Lord and cursed myself for being so arseholic. What was I thinking?

As I began to get my breath back and relax, I decided that I really should check that John was still OK. I made my way back to the flat. I was surprised at this as my sense of direction is pathetic. I can get lost in a two-bedroomed house.

I stood in the doorway to the room where John was still asleep. I shouted at him to make sure he was still alive.

The covers moved slightly, and his head appeared for a very

brief moment. He then disappeared again. I heard him snoring and again headed for the door.

I walked down the street, thinking that, as football had created this scenario, I should be able to generate some interest.

I kicked the ball off walls, cars, bus stops, fences and continued down the road. I passed a pub where there were a lot of people sitting out in the evening sun enjoying a beer and some snacks. At a table, four people were sitting. One of the guys was signalling to me. He beckoned me with his hand. Come here he was saying as I walked over to their table, ball under my arm.

'What are you doing?' He said in really broken English.

'I'm just kicking a football around' I said.

We eventually got an understanding going, his friends spoke no English whatsoever, so he was translating for them.

As the message got through that, I was here to help Ukrainian orphans the others in the group started to respond in a very warm, kind way. They invited me to sit with them and tell them a bit more. As we sat and had a pint or two the main guy went to the bar, he came back with a snack for everyone. I was confused. It was a big, long dry fish. Apparently dried pike is one of the go-to snacks for Ukrainians. They passed it around the table where they were all picking and pulling chunks off it. It looked horrible. It made its way to me, and for some reason, I stuck my finger into the eye socket. It was still moist.

I almost boked. Moist eye socket was definitely not on my list of snacks. The two lagers had made me feel merry, and after drying my wet finger on my green socks, I decided it was time to go. I picked my ball up and headed into the city centre. I must have passed the ball to a hundred people that night, I would kick the ball to them, hoping they'd pass it back and that's precisely what happened most of the time. As it got later and later I was running out of energy and places to go.

I decided to head back to the flat, but as I looked around, I had no idea where I was. There was a group of young adults dancing to some music near a bridge. I headed over to them. By this time I'd popped into a couple of bars and had about four or five pints.

I kicked the ball in their direction, and it came back immediately right to my feet. I did it again with the same response. As I got closer to the dark underside of the bridge, I kicked it again. I saw a young woman trap the ball with her high heels on and kick it back to me.

I was gob-smacked. She was wearing what I can only describe as a beautiful red ball-gown with the most elegant black high heels on. I kicked the ball in her direction again just to make sure I saw what I thought I'd seen and sure enough. She trapped it and passed it right back to me. As I kicked it again, a few of the guys who were standing around took the ball and started to kick it around between them. One of the biggest guys approached me and put his arm around my neck.

'You like zee football?' He said.

'Yeah, I love it' I said.

He got a couple of his pals to come over, and they all introduced themselves to me. They handed me a can of beer from the stack they had sitting in a bucket of cold water. We kicked the ball around for a good twenty minutes, nobody saying much at all. I loved it. This is precisely what I was hoping for when I first went out. After a few more beers and with the kick about getting more serious, the young woman in the red dress approached me.

'I think you better go' she said.

'Why' I said.

'They are saying they are going to jump on you and take your ball'.

'They can have my ball' I said. 'I don't need it'.

'No. You should go. They are getting angry that you are here.

I'm sorry, but you must go. Now'.

I'd no idea what was happening, but for some reason, the dynamic had changed, and not in my favour.

I thanked her for her help, picked up my ball and ran as fast as I could towards the flat, at least I thought it was the right direction. It just felt right. It was actually way wrong. Almost the opposite direction of where I should have been heading.

I ran and ran as far and as fast as I could. I had no idea where I was heading but just ran until my lungs hurt. After a while, I got to the highest point I could find and looked around for some landmark.

Thankfully I spotted the weird cactus-shaped building that was close to our apartment. I headed towards it and eventually it took me back to the right place. I was so relieved. I went straight to the room where John was sleeping and checked he was OK. He was snoring loudly. I made a cup of blackcurrant tea and headed to my kip. As soon as my noggin headed for the pillow, I was gone.

I was awoken by a loud banging on the door.

I sprung up in a single dream-like Ninja move to find Natalia and Ira waiting impatiently.

'You are ready?' Natalia said.

I'd completely forgotten that we were meant to be going on a road trip to the interior of the country to check out a new orphanage that had desperately asked for our help.

As they walked in, I could see them looking at me questioningly. I still had my full Hibs kit on.

'I'll be a couple of minutes' I said.

I got dressed and splashed some cold water on my face and rubbed the fur off my teeth with my toothbrush.

As I went through to the living room, Natalia and Ira were standing at the door of John's room looking in.

John's head was barely visible above the covers.

I tried to wake him.

'Are you coming with us?' I said.

Natalie and Ira looked at me.

'I do not think he will be ready to go anywhere until tomorrow' Natalia said.

'Are you OK?' I asked him.

'Yeah. No. I feel crap. You just go without me' he said.

I put a litre bottle of water next to his kip and closed the door quietly.

The three of us went downstairs and into the minibus. After a good three hours drive, we got to the new orphanage. I could see straight away that they really needed our help. The woman who was running the place was an absolute angel. She'd spent her life and everything she'd ever owned on looking after these poor kids. I felt that old lump in my throat coming back to life again. Four of the little kids who were waiting for us in the garden did an acrobatics act for us, and one wee lad was doing these incredible handstands over and over again. It was great to see such honesty and purity where only poverty existed. I looked at the clothes they had on and almost wept. By the food traces on their clothes, you could see what they'd eaten for the last month, The woman, Christina, who was running the place, was getting help from nobody, she was using her life-force to feed, house and clothe these kids. When we told her that we would supply her with enough money and funding to help her run the place, she was overwhelmed.

'Why are you doing this?' She said to Ira in Ukrainian.

They could not understand why people from a country thousands of miles away were helping people they didn't know.

Ira put her hands up and said' They just want to help.'

We got a grand tour and a bite to eat, thankfully there was no vodka on show.

We got back to the apartment, and by this time, John was

recovering well enough. I told him how it had gone, and he was delighted.

We were heading home that night, and as it was a Sunday, no trains were going from Dnipropetrovsk to Kiev Airport. It meant we had to get a taxi. Kiev is around eight hours from Dnipro, and a cab was going to be very expensive. After much deliberation we got Ira to organise a taxi for us, agreeing on a reasonable fee with the firm as we did not want to pay any 'special tax'.

Sure enough, the cab turned up on time. We said our goodbye's to Ira, Natalia and Masha. It was a long drive, especially after all of the hard work and emotional stuff that we'd dealt with over the period. We were silent for the whole journey, just looking forward to getting home.

As we approached the airport, we were so relieved. We had about an hour to get checked in and through the gates. I had the money ready for the driver. Wearily we got out of the cab, I said thanks to the guy for getting us there on time. I then handed the money over to him, adding a generous tip.

'Not enough,' he said.

I was confused.

It was about two thousand Ukrainian hryvnias equivalent to about eighty quid.

'What do you mean not enough?' I said. I could feel my blood pressure increasing.

'You said two thousand'?

'Each' He said.

'You never said anything about that' I shouted at him.

I was absolutely raging. I was thinking about how he was ripping us off while that money could have been going to the kids.

'Normally, John can go into a rage that most people would

shy away from. This time it was me. I was incandescent. I was about to go for the guy.

'Stay calm Jim,' John said.

'Look over there'.

In the distance there was a gang of men approaching us, they'd obviously heard the commotion and were ready to back their pal up.

The guy refused to open the boot with our suitcases in it until we'd paid the full fare of four thousand hryvnias.

Reluctantly I dipped into my wallet and handed the money over. Thumping each note into the guy's palm, hoping I hurt him with each smack. He eventually released the catch on his car boot, and we greedily hoisted the cases out and ran towards the airport.

After the usual checks and delays, we got onto the plane and headed for home. We'd had a really brilliant trip. It was the first time in decades we'd spent that much time together, but even through all that time, nothing had changed. I was still the immature kid while John was sensible and grown-up about everything.

We landed at Edinburgh airport in the early hours of the morning and shared a taxi.

I dropped John at his farmhouse near Dalkeith before I headed to Newtongrange.

Just before the taxi pulled away to take me home, John stopped me.

'Something's been bothering me Jim' he said.

'What's that ?' I said.

'You know when I was out cold for sixteen hours?

I think I was awake for thirty seconds out of that whole time and, correct me if I'm wrong, but I think I was dreaming. I woke up for that short time and was convinced that you were

standing in the doorway with a full Hibs strip on. How weird is that?'
I looked at him and laughed.

As I shut the taxi door, he stood there pointing at me with a very uncertain look in his eye.

BILL BAILEY

I'M STANDING WITH TRISH on the shores of balmy Lake Garda in Italy. On our annual summer holiday. It's been so long in coming for us as we've been working our socks off and training hard for months. The sun is beating down, but I'm not happy, not in the slightest. The phone goes, and it's my brother Gordon calling from our offices at the Scottish Mining Museum in Newtongrange.

'Bill Bailey, the comedian, has been in touch and wants us to design and produce his first songbook,' he says excitedly.

I'm not really listening though, I'm so mad with what's just happened that I think he means Bill Barclay, a lesser-known beardy Scottish comedian.

'Whatever', I say, 'let me know how it goes.'

Gordon seems a bit put out by my lack of response but not as put out as me. I've just had a real argument with the German receptionist in the Motel of what was supposed to be a hotel and a good hotel at that.

'But we've upgraded you twice Mr Deveen' she says.

'Divine' I say for the third time, getting more than slightly annoyed.

'I'm not interested in upgrading' I tell her.

'We were expecting a four-star hotel suite, not two-star Butlitz accommodation - (a cross between Butlins holiday camp and Colditz prison camp). Our travel rep definitely said it would be four stars. I could see she was scoobied by the word Butlitz. I didn't bother to expand on it.

Trish had, for the first time ever, gone against her instinct and let a travel expert sort our holiday for us. This woman had arranged many holidays for our friends who swore she was

the best. We looked at where we wanted to go, what type of accommodation, what facilities and amenities we liked and so on. The rep came up with a two-week break at Lake Garda, she showed us some cracking images, and we loved it.
Fast forward a month or so, and that's where we are now.
As Trish and I are both very understanding and accommodating folk, we decided to give the rep the benefit of the doubt.
'Let's take a stroll around to see if the amenities will make up for lack of class in the accommodation' Trish says. After a few minutes walking and having to run for our lives over the motorway as there is no footpath nearby, we decide that it's completely farcical.

I decide to go back into the Motel and give that ignorant German receptionist another piece of my mind. In the meantime, Trish is on the phone to the rep who says she can't do anything till the morning,
'You'll have to spend the night there while I sort out somewhere else' she tells us. Not happy bunnies, I can tell you. I make an appointment with the manager of the Motel as I am getting so pissed off with the German receptionist. She's already called me a liar twice and Meester Deveen four times, seems the customer is never right. Herr Basil Fawlty comes to mind, but I bite my tongue.
I take a look around the bar area it looks OK, not good enough to eat in but OK for a beer, compliments of the manager who's just turned up.
'What seems to be the problem, she says'.
I ask her to take a walk to the room with me and explain that we've saved up hard for this break and are not happy with the level of discomfort.
'Would you stay here for your main holiday?' I say.
'No' she says. 'I work here, I would not holiday where I work.'

She misses the point by a mile, I let it go, explain that we're after four-star accommodation and not stardust. She eventually gets it. Fair do's to her she says we can stay the night and go find somewhere else tomorrow, no charge and a free drink. Things are looking a bit brighter.

Trish is worried that we'll be charged for the two weeks accommodation as we've paid it upfront. I ask her to get me the number of the rep and give her a call. I get her right away, and she says she'll see what she can do.

'Sleep on it' she says. Things will look different in the morning.

'I used to do that with my inflatable doll' I say trying to lighten the mood. 'Things were always a bit flatter in the morning'.

She kind of coughed, maybe stifling her laughter but I doubt it.

As we're sipping our complimentary beer, I pick up one of the travel books in the small library. It's all about Lake Garda, there are so many amazing places around it.

After our drink, we went for a wander to find something to eat. There was nowhere obvious. I spotted some coloured lights in the distance, but it meant we'd have to cross that busy road again. After a lot of waiting and running, we made it. We reached the coloured lights, and it turns out it was a pizza place, the only place within a mile of the Motel where we could eat. It looked like Portobello promenade. It had six plastic tables and one guy behind the counter, making the food and serving it. The pepperoni pizza looked OK, so we ordered that and a bowl of spaghetti.

As we ate, I was flicking through the book I'd borrowed from the library. The place on the lake that jumped out was called Sirmione. It looked idyllic.

'Right Trish', I said. 'Listen to this.

'Sirmione is a resort town on the southern bank of Lake Garda,

in northern Italy. It's known for its thermal baths and Rocca Scaligera, a medieval castle overlooking the lake. Set at the tip of a peninsula, the Archaeological Site of Grotte di Catullo encompasses a Roman villa, a museum and olive trees. Just below the ruins is the rocky Jamaica Beach. The church of San Pietro in Mavino is adorned with frescoes. There are multiple high-quality restaurants and a multitude of bars and ice cream shops. There are very few cars on the roads as it's a designated pedestrianised area.'

'Wow!' She said. 'Sounds amazing'.
'I have a plan' I said. We leave the Motel at nine tomorrow morning, and we're going straight to this place, don't worry about the cost, if we have to pay for that shitty Motel we'll deal with it later, the most important thing we need right now is a two week holiday.'
I showed her a couple of images, and she was sold.
The next morning we got up, had a quick bite to eat and headed out of the Motel towards the taxi rank. Plenty were waiting. We told the driver all about our shitty experience so far, and he was very helpful. He was on his phone to someone possibly talking about us. He dropped us off at the tourist information.
By the time we'd approached the window, the girl behind the desk had heard about our plight.
'OK,' she said. ' I have two suggestions for you'.
Suffice to say we ended up at this stunning hotel. Marble balcony overlooking the small yacht collection on Lake Garda. It was a dream.
We unpacked and headed for a very welcome lunch of spaghetti carbonara, garlic bread and a bottle of Gavi. Bliss.
The weather was mid-twenties, the birds were singing life was all of a sudden, great.
I think we got drunk on the wine, but we were probably

delirious with relief. The day passed quickly into the evening, and we sighed happily at our weird situation. As dusk approached, we headed off to our kip for the deepest and peaceful sleep, we'd had in ages.

We awoke the next morning to a glorious sunrise, the lace curtains on the balcony blew to and fro with the light, warm breeze drifting in through the open doors, the sound of laughter rose up from the decking platform below where breakfast was being served. We looked at each other, really appreciated our luck.

As we sat at the sparsely populated area after ordering our breakfast, a voice called out.

'I recognise that accent'.

An English guy and his partner were sitting a few tables away.

'Edinburgh, if I'm not mistaken?'

'Close?' Trish said, 'Dalkeith to be exact'.

'That's not bad though is it?' He said.

'Ten miles or so out'.

'Very impressive, where are you guys from I said'.

'Guess?' He replied.

I'm pretty good at guessing accents and said 'Surrey?'

'Not even close,' try nearer Scotland' he said.

'No way?' I said. You don't sound remotely Scottish'.

'Why don't you come and join us?' I suggested as we'd clearly both just started breakfast.

They did. 'Steve' he said, shaking my hand 'and my wife, Sandi'.

'Jim' I replied 'and' 'Trish' she said, leaning over shaking his hand.

We got on like the proverbial house on fire and sat gabbing all morning and agreed to meet up for lunch the following day. Trish and I headed for a stunning wee village at the top of Lake Garda called Riva. As we wandered around the market in the glorious sunshine who should we see walking around in front of us but Steve and Sandi. They were headed for the same ice cream parlour as us. We let onto them, and two minutes later, Steve had bought us all ice cream. I tell you it was such a treat in that heat.

The following morning we met at breakfast again, sat together, we got on so incredibly easy. Sandi worked for the LTA (Lawn Tennis Association), and Steve had retired from Texaco Oil a few years previously due to ill health, he looked fine to us though. We ended up meeting most days, and it was a real bonus to meet such lovely people who had similar interests. It seemed we had been on the same trail for many weeks without ever noticing. Steve and Sandi had been to the Edinburgh Festival for a week or so, from there they'd gone to Venice at the same time as us and ended up in the same hotel in Lake Garda. We got on so well, and we ended up spending almost every night with them. When it was time to go, we agreed that we would definitely meet up in London and Edinburgh.

On our return from a brilliant holiday, I went into the office on the Monday. Gordon had been on his own for two weeks and had done an incredible job on the Bill Bailey songbook. We sat down for an hour to go over everything that he'd been doing and sure enough, as soon as I saw his work I realised it was Bill Bailey and not Bill Barclay. This guy was a big hitter on the comedy scene. I'd seen some of his work on various TV shows and really liked him, despite not realising who he was. It must have been the red mist brought on by that German. Apparently, Bill had been trying to find a design company that could come up with the right look and feel for his first songbook, he'd been trying for a while and when someone suggested us we made it happen, at least one of us did. It was a really wacky design as you'd expect if you know anything about Mr Bailey.

We were to be in London the following week with some proofs to show him, and from there it was a question of getting the songs and illustrations finalised and sent to the printer and binder.

We arrived in Heathrow on Friday mid-morning and headed into Central London. We were due to meet Bill at three o'clock and went over the work we'd done for him, we spoke about making a few amends here and there but were generally very happy with it.

When we got to the restaurant, Bill was there, surrounded by a big group of people. A small, attractive young woman came over to us and introduced herself.

'Hi, I'm Chris, Bill's wife' she said, shaking our hands. 'You must be the Divine boys'.

'By name and nature,' I said.

'Really?' She said.

'Nah. Just name' Gordon said.

She laughed and asked if we wanted a beer while her husband was dealing with a lot of other things.

It felt really nice, none of this big showbiz stuff.

After about half an hour, Bill came over to where we were sitting, finishing our beer and introduced himself to us. Like his wife, he was also very welcoming.

'Right boys, let's see what we've got,' he said, rubbing his hands in anticipation.

We'd mounted the spreads onto boards, it looks much better presenting things this way.

He went through them, 'Uhu, Mhm, Yeah, love it' and so on.

'Well, I can say categorically that I'm delighted with that. When can we go to print?'

'Well if you're happy with this, we'll get finished artwork to you middle of next week, and when you sign it off, we'll go straight to print. How does that sound?' I said.

'Stunning' he said. 'Must go, the wife's calling me'.

That was brilliant Gordon, outstanding work I said. He was chuffed as he'd been a Bill Bailey fan for years.

We sat and had something to eat and another beer, this was the kind of client we needed, high profile yet very happy with the work we produced. It felt great.

As we sat eating, Bill's wife came over to us again.

'Are you guys coming to the show tonight?' She said.

'What show's that?' Gordon asked.

'Bill's having a pre-tour show at the London Hammersmith theatre'.

'Yeah, that would be brilliant' we both said.

'Cool, can you find your way there or would you like a lift down with us?'

'A lift would be great' I said. 'We don't really know London that well'.

'Where are you staying tonight?' She said.

'We're actually staying in this hotel'.

'Even better' she said. 'See you in the car park at six-thirty?'

'Thanks, Chris,' I said.

Gordon loved this.

Before we left for London, Bill's agent had called us up to see if we could come up with any ideas for Bill's up and coming world tour, the Tinselworm tour.

'Yeah, of course, we can, what kind of thing are you looking for' I said.

'We're not really sure, can you guys throw a few ideas around and maybe show Bill them when you're down in London?'

'Yeah, no problem,' I said we're onto it.

We did three or four spreads with some ideas and put them in with the songbook stuff.

Bill and Chris and their wee boy Dax were waiting for us as we headed into the car park.

'Evening lads' Bill said.

'Ready for a big night out?'

'Big Night?' I said. 'I thought it was a pre-tour test show?'

'It is, but there's about two thousand folk who have bought tickets'.

'Wow.' That's impressive pulling power,' I said.

'You ain't seen nuthin yet,' he said.

'Hold onto your hats'.

We got to the theatre, and sure enough, there were queues all around the corner, and this was a good forty minutes before it was due to start.

Chris had reserved front row seats for Gordon and me, what a real treat this was turning into.

After almost two hours of standing on stage on his own with some musical instruments and a couple of strange-looking objects, Bill closed the show. It was superb and finished with a well-deserved standing ovation from the crowd.

As they dispersed, there were a group of people hanging back for autographs. As you'd expect, Bill signed everything and was generous with his time. When everyone had gone, he sat on the chair on stage and gave out a massive sigh of relief. He looked knackered.

Gordon and I went onto the stage and congratulated him on his fantastic work.

'Are you lads coming to the after-show party?' He said.

'Yeah, sure, of course' we said.

'Where is it?'

He pointed to the back of the stage.

'Behind that curtain,' he said.

'We walked over to it, and Chris was there with Dax, he was asleep in his carry-cot. On the small table was a bucket full of

Thunder At One AM

ice and bottles of beer. There was nobody else there.

'Is this it?' I said, bemused.

'Yeah, we like to have quiet nights when we can, but don't worry after the big show at the O2 Arena, it'll be a different sort of after-show party'.

As we sat there talking about the show, Chris jumped up.

'Have you found your passport yet?' She said to Bill.

'No, I thought you were looking for it?'

There was a slight domestic going on here.

'Bill, if you don't find it by tomorrow Dax and I are heading on holiday without you, I told you to look for it ages ago,' she said, obviously exasperated.

'Well, I've been busy,' he said.

'Hi guys', Gordon said.

'Jim and I need to get some shots of you for a couple of ideas, could we take ten minutes and do it now?'

By this time it must have been around half-past ten, we were all pretty tired and hadn't eaten much.

'Yeah, sure thing,' Bill said.

We headed back onto the empty stage and got some photos of him mucking about. It was incredible the energy he had, especially given that he'd just put on an incredibly tiring one-man-show.

After we'd finished, we headed back through to where Chris was sitting.

'Are we ready for something to eat yet guys?' She said.

'Yeah, of course,' I said. I really was hungry now.

As we were heading out, Bill stopped dead.

'Hold on a minute?' He said.

'I think I know where my passport might be'.

He pulled out his mobile phone and Gordon, and I stood there looking at it. It was mesmerising.

'What's that? I said, mouth hanging open. 'Is it one of those new iPhone thingy's?'

'Yip, just got it delivered this week' Bill said.

He came over to us and started flicking through his photo library, then spread his fingers on the screen and the image zoomed in. It was incredible.

Chris looked at him.

'Well?'

'Oh, yes?' He said. 'My passport'.

He called somebody called Alfie.

We heard one side of the conversation. Seemed like Bill had sold his old car to an old Norwegian guy, Bill thought his passport was in the glove compartment and that he could get Alfie to find this guy and recover his passport.

'Damn?' He said. Putting his phone away.

'Is that a no then?' Chris said.

'Unfortunately, it seems the old guy I sold my car to, sold it to a scrapyard. Alfie says the old boy got more money than he paid me for the car from the scrappie'.

'Well, it looks like Dax and I are on holiday by ourselves then?' She said.

'Not at all' Bill said.

'I have a cunning plan'.

'Well, let's hear it then?' Chris said.

'I've thought about it, and I remembered that my passport wasn't actually in the glove compartment. Before I sold the car, I remember taking everything out of it and putting it into a box and taking it to one of those 24/7 safe and secure lock-ups,' he said triumphantly, pointing a finger in a victorious salutation.

'Let's go,' he said.

We headed out to the car. I got into the front seat while Bill drove. Chris, Gordon and Dax were in the back.

'Right, here goes,' Bill said, starting the car up.

'Where are we off to?' Chris said.

Bill was flummoxed. 'You know, I can't quite remember,' he

said. 'I think I have three of those places with stuff in them'.
He got his phone out again, called Alfie.
After a few uh huh's and mhm's he put the phone down.
'Looks like there are only two possibilities,' he said.
We drove for a good half hour and reached a big warehouse
with a security gate at the front. There was a vast ten-foot
wire fence all around it. Although it was meant to be 24/7, it
seemed you had to give them 24 hours notice, the sign on the
wall stated this categorically.
Bill looked around and Chris and smiled sheepishly.
'You know what?' He said.
'I don't actually think it's in this one, it's in the other one'.
'And where exactly is that?' Chris said, getting a tad irritated.
And who could blame her?
He pulled out his phone and called Alfie again.
He tapped something into the map on his phone, and we
headed off into the night.
Again, after a half hour's drive, we ended up at another big
warehouse. This time there was no fence around it but a series
of wooden gates but no sign of any security guard.
Two weeks previously, Gordon had taken part in the World
Tae Kwon Do championships with his Scottish team, and
they'd won gold for a thing called 'Destruction,' I think it was
the event where you had to destroy planks of wood, and stone
all piled up.
Earlier in the day, Bill had been asking what else we did apart
from design and we'd told him, Gordon mentioned his latest
medal.
Bill, Gordon and I got out of the car, while Chris sat with
Dax, who was now starting to wake up, probably heard our
stomach's rumbling.
We walked around the place, looking for weaknesses, we were
looking to find a way in as Bill was getting pretty desperate
by this point, he'd worked so hard and didn't want to miss his

holiday.

'Gordon,' he said, pausing for a moment.

'Do you think you could tae kwon do one of those gates?'

'Easy' he said.

'But when I've broken it, do you know exactly where your unit is and how do we get into the box, do you have your padlock with you?'

'Nope,' Bill said.

The car window wound down.

'Bill, do you know exactly where your box is' Chris shouted.

'We've just had that discussion,' he said, in a low voice.

'Right, back in the car boys.' He said.

'Looks like I'll have to think of another solution'.

We drove back to Hammersmith, near to their house and stopped outside an Egyptian restaurant.

'Are you boys OK with Falafel and such like?' He said.

I'm pretty fussy, but by this time I would've eaten anything.

We were all out of the car before we could answer.

We sat there stuffing our faces, it was way past midnight now, and we still had to get back to Central London.

Bill dropped Chris and Dax off at their house and gave us a lift to our hotel.

'Are you guys OK to discuss the tour programme tomorrow morning?' He said.

'Yeah, we've got a few spreads prepared' I said.

'Hopefully, you'll like the ideas'.

We said goodnight and arranged to meet for breakfast at a coffee shop in Hammersmith at eleven.

We were knackered by this stage, and I fell into a deep sleep.

The next morning we got a train right to the front door of the cafe. Bill and Chris were waiting for us. They'd ordered us some breakfast. It was a glorious sunny morning, and we sat outside.

'That was some night lads, eh?' Bill said, laughing.

Thunder At One AM

'Did you find your passport' I said.

'Nope, still no sign' he said. Looking at Chris.

'What are you going to do then?' Gordon asked.

'Apparently, I can apply for an emergency passport as I'm a celebrity' he said laughing. 'It'll take a couple of days to get here, but at least I'll be getting that much-needed rest'.

'What's going to happen with you and Dax Chris?' I asked.

'We've no choice, we have to head out tomorrow morning as the tickets and hotel are all booked. Bill will have to join us when he gets his passport sorted'.

'Where are you going?' I asked.

'We're off to an isolated little island in Sumatra where there are no mobile phone signals, TV or internet.' She said. The only communication is by conventional telephone or 56k modem and Fax machine'.

'Fax machine?' I said. 'Bill, when exactly do you need this tour brochure?'

'Well the tour starts in six weeks, so we'll need the brochure in three or four weeks' he said.

My heart jumped.

'How long are you on holiday?' I said.

'Three weeks from tomorrow. Why?'

'So, in effect, that only gives us one to two weeks to design, write, proof, test, print, finish and deliver the brochure?'

'Yeah... Ah. I see where you're going with this,' he said.

'How big is this brochure going to be?' Gordon asked.

'Apparently, it's got to be at least thirty-six pages, but my tour manager is recommending we go for a forty-eight pager'.

'Jeez, that's a really tough call' I said.

'Don't worry' he said. I've lined up a copywriter for you to work with, you guys can do this at a canter'.

I sat there and took in the gravity of the situation. This really was a big ask and given that we'd not even shown him one design yet.

'Bill, do you realise that sending an A3 spread full of illustrations and fine text halfway around the world on a 56k modem/Fax machine will take a good few hours and if we're doing twenty-four of these spreads that's a lot of time that we really haven't got.

'Don't worry, you can do it,' he said.

'Right let's see your initial ideas'.

Thankfully, he really liked the work we did. The only problem was that it was 'too clean,' he wanted a dirty, grungy feel to the tour brochure. Gordon and I sat and did a couple of sketches based on what he'd said, and he loved them.

Right, that was the basic style agreed, now all we had to figure out was the content, illustrations, photograph, and copy.

'By the way' he said, handing a big cardboard box over.

'Here are all of my photos from the past twenty years, use what you can, make sure you look after them though.'

We said our goodbye's and headed back to the hotel to pick our things up and then head straight home, there was definitely no time to waste.

The copywriter Bill had organised for us to work with us. Was a guy called Dave, as the time line was so tight it meant he had to come up to Newtongrange for a week to ensure we got the words sorted and put into the brochure as soon as possible? We also had access to an illustrator called Max, from Manchester who produced these incredible illustrations of all kind of weird things that were in Bill's head. So, that was us, a team all set to get this thing designed. If we had been given more time, it would have been one of the best things ever to work on as Bill was such a wacky, zany guy and we could do absolutely anything. There are not many opportunities to do stuff like this, it's basically a license to have fun and play while getting paid. But under the circumstances, we had no time to waste so the pressure would be on until we delivered the finished item. We organised a B&B for Dave and arranged to pick him up from Edinburgh airport in two days, this would give him enough time to get his research on Bill sorted and also give Gordon and I a chance to assemble all the pages and layout basics. We also had to brief the printer about the quantities that we'd be buying. He stopped breathing for a minute when I told him the deadline. 'I'm not sure that will be possible, but we'll give it our best go,' he said.

I knew I could squeeze him for a time if I had to so I wasn't anxious about the deadline, as long as I had the final copy to him by in eighteen days he would be fine.

By the time Dave had arrived we were in excellent shape, we knew the layout was working, and it was merely a matter of filling it up with stories, competitions, anecdotes, images, illustrations and other wee bits and pieces to entertain the Bill Bailey fan club. Three days into it and we were really starting to motor. 'Right guys' I said, as we were about to leave the office for the night. 'I'll fax these over to Bill tonight, that way we'll be able to test the line speed, and hopefully, it'll get there, and we will have a response from him by the time we get in tomorrow. As you'd expect the fax number he gave us for the hotel didn't work. 'Shit, what are we going to do Dave said,' they're about seven hours ahead of us so it'll be about one in the morning, there's no way Bill will be awake at this time.' 'Surely the hotel staff will be up though' I said. 'Give me the number Dave'.

I called them up and explained who I was and what I was trying to do. They were great. It seemed Bill had the right number, but there was an extension number required for the fax.

'Do you mind if I send a quick test through to ensure it's working?' I said.

'No problem' the receptionist replied. I sent through a plain sheet of paper with the words Bill Bailey.

I waited with bated breath.

'Beel Beelay' the guy said.

'Brilliant' I said, 'Fantastic,' I was so relieved.

We set the fax to work and headed out for the evening.

The next morning, was glorious, sunny and warm. I met Gordon, and we went to pick Dave up from his B&B. Headed off to the Mining museum for breakfast and then straight up to the office to hopefully see a fax on the machine from Bill. I opened the door, and Gordon opened the windows.

'Yess.' Dave came through with a sheet of paper in his hand. 'He loves it,' he said.

The three of us bent over a tabletop as we tried to decipher Bill's scribbles. Basically, there were only a couple of words he wanted, but the first spread was ready to go.

There was palpable relief in the room but also an acknowledgement that we were on the right track. That day we managed to finalise four or five spreads and get them off to Sumatra. The days flew in, and it really was a brilliant time for all three of us. Max kept coming up with incredible illustrations, and the whole thing was coming together beautifully.

After a good thirteen or fourteen days, we had the complete brochure sitting in front of us, as a mock-up, which is a test print to make sure everything is working together and all the pages and stories are in the right order.

It looked great.

'Well, Bill's home in a few days so let's get a high-quality mock-up made, and we'll head down to London to see him,' I suggested.

We arranged flights and headed down the next day, planning on Gordon and I coming home the same night.

We met Bill and Chris at the same coffee shop in

Hammersmith, they both looked so relaxed, Chris had a lovely colour about her while Bill looked the same.

'Not much of a tan Bill' Gordon said.

'No, I'm not a tan kind of guy,' Bill said.

'I'd rather be watching birds in the undergrowth or swimming with dolphins'.

They showed us some of their pictures, it looked incredible.

'Anyway, onto business,' Bill said after a bit.

'Do you know something?' He said.

'I loved that experience. I used to go for a short swim, get my coffee and croissant, head to the fax machine and pick up my spreads for the day. It was great to see that stuff roll-off, and it gave me a chance to think about the spreads. I've never had so much enjoyment doing a brochure. Thanks, guys, I really appreciate your work'.

We all felt great when he said that.

'So what's the next step?' He said.

'Well, if you and Chris take some time to go over this mock-up you can get back to us with any final amends, from there we'll get it made into finished art and off to the printer for a final proof, from there we'll be going to print,' I said.

We finished our breakfast, gave hugs all around and we were off.

Over the next ten days or so, we got everything finalised approved and printed. I think we got around ten thousand brochures printed and also three thousand songbooks. They were going to be the main piece of merchandise for Bill's world tour. A week or two passed and we were ready to head to the first of two Scottish shows, first one in Glasgow and the second, a day later in Edinburgh. Bill gave Gordon and me special passes for our wives and us. The first thing we did on arrival at the Glasgow show was to head for the merchandise stalls to ensure everything was laid out correctly, it all looked great.

The show went down amazingly well and again we were invited to the after-show party. There were about nine people there. The Edinburgh show again went down well, and then he was off to tour the country. We would next meet at his final concert in the O2 Arena in London in a couple of months. I could not believe the support he had. He filled the O2 arena three nights in a row with around ten thousand people per night. What a guy. Gordon couldn't make the final show, so I went with my mate Chris who was a fan. Trish and Chris's wife Anne had decided to go to see Take That who were on at the main O2. We were happy to just go along to the gig and have a blast. It was a fantastic experience to see that many people were mesmerised by one man and a lot of musical instruments. After the show, Chris and I headed to the after-show party, which was quite a bit away from the arena. We jumped into a taxi and told the guy where we were heading. English was not his first language, you could argue that it wasn't ours either. It took a long time to explain to him but eventually we thought we'd done it. Twenty minutes later we found ourselves in the back of the taxi under a bridge somewhere in a dodgy area of London. By this time, I'd had a lot to drink and could feel my stomach gurgling. The guy had no idea where he was meant to take us, and it looked like he had decided to take us back to his clan's lair. Six big guys were lurking outside the taxi. The guy was insisting we paid him.

'No way pal,' Chris said. 'All you've done is taken us on a wild goose chase, and we're further away from the hotel than when we started off'.

'You better open the door,' I said threateningly, holding my hand over my mouth. I was getting close to the moment of no return.

'Money,' the guy said.

I couldn't hold it in any longer. I sprayed the inside of the taxi with a colourful stomach full of mixed drinks. The door immediately popped open. The guy was going mental.

Chris and I bolted out, ran under the bridge and away, being chased by his pals. After a while we stopped breathlessly, we were pissing ourselves laughing, but there was a real tension as we had no idea where the guys were or if we'd bump into them. After what seemed like hours, we eventually got to the hotel where the party was.

This time at the after-show party, it really was an after-show party. Hundreds of people were there quaffing champagne and sausage rolls. Famous people you'd seen on TV and films, actors, comedians, singers, whatever.

After an hour of no show, Bill eventually turned up to great applause, he was wearing a white cowboy outfit and looked really happy with himself.

Eventually, he got around to chatting with us. 'That was the best show yet Bill' I said.

'Yeah it was something special wasn't it' he said.

'Now for the rest of the world (he was heading to Australia, New Zealand and many other places).

Thanks again for all of your hard work, this is definitely the best tour brochure I've ever had.

I'll see you around pal'.

MY ADVERTISING & DESIGN Company, 21nine
Advertising & Design had now been going for around eight
years. I was just about making a wage and getting some decent
clients.

I started it back in January 2000. I'd been with Marr for too
long and needed change in my working life. It was no longer
enjoyable, I was not getting out of bed with that tremendous
sense of excitement and energy that I'd always had. It was
becoming like a job, and that was one thing I had no intention
of carrying on with. Each day it was getting harder and
harder for me to motivate myself. I could feel myself feigning
illness just to live another day out of the office. (When I got
a skive day off I'd genuinely watch old stuff like Mr Benn and
Bagpuss). It reminded me of calmer, more relaxed, hassle and
care-free times in my life.

The highly coloured path of my life was now fading to black
and white and was in danger of fading away altogether. Since
we'd won all of those awards over the years, we were buying in
staff who only wanted to win awards and to hell with the day-
to-day work that had to be done to keep the company stable.
I could see the business had taken its foot off the accelerator
and was counting on the momentum we'd gained through
years of hard work and hundreds of awards to see us into the
future. We lost a few accounts in a very short time, the whole
tapestry of Marr Associates seemed to be unravelling, thread
by thread. One of the first casualties was Phill. I remember it
as if it was yesterday.
Phill came into the office, buzzing like a hungry bee through
an open window, it was his birthday, and Phill loved his

birthday. We were planning to go out for a little celebration at lunchtime probably downstairs to the Malt & Shovel for a couple of beers and some of their scrumptious fish & chips. He'd just made us a coffee when our phone rang, I picked it up. It was Liz.

'Can Phill pop up to see Colin in his room?' She said monotonously. (Which was very unlike her).

I relayed the message to him. He jumped up, rubbing his hands with glee.

'That'll be the wage rise I was after' he said.

'Looks like beer and food will be my treat today'.

And with that, he bounded upstairs......

Fifteen minutes later and he virtually crawled through the door.

'What's wrong?' I said.

'I've been laid off' he said, trying to force a laugh.

'Eh?' I was gob-smacked, nobody had told me, or even hinted that my partner in crime was being made redundant.

'Are you sure?' I said, really not believing it.

'Of course, I'm bloody sure he said' laughing.

'It's not the kind of thing you don't hear with 100% accuracy'.

'What happened?' I said. I was stunned. Disappointed. Angry.

'I went in expecting a birthday pay rise as you know, and Colin didn't beat about the bush. He said he had to let me go'. I've never seen him looking so severe.

As Phill replayed this, he started to go into hysterical laughter at the irony of the situation.

I sat there, shocked and unwilling to believe it. Deep down I knew Phill would get a job quickly as he really was a talented guy, and not just in copy-writing, he could turn his hand to a lot of different things; illustration, design, writing for radio...

As it turned out, he headed back to London and since Marr he's had a series of very successful agencies.
I was now a team of one.

It took a long time to sink in, but like any change, I got used to the new 'norm'.

Weeks later, I sat at lunchtime reading a National Geographic magazine, the article was about the Caspian sea, the only land-locked sea in the world. I'd always thought of a sea as a vast, uncontainable, unfathomable raging, beautiful beast, yet here was a sea trapped within the confines of a country and for some reason, it resonated with how I was feeling right now. I was this vast force of energy and creative ideas looking for something to focus it on, yet I was utterly trapped. I had to get my creative thinking cap on and get me a way out of this situation.

Over the years at Marr, I'd introduced all of our new computers in the hope of keeping us at the forefront of technology. We were still miles behind the curve, but personally I understood much of what was going on, Colin just didn't want to pay for me to buy anything significant as he didn't believe in the internet.

I made the decision to leave Marr and set up on my own. I had developed the skills to enable me to do everything from creating the concept right up to delivering the finished product. I talked it over with Trish, and she was right behind me as always.

It took a long time to come up with the name, we tried many different ideas: The Blue Dog, The Green Armadillo, James Dean Design, and so on. Eventually one day I was sitting at tea, and I just said,

'How about 21Nine?'

I like it' Trish said. We agreed, it sounded just right. It was now a case of me getting my finger out and setting up an office/studio in our reasonably large attic.

When we first moved into Newtongrange, (a move I was not too enamoured with) as always, I trusted inherently the vision that my wife possessed by the bucket-load.

After selling our flat in Leith and purchasing the house in Nitten, we settled in quickly, it was a real eye-opener moving from a one bedroomed top floor flat to a three bedroomed semi-detached cottage with a good front and back garden. All of our worldly possessions barely filled one room.
The neighbours were brilliant, mostly old ex-miners who'd rented their homes since time immemorial but were sadly on their last legs.

Our next-door neighbour Nancy was in her late eighties and over the couple of years we knew her, we learned that she'd lost her fiancée in the first world war and had never looked at another man since. The faded picture she had of him still stood proudly on the little table next to her bed in a basic silver frame. He was a young man, probably in his late teens, dressed in a Tommie's uniform, his moustache bent upwards as he smiled uncertainly at the camera. He was about to head to a place called Passchendaele. I wondered if he knew the full horror of what was waiting for him, would he still have gone? Seeing that picture brought home to me, a real sense of sadness and a life unfulfilled every time I visited her, which was most days. The day came when Trish and I returned from work to find the house empty. Nancy had fallen and broken her hip. We'd never see her again as she died a short time later. I prayed that she would now be reunited with that young man who'd sat at the side of her bed smiling at her for the past sixty or so years.

Back in 2008, my business was failing miserably, I was racking my brains to try to find a solution. Clients were leaving me quicker than lice off a drowning pigeon. I'd tried everything to keep my business going. I hated SKY News for putting up that big, black 'RECESSION' banner every morning. They made it look like it had been sprayed onto the screen by some vigilante, anti-establishment group. The reason I hated it was that every morning, clients or potential clients would be sitting with their cornflakes looking at this and thinking there's no way I'm spending any money on advertising or design. Well, thanks to SKY, it worked. In my opinion, you helped us believe this was real and the impact it had on thousands of businesses, big and small was terrible. So many lives ruined and it would take years to get back to anywhere near the level we were at before. It was undoubtedly the toughest time I'd ever experienced in my entire life.

Pre-recession my life was excellent. I had a small business that was giving me and my brother Gordon a living. We had great clients and great fun. Once it all started to crumble, there was no stopping it. I had a big overdraft that I never used. I went to see my bank manager to get her advice on whether I should tap into it as I was getting money from nobody at this point. 'That's what an overdraft is there for' she said. 'To tide you over when cash-flow is not as good as it could be'.
This was a massive relief to me. I started paying my debts off and paying myself a small wage from my overdraft, just to help me, hoping that when the tide turned, I'd easily be able to top up the overdraft and be back on an even keel. I decided not to tell Trish this was my plan as I didn't want to worry her, and anyway, everything would all be back to normal before you could say 'you're on your own pal'.
This 'tiding over' thing went on for over a year. One of the

Thunder At One AM

toughest things was having to pay Gordon off. I should have paid him off in September but as Christmas was approaching and he had a wife and three kids to look after I couldn't bring myself to do it. I waited until January before telling him, he was great. He completely got it. By then I'd almost completely reached the bottom of the barrel. I went to the bank manager again to see if she could top it up. She was not even slightly interested in my plight. All she could talk about was how unfairly she'd been treated by the bank, they were not going to give her early redundancy. I didn't give a fuck about her situation, all I was interested in was how in hell's name was I going to get through the next couple of months. Could she at least stop sending me demands for the interest on my large overdraft payments?

'No. There's nothing we can do, you agreed to the terms, and you're going to have to stick by them'.

I was incandescent with rage. 'But you said'...

'It doesn't matter. Things have changed. It's a different world from a few months ago. There's nothing I can do'.

I stormed out of her office. Utterly clueless as to what to do next. I'd never been in a situation like this in my life.

I went around all of my old clients offering sixty, seventy, eighty per cent discounts on their work, all to no avail.

I was snookered, out on a limb, up a gum tree and in so much of a pickle that I could taste the vinegar in my mouth.

I stumbled my way back to my office. I had two rooms in the National Mining Museum, one to work in, the other as a board room. I had to get shot of these as quickly as possible. I had no money and decided to come clean and tell them the situation. I was out of there by the end of the week owing them a good few months rent. All this time, Trish kept asking how business was, and I consistently lied and bluffed my way to make her believe that everything was OK, tough, but OK.

I hated myself for doing this. Why hadn't I told her about it early on? It was too late now, she'd never forgive me.

I moved the business (or what little there was left of it) back into my attic studio. I hoped that I could re-establish myself, a one-man-band again, flying by the seat of his pants.

Month after month, I sat up there, trying my damnedest to generate income, but I was getting nowhere.

In desperation, I got in touch with my old copywriter Phill who'd set up his own business in London and told him I was desperate for work but not going into to much detail.

'Sure' he said. 'I'm sure we can get you some work down here, there's always too much to do and not enough people to do it,' I was ecstatic. That night I went for dinner to our local hostelry with Trish and our friend Fran. Fran was buying, and Trish had no idea how grateful I was for this as by this time I had dug a super black hole of debt in my account and had barely a couple of hundred pounds to last me.

As we chatted, I floated the idea of moving to London for a while on them. I explained that Phill had some work for me and I'd also found out that a job I'd been working away at had come to fruition and that was also based in London. Things were starting to look up.

They both thought it was a great idea. It could really help break me into the bigger advertising scene. I'd done a lot of really nice work, but when you're in a goldfish bowl, you are not really sure of your depth or horizons.

I got in touch with Steve and Sandi the next day to see if they would be willing to put me up for a while. They could not have been sweeter.

'Of course, you can come and stay with us' Steve said, sounding enthusiastic over the phone.

Steve and I were massively into football, he was a Burnley fan, and they were hovering about the promotion areas of the second tier of English football.

We agreed that I could stay with them for up to three months, depending on if I got work. They had a big house in South Croydon, it had a sprawling garden that could take a couple of days to mow. I'd been down a few times before and loved it. Had things suddenly taken a turn for the better? I certainly hoped so, it really seemed like it.

Unbeknown to anyone, I'd been wakening up at two-thirty every morning in a cold sweat. The realisation of how much money I owed the bank struck my heart like an ice-cold dagger. Night after night after night.

I was a wreck.

I actually began to pray using my hands in a praying position, trying to make them act like some kind of antenna that would send a signal out to the world that I was desperate. I needed help and guidance like never before. I used to sneak off to our spare bedroom as the tension would make me toss and turn all night. I felt the pressure of my world crushing me into a small, terrified creature that longed-for release. This feeling stayed with me for years. I was also being crushed by the pressure of lying to the person I loved most in the world. I reasoned that I was doing it to protect Trish from the onslaught of pain that I was going through, I genuinely thought I was her shield. What a fool I was.

I cursed myself so many times for not being honest way back, it was now blatantly too late. I knew for a fact that if she found out how much I'd deceived her, it was all over. I couldn't bear the thought of that. I'd been responsible for turning our lovely life into a nightmare. I was putting myself down a hundred times a day before breakfast.

We agreed on a date for me to travel down to London. From memory, I think it was around November 2012. I decided that I was going to go down there as an independent, stand-alone, one-man advertising and design company. I took all of my equipment with me, packed it into the back of the Mini along with enough clothes to last me a month. Trish was so excited for me. At long last, it looked like the gods had shone a light in my direction. Little did she know.

We'd shared a bottle of red wine along with a nice dinner the night before and spoke only of hope and the good things that would come along. I even started to believe it myself.

As I said goodbye to her, I knew that this was going to be the most significant make or break time of my life.

I took a deep breath and walked out to the car. I started the engine and put the Mini into first gear and drove off into the distance.

SOUTH CROYDON

I TOOK A BREAK from driving after around four and a half hours. Trish had given me an envelope with a hundred pounds in it. It was more welcome than she could ever imagine as, by this stage, I had two hundred pounds of my overdraft left.

Part of me getting away was to escape the oppressive world I had got myself into. The weekly letters from RBS demanding incredible interest payments on the colossal overdraft I'd accumulated and had no chance of paying. I would no longer have to tremble at the postman's delivery as I'd given them no forwarding address. I'd hated going into my office and physically avoided looking at the postal pigeon holes. If I didn't look, the letters didn't exist. It was a massive self-deception, but it worked for me. It had to, I had no other mechanism for dealing with my life other than pretending it didn't exist.

After a long and enjoyable road trip, I rolled up to Steve and Sandi's house nine hours after I'd set off, one tank of fuel. I was delighted to be there and see them again. They treated me like a long-lost son, it felt magical, maybe there really was hope for me?

It was a Friday evening, and they'd decided to take me out for a slap-up meal. It was lovely. I could not believe their generosity, they'd decided that they were not going to charge me anything for accommodation or meals. I was so happy I cried. I didn't let them see me do this of course. They'd just given me a get-out-of-jail card. Everything I earned in London could now go towards paying off my overdraft. I did some work with Steve on the following days, helping to weed his garden and a lot of other physical tasks that he was now no longer able to do. I was just happy to be somewhere where the sun shone, and the pressure was away in the distance. I had my own room and bathroom, I was able to come and go as I pleased. I honestly felt the world was shining for me.

I got in touch with Phill and Pete, who'd also promised me work. Phill said I could come into the office Wednesday as they were working on a top-secret project and could do with my expertise.

Pete said I could begin immediately on Monday morning. I'd met Pete in Edinburgh through a friend. Pete's company were developing nutritional fruit drinks that were cold-compressed, meaning that they held more nutritional value than most other fruit drinks. My role was to help them develop some new imagery for their labels and marketing. I was buzzing. I turned up at his office at the Gherkin, I'd never seen it up close before but was instantly mesmerised by its beauty. Wow, this really was a piece of work.

The interior of the office bright yellow and I mean BRIGHT. I felt like I should have taken my sunglasses, I now knew how rhubarb felt when it was dropped into a bowl of custard.

I set my equipment up and got on with the brief he'd given to me. I spent a couple of successful days there, Pete's boss was delighted with what I'd produced, and they paid me the next day. This really was beginning to feel like a turnaround.

Two days later I turned up at Phill's office. We went for a coffee and some kind of fried breakfast. It was great seeing him again. We'd always been close, ever since the 'plaice' incident in Marr Associates years back.

'The thing is Jim' Phill said. 'We'll have to charge you for desk space, two hundred quid a week, how does that sound?'

'I'm sure you know that if it was up to me, you could have it for free, in fact, that's what I was pushing for as I knew your situation.'

'Can you guarantee me any work though?' I said.

'If you're giving me enough work, then paying for desk-space is not going to be a problem'.

'Well, that's the other problem' he said. Scratching his chin. 'It seems like you attached the recession to the back of your car and dragged it down here. Things were looking pretty busy last week, but right now we've had so many people pulling out of deals that I'll be lucky to get you anything. I'm sorry,' and I could see that he really was. When you promise pal work, you want to deliver.

I was floored.

'Can I pay you desk space when I get money in the door?' I said, hopefully.

'Sure, leave it with me, I'll have a word with the boss'.

The next day I set off for his office in Trafalgar Square. I had to drive in with the equipment as it was too heavy to carry on the train. I got there and set it all up. I was in the design department and was welcomed by a real group of nice guys. After setting up, I parked the mini away somewhere where I didn't have to pay for parking. I got back to the office after a good hour's walk. It took a couple of hours to set the equipment up, obtaining the passwords and accreditations I needed should work arise. I loved being in there. The office was buzzing within energy and hope.

I spent the next couple of weeks there, getting the occasional bit of work, going for lunch with the guys; Joe, Gary and Matt, we went to Soho most days and generally I had a feeling that things were turning. It was now heading towards Christmas. The mining Museum had sent me a package as I was no longer at their address. In it was a bundle of letters from RBS demanding payment on my overdraft which had by this time all but burned out. The sums on the statements were astronomical and what made it worse was that at the front of this enormous figure was a (-) which meant minus, in other words, I owed them more money than I'd ever heard of. I was flattened again. The image from Star Wars, where, the gang are trapped in the disposal machine waiting to be crushed came to me. It's precisely how I felt, it was merely a matter of time before I succumbed to a slow, painful death. In fact, for the first time in my life, I actually wished I could curl up and die. Trish was coming down to visit me, Sandi and Steve before Christmas, on what she thought would be a magical, London experience.

The day before she arrived, Phill informed me that there was no work left for me. He'd paid for my desk space from his own pocket for the next month, which was an act of generosity that brought a lump to my throat.

We'd sat down at a cafe the evening before, and he'd asked me how things really were. I was open and struggling to hold back the emotion of my failure.

'At least perhaps that month will allow you to look for work or tidy up your CV' he said. I was grateful for his help.

'The good news is' he said.,

'You're invited to our Christmas party tonight, food, drink, clubs, everything on us, can you make it?'

'I'll see how I feel Phill, thanks for thinking about me.'

I left work early and headed back to Steve and Sandi's to get changed. I'd brought a nice trendy shirt down with me for such an occasion, and Trish had left me a Christmas present of a beautiful pair of Italian leather shoes. I got showered, ironed the shirt and generally felt better than I'd felt in a long time. I was looking pretty hot and was really up for a great night, especially if it wasn't going to cost me. I got back to Leicester Square and caught up with the guys I'd worked beside for the past few months. We started off in a karaoke bar in Soho, Phill loves karaoke more than anyone I've ever known. He sings like he means it, let's leave it at that.

From there, we went to a dozen different places, and as the night grew longer, my worries disappeared. I looked at my watch, and I had no more than ten minutes to get to the train station for the last train. I said my goodbye's and legged it. I made it to Leicester Square station with barely a minute to spare. Relieved, I settled into the compartment and semi-dozed. The train juddered to a halt at East Croydon station. I got off and was faced with that long, horrible thirty or forty-minute walk to South Croydon. As I walked, the heels of those new Italian shoes were now eating into the skin of my heels, biting away at me as if the cow who'd given its life for the leather was getting its revenge on humanity.

Before too long I was hobbling like I was on hot coals. South Croydon was a long, painful way away at this rate. I had no option. I tried taking the bloody things off, but the ground was cold with ice. My socks turned into slush puppies. The temperature had dropped significantly, and I was now in real danger of hypothermia. I'd only worn that light shirt and a jacket that would surely have ripped if the wind had been a tad stronger. Like a true athlete, I concentrated on a goal. My focus was on getting my arse to Steve and Sandi's house where a lovely comfy bed with a big warm, fluffy duvet was waiting for me. At the thought of this, I instinctively put my hand into the left-hand pocket of my trousers. This is where I always kept the house key. There was nothing there. Shit. I remembered laying it down on the bed as I removed my jeans and put on these fancy pants that I was wearing now. I just hoped that Steve or Sandi would still be awake when I completed my long, arduous, Antarctic journey. I'm not exaggerating when I say this, but it seemed like I'd been hobbling along for a week, my heels were so bloody and sore, my ribs were aching from shivering in the cold. I was basically a total wreck with one aim, get to the house, get to the house, get to the house. As the street they lived in came into view, I sighed with relief, and the pain eased a bit. I got to the door and rung the bell.

Nothing. I rung again, the same result.

'Fuck' I cursed my self for being so stupid, leaving my key on the bed. I knocked this time, as hard as I could. Nothing. They were dead to the world.

I walked over the road to the park and got a handful of stones, threw them at the window. Still nothing.

By this time, my body was beginning to shut down, my extremities were blue, I was shaking like a jakey. What the fuck was I going to do, this was serious shit?

I thought I'll get a cheap hotel or B&B, that's the only option even though I had no money. I walked around, and there was nothing. It was now about two in the morning. After walking around like a zombie trying to figure out where I could find shelter to avoid dying, I remembered Steve and Sandi had a shed in the garden, surely there would be some sort of bedding or cushions in there? I felt relieved, I'd solved the problem, there was a kind of euphoria deep within me. I got to the side gate, and it was all locked up. When the hell did they put a padlock there, I said out loud.

The only thing to do was climb over. I'd jumped over a thousand fences like it when I was a kid, this should be a breeze. As I clambered onto the large plastic bins I got a good foothold and climbed over the fence, there was nothing to lean on or rest my foot onto. I decided to go for it and tried to leap over. My lovely Italian shoes slipped on the top of the fence, and I landed directly on top of it, one bollock either side. It was so painful that I could not even register a noise. Perhaps it was so high that only dogs and scavenging foxes could hear it. I fell over into the garden, lay for a few minutes massaging the area very gently and made my way to the shed. My coccyx was absolutely throbbing. I'd landed on the

Thunder At One AM

blasted thing, straight onto the top of the fence. I cursed, God, I cursed Charles Darwin, I cursed Captain Caveman. Why the fuck did we have a fucking tail in the first place? I'd first experienced this pain many years ago, trying to slide down a hill that was covered in ice, without a sledge. It took a long time to heal.

As I got to the shed, I noticed a couple of shiny shapes on the door, was that a...Padlock? You must be fucking joking when the hell did they put them on? Fuck. I now had to get back over that fucking fence, and it was much higher from this side, especially as there were no buckets to clamber onto. After much sliding, scraping and yelping I eventually got over. I can tell you if my tail was still working there was no way I'd be wagging the damn thing. I was so angry that I didn't give a fuck about swearing to myself.

'What the fuck next, I thought.

I tried knocking and ringing again but got the same response. I wandered about the area looking for a solution. I also suspected that someone would be watching this suspicious-looking guy walking around an affluent area with more than a modicum of concern. It didn't concern me at all though as I was into survival mode by this point. At times like these, instinct takes over.

As I grew colder and more desperate, it was as if my brain was taking over, telling my body to get the fuck out of the way and let the adults get on with it. I suddenly remembered that there was a pensioner's home at the back of Steve and Sandi's house. Pensioners homes were always warm, too warm, so I figured I'd be able to sneak in and get a bed for the night. I wandered, and like Steve and Sandi, they were all dead to the world. All was not lost as I spotted a couple of pensioner minibuses in the courtyard. I hobbled over. Hallelujah the doors were open, somebody was looking out for me after all. They must have blankets and covers in here? As I scrambled around, I found a big bag in one of the overhead lockers, looked like a duvet bag. 'Yesss' I said as I pulled it down, I was saved.

I opened it up, and to my utter disbelief, it was full of pensioners nappies. I was so tired, desperate and cold that I sat in the back seat and tried to cover myself with them. It was pointless. They were so small and flimsy.

I then thought about the consequences of what would happen in the morning when they found a frozen dead Scottish guy on the back seat of a pensioner bus covered in nappies with sickness all down his shirt, blood on his face and his heels cut to ribbons.

I could imagine how the stories would grow arms and legs;

'Yeah he was found in a minibus with used pensioners nappies all over his head; apparently, he was intae that kind of thing. Fuckin' perv'.

I couldn't do that to Trish, I'd embarrassed her enough over the years, and the thought of appearing in the **Darwin Awards spurred me to get the hell out of the bus.

I got out of there and decided to head back to the train station. It was a long, painful hobble, but I really had no option. I gritted my teeth, pulled my bloody socks up and headed to East Croydon station once more. As I walked I spotted a Premier Inn, I must have passed it a hundred times but had never noticed it. Surely they would have rooms?

I went into the reception, and there was a night porter on duty. He fussed around behind the reception desk for a bit ignoring me, making himself feel important, I was happy with the arrangement as there was a terrific heat coming from the glass-fronted gas fire in the bar area, I was warming up nicely, so much so that I could have fallen asleep on the spot.

**The Darwin Awards are a tongue-in-cheek honour and

recognise individuals who have supposedly contributed to human evolution by selecting themselves out of the gene pool via death by their own stupidity.

After a few minutes faffing, he was in the frame of mind to speak.
'And what can we do for you, sir?' He said in a tone that was so close to contempt.
I was ready to fall down and could not give a toss about his attitude, all I wanted was permission to collapse in a warm environment. I explained my situation to him, showing him the blood and my heels and my bruised coccyx.
'I'll see what I can do he said,' I thought he'd take the gravity of my situation into account and actually pity me and give me a room for free after all this was potentially a life or death situation.
I waited anxiously, figuring out what I could afford to pay.
In my mind, I settled on the figure of £70. I definitely couldn't afford to give that much money away, but it was all I had left, and it was now getting to three in the morning, and I'd been up for over twenty hours.
As I waited, hoping, I was trying my Jedi mind trick to get him to say something like,
'Well sir, it looks like you can have it for free, as it's so late and there's no chance of anyone else occupying it tonight'.
He didn't. He looked up at me.
'The good news is' he said. 'We have a room'.
'Great' I said. 'How much?'
'£200'
'What? £200 for a room that I'll be using for a couple of hours? No chance. Is there any way you can get me something for £70?'
'Sorry sir, that's all we have'.
'But there's no chance of anyone coming in at this time for a

room is there?' I pleaded.

'You're asking for a room now' He said cheekily.

I had to admit, he had a point. Twat.

My hopes were dashed.

'Can I sit by your fire to heat up for a bit then?' I said, desperately.

'I'm sorry sir, that's for guests only'.

'But I'm desperate?' I said.

He looked away and continued playing with the computer keyboard. Totally ignoring me.

I walked away, I was floored.

I had hardly any overdraft money left never mind £200 quid for a couple of hours kip.

I went back outside into that bitterly cold night wondering what the hell I was going to do and if in fact, I'd survive it. I had visions of me as the little match girl, lighting up matches to keep me warm, anything to endure another moment. There was nothing else for it. I had to get back to East Croydon station and catch the last train to London, I reckoned I had an hour to get there which should be plenty of time even for a guy who was walking like a gimp and shaking as if he'd spent a full day on top of a washing machine on spin cycle. I made my way painfully to East Croydon station and sat freezing in the waiting room for a good half hour. I really wondered how these homeless people survived. We go on about how tough the SAS and guys like Ant Middleton and Bear Grylls are, but these guys are in a different league. My respect for them jumped many fold after that night. I'm not sure at what point I didn't feel the cold anymore, you can only shake so much before your body forgets that it's actually shaking.

My eyelids must have fluttered a million times as sleep threatened to consume me. I battled those damned eye covers as they were being pulled down by the weight of a heavy

Thunder At One AM

night. Thankfully the noise of a train brought me to my senses, and I was compos mentis for a few minutes. It came to a stop a few feet from me, and I stumbled on board. The pleasant heat that enveloped me almost made me faint with pleasure. As I sat there in total bliss, I could feel pain in my fingers and toes as the warmth crept back into the extremities. I was conscious that I may have been in the early stages of hypothermia and made sure I wiggled all my moving parts. Before I knew it, I'd conked out. The change in temperature was too much for my fragile state. I was in a glorious dream in some far away location, lying on a sun-bed with that big golden beauty throwing his life-giving arrows directly onto my grateful skin.

I awoke god knows how many stops later but it was certainly more than I'd bargained for, or had paid for, for that matter. I aimed to get back to Leicester Square and go back to Phill's office to kip there until morning. I got off at London Bridge station. I had no idea where to go from here. I decided to walk towards Charing Cross the pain from my feet and arse started up again. It was too much. That dream had me all cosy and content. I didn't know if I had the energy to go on. As I walked past London Bridge, there was a small cubby hole in a wall. There was a warm vent of air coming from an outlet, It looked so comfy, it was beckoning me, tempting me back into that blissful dream. I sat down for a moment and was drifting off. I suddenly realised with certainty that if I stayed there and fell asleep, I would not waken up.

The thoughts of the past few years came back to me, the pain I'd put Trish through, the complete fuck up I'd made of my life and hers, was it worth carrying on? I contemplated my situation and really wondered if this would be the solution to our problems. I was insured after all so my life was worth something and Trish would be free of this fuck-up of a husband. What is it with us men? If I'd admitted to Trish that my business was going to shit years ago, I would have avoided this whole thing. I wasn't being blasé or arrogant, I really believed that I could get myself out of this mess, and at some point, business would come flooding back. It was apparent now that I'd gone into some kind of depression and suspension of reality. I'd never suffered anything like this in my life before, sure I'd been under the weather and feeling down, but this was a whole new downward level. I realised what depression felt like, I think? I was physically in a hole. I pictured it like this; My life always had a visible horizon point, I could look ahead and see what was coming up. It had always been that way. Trish and I always had something to look forward to; running events, holidays, dinner dates, sports events, concerts, cinema, theatre performances whatever. There was always something to look forward to or aim for. Recently that was not the case as I had no money to fund any of them and kept pretending that I didn't want to go to any, hoping that Trish wouldn't realise it was all about my lack of money. I was in this self-made hole, which felt tiny and constrained. My own thoughts and feelings occupied this small space, and I was too scared to put my head above the parapet in case the shrapnel of my disintegrating life hit me. The only horizon I could see was the rim of this hole, this depression. I'd been in there for years unbeknownst to Trish as I always tried to bluff that everything was OK. That small space was still waiting for me as soon as I woke up and I fell into it quickly. I hunkered down into the recess of my world, terrified at what the day would bring. I now understood what depression was, at least I think I did. I could see no way out. Every turn I took led me to the same conclusion, no escape. To me, money was the only ladder that would allow me to climb out of this place.

I thought about the thousands of men who took their own

lives every year thinking there was no way out, that the only conclusion was to end it all. I really did know and appreciate their way of thinking. Who did you talk to and trust at this most desperate time? Your brother, your best mate? A helpline? I have a brilliant set of friends, family and colleagues but I felt so stupid even thinking about trying to tell them my problems as it was embarrassing and my own stupid fault. I would never contemplate committing suicide, but the position I was in right now felt like a warm tunnel that would take me away from the problems I'd created.

I sat there and really considered the thought. After a moment, clarity appeared. I was a survivor. I was sure of it, and I stood up, shook myself down and headed purposefully towards Charing Cross station.

From Charing Cross, I knew the office was only a two-minute walk away. I hoped the cleaners would be there and would recognise me. It was now just after two in the morning. There were surprisingly very few people about, and this is the heart of London. I got to the office and whooped inwardly as I saw the office lights were on. I rung the bell, again and again, and again. No reaction. This was hopeless. My head dropped like the batteries had died. I was back to square one. I had no option. I did a few painful star jumps, had to get heat into those damned limbs of mine. It gave me the boost I needed. I had no option. I headed back to Charing Cross and wished with all my heart that there would be a train waiting to take me back to South Croydon. It never happened. I looked at the clock on the notice board, it's two forty-five. I look around, and there's only one place to sit, there's a metal bench, but it seems like this homeless guy has most of the real estate. There's no option, I sit on the bench next to him, and I can feel myself drifting away...

As I'm coming to, slowly awakening, I get the awful stench

of days-old urine. My nostrils are stung with the same intensity as smelling salts. My head jerks upwards, I recoil as I realise I've been sleeping with my head on a homeless man's shoulder. There's absolute silence, save the mechanical drone of a diesel engine somewhere in the distance. The side of my face, nose and lips are covered with frozen saliva, I've got a horrible metallic taste in my mouth. My cheek aches, I dab my finger to it, there's blood, I look at the guy's shoulder, there's blood there too, and I realise that my jaw must have frozen to his coat during the night and my abrupt awakening must have torn it.

The overriding feeling is one of desperation, I must catch that train. By now, my energy is lower than a politician's morals. I'm totally drained. I somehow manage to get myself onto the train, again the heat hits me, bliss. I check to see where it's destination station is and realise it's going to Brighton, via East Croydon. I better make sure I get off at the right stop otherwise I'm in shit so deep, I'll be picking it out of my ears for the foreseeable. As I sit in the seat anticipating the journey and the third painful walk to East Croydon in less than a day, I heave a deep sigh. I can feel those eyelids putting on weight again and fight as hard as I can to resist, voices in my head lure me into oblivion, and I disappear into their void. Blissful, warm, relaxed...

I then feel that involuntary jolt of the head, followed by a brief realisation that I've no idea where I am. As my focus returns, I realise I'm still sitting on the train, in Charing Cross. There's a couple of people now on board, and I ask one of them when the train is leaving.
'Not for another two hours,' the guy says. My eyes and mouth widen, and I try saying words of the incredulous type, but my voice-box is not interested in engaging, it's way too tired,

I open my mouth, and close it again. I look at my iPhone to check the time and realise that it lost its power way before I did, many hours ago. I realise that I've not called Trish, or Sandi, or Steve, who would no doubt be worried about me if they were still awake. Two hours waiting is more than I can handle right now, staying awake that long is impossible. I have no option but to sink into the material of the seat. I merge with the damn thing on what seems like a molecular level. We are one. The crumbs, the shitty pattern, the fluff and I bond like a human and train upholstery have never bonded before. I'm gone, even forgetting that I could end up in Brighton, at least that problem, if it should ever arise, is hours away, a good two, warm, cosy hours away.

As I disappear off to that land, the one I've craved for the past few hours, the train finally pulls out and is now on the way. Miraculously my eyes open as we're two minutes away from East Croydon station. Looks like the big man upstairs has had enough of yanking my chain and has decided to give me a break. I get off the train feeling stiffer than a teenage boy's bedsheets. The stiffness eases off as I walk along the platform, daylight is kicking in, and it looks like there could be a lovely sunrise just over the horizon. By this time, the journey to South Croydon is like the hallway in a Tom & Jerry movie; never-ending, repetition. I've done it a hundred times and know that when I get to Steve and Sandi's, they'll be awake, as I know for a fact Sandi has a board meeting at the LTA at ten, and she'll have to leave in the next hour.

I get to the front door and ring the bell. Steve's there in a split second.

'Where have you been?'

'I..'

'You look terrible' he says.

'Trish has been so worried about you'.

'Is that Jim?' Sandi shouts from the kitchen.

'Yes,' Steve says.

'Come in, how are you feeling? Where have you been all this time?'

'It's a long story' I say.

'You look like you're hypothermic' Steve says.

'Sorry Steve, I've got to sleep,' I say.

'I'll bring you some tea,' he says. I wave my hand.

'Sleep' I say, I just need sleep'.

Sandi comes through with a warm blanket and puts it over my shoulder as I head upstairs.

I pull my shoes off without bending down or untying the laces and wince as I feel the blisters reintroducing themselves, get into bed, under the duvet, I get into the foetal position, shiver, yawn and roll about until sleep bludgeons me. It's a long restless journey to get to the dream, but I must have got there at some point as I wake up a good twelve hours later.

All the months I'd been down south, I could not find work, happiness or contentment. The long, unhappy train journeys back from the office every night provided me with a half-hour walk back to South Croydon. Many times as I walked back a total failure, I longed for it to rain as I was so low that my only pressure release was to cry out loud. The rain hid my tears so well. I walked many times past the pubs and supermarkets in the pouring rain, passing people who had no idea of the hell I was going through, wondering when I would eventually have to tell that beautiful wee wife of mine that I'd ruined our future, the future we'd so carefully planned and dreamed about. How could she have been so stupid as to have hooked up and believed such a fucking loser? I was down, down, down. I laughed for a few seconds as I thought about Status Quo.

There were many times I got back to the house where Steve would be waiting with a cup of tea ready for me. Hoping that things had gone well. I really felt for him, but he was no mug. I sometimes pretended that it had been a brilliant day others not so good, but he was too savvy for my amateur performances. Most days I'd cry from East Croydon and give myself ten minutes to get over the pathetic tears ten minutes from their house. This would give me enough time to dry my eyes and get my 'everything's OK' act ready as I walked through the door. In the end, I couldn't pretend any more. Steve was devastated for me as was Sandi. There was nothing they could do, they'd helped me so much that I could never repay them.

Trish arrived in London for a weekend trip and was full of life as always. I was so low that I could not see any further than the next RBS statement. I was beaten, dead to the world and had to somehow find the energy to bluff my way to being upbeat.

It was a horrible weekend. Trish was annoyed that I was so flat, she said it was like I was a dead man. How perceptive. I had no energy to pretend any more but didn't want to burden anyone with my self-created woes.

She left on the Monday, and as she headed into the taxi to go to the airport, I took hold of her hand and did not say a word. I thought this may be the last time I ever saw those lovely green eyes. I was sure that this was the end of us. I felt guilty letting her down like that if ever the term damp squib was appropriate this was the time. I was gone.

That night Trish called me on my mobile. I'd just gone to bed even though it was only just past eight.

'What the HELL is going on Jim?'

'What do you mean' I said trying to bluff it as I'd done for the past few years.

'There's something you're not telling me, I've never known

you to be like this'.

'Like what?' I protested.

'Like you're fucking dead,' she said.

I put the phone to my side and lowered my head in shame.

I could hear her talking on the other end and ignored her for a minute or so trying to gather my thoughts.

'Well,' she said. 'How bad is it?'

I took a deep breath, preparing to say the words that would commit me to Hell.

'Really bad, I mean really, really bad,' I said.

A massive lump coming to my throat, it was so big that I could hardly draw breath. This could be it, the moment I'd been dreading for years, the moment when she said it was all over.

'How bad?'

I told her how much I owed. There was silence. I could hear her crying on the other end of the phone.

I waited on her saying the words that I'd long dreaded...my mind drifted....

I'd gone up to visit our friends Phil and Rachel in Solihull a month previously. These guys had only got together because of Trish. Trish was working for Standard Life in the sales division at the time. She had a team of four people. Oli, Phil, Amanda and Rachel. It was on their Christmas party that they'd got together. I arrived to pick Trish up the morning after the party, the atmosphere was strangely muted. They were always bubbling with enthusiasm and energy, something had obviously happened last night.

She told me that Oli had grabbed her during the evening and led her to a broom cupboard, upon opening it she discovered Phil and Rachel snogging. Trish was not happy, she'd taken a long time to assemble this incredible team, and any internal shenanigans would simply muck the whole group dynamic up, she was furious and told them both.

As it turned out, they got married a year or two later and now have three beautiful kids.

As I got to Birmingham train station, I could see Phil and his daughter Amy waiting for me. I felt apprehensive as they were such good friends and I'd decided to tell them the truth. We got back to their house, and after the babysitter arrived, we headed out for a bite and beer.

Half an hour or so, I opened up to them and came clean.

'Why didn't you just tell her?' Phil said.

'I wanted to protect her, but all I've done is the opposite' I said, head-rolling to the floor.

'Just tell her the truth' Rachel said. 'If anyone will understand it's Trish'.

'Yeah, you're both right, but I honestly feel that if I tell her, she'll walk away'.

'Do you honestly believe that? ' Phil said.

Yeah, I do'.

'Listen,' Rachel said. 'I guarantee you that when you tell her the truth, she'll be right behind you. In a year or two, we'll all be sitting somewhere laughing about how serious this all seemed'.

I so wanted to believe them both, but I'd gone so far down that negativity line that I'd probably even find it hard to believe that birds could fly. They convinced me to tell her and before I left on the train back to London that night I promised I'd tell her soon. The thought brought a real tightness in my stomach, but I'd lived with that feeling for a long time, so I knew how to shrug it off.

'Are you there Jim? Hello, hell..'

'I'm here' I said.

'I'm really sorry Trish, I mean, REALLY sorry. I'll completely understand if you want to walk away. I've really mucked our lives up'.

I could hear her gasping for air through her tears. 'I'll have to call you back she said' and hung up.

I put the phone down on the cabinet at the side of my bed and crawled under the duvet hugging myself into as small a ball as I could make. It was over, that much was obvious. I just lay there, thoughts going a thousand miles an hour, wondering where I could go to live, who did I know that would put me up? My nails were bitten down to the quick, and I was shaking like a Welsh Elvis tribute act. I laughed at the thought of Shaking Stevens, shaking as much as I was under the bed covers. It was mental. I'd heard of people breaking into laughter at funerals due to uncontrollable nerves, and I reckoned this was what was happening to me.

I waited and waited.

The iPhone lit up, and I grabbed it.

'Hi honey' I said, 'I'm...'

'Stop' she said.

'You don't have to apologise, why didn't you tell me?' Her voice was so concerned and soothing that I burst into tears, uncontrollable sobbing, relief, the lump in my throat had increased in size, and I was actually struggling to get air into my lungs as the tears kept on coming.

'Can I call you back?' I said. I was fighting to get words out of my mouth, in fact, I was conscious that the words were coming from my stomach but couldn't get past the lump in my throat.

'Sure, just call me back when you're ready'.

I managed a grovelling 'Thank you Trish' before melting into a mess on the bed.

I lay there, crying for a long time. There was a knock on the door.

It was from Steve. 'Are you OK in there Jim'.

I managed to make a noise in the affirmative.

'OK, then, goodnight, and remember if you need to talk we're right down the hall'.

Again, I could say nothing. The generosity of everyone was crushing me. I felt so wimpy, if a butterfly had fluttered into the room, I would have wept at its beauty.

The relief was completely overwhelming me. I called Trish and thanked her, giving her a brief overview of how I thought my life was over and told her that she had rescued me.

'Don't be daft' she said, you think I'd leave you because of money? I've spoken to my mum and dad, and they're going to help us out if they can'.

When I heard this, another flood of tears came.

'Jeesus, how much water do tear ducts hold ?' I thought.

'Call me tomorrow' she said. 'Hopefully, you'll get a good night's sleep. Night' honey.

That night I slept like never before, a deep, peaceful and dream-free sleep. That tyrannical voice in my head who'd been putting those thoughts of despair and disaster into my head for such a long time was utterly silent.

Not a peep. I hoped he'd fucked off forever.

I woke up, feeling absolutely shattered. The relief after all those years of stress; waking up at two in the morning, dreading any letters that came through the post, quivering when I saw an HMRC ad on TV or bill poster. They all accumulated to make me fear the world I was living in and to make things even better, I still had a wife who loved me.

I felt fantastic. I bounded downstairs with an energy that had been lost in action years ago.

'Morning' I said to Steve who was sitting at the kitchen worktop reading his Times.

'Good morning young man. You seem to be full of the joys?'
'I am indeed Steve, I am indeed'.

'I spoke to Trish last night and was completely open and honest with her'.
'And she still loves you, right?' He said not taking his eyes off the newspaper, munching into his buttered toast
'Right,' I admitted.
'What did I tell you?' He said looking really smug with himself and happy for me. He ruffled my hair and pretended to shadow box with me. He was as relieved as me.
I felt fabulous. I now could not wait to get into the Mini and head home. I was really sad to be leaving South Croydon as apart from the lack of work, I'd really enjoyed Steve and Sandi's company although admittedly I spent most of my time with Steve as he was in the house most of the time. We'd sit and watch his favourite programmes, Poirot, Downton Abbey and Death in Paradise. When I was watching those programmes with Steve, my troubles disappeared somewhere into the background, and I was able to enjoy the escape. As soon as the programme was finished though, I'd be back to my old self. It now looked like that was all over and done with. I sat and had some toast and tea, They had an AGA, and I'd learned how to make toast by using a kind of fish griller, it was the best toast I ever had. Happy, sappy thoughts were running through my head. Life was good, the sun was shining, and I was on my way back to Scotland for the first time in three months (I don't want to include that trip back for Christmas where I bluffed my way through the celebrations, pretending to everyone that I was happy in London and business was good, this included duping my wife. I've blanked that part of my life out).
Steve and I sat there in silence, eating and reading. Steve glanced at me a couple of times with a big grin. He loved Trish

and was absolutely made up that she, as well as me, would be happy again.

As I got up to head to the shower, he shook my hand. 'I'm really chuffed for you mate, both of you'.
'Thanks Steve' I said, I really appreciate everything you've done for me, I'll never forget it, I hope I can pay you back some time'.
'There's no chance of that, I'll be gone in a year or two,' he laughed.
I'd hated it when he talked like that. It was true enough though. He'd had cancer since he was a kid of around nine or ten, and had so many operations to divert blood and nerves to all kinds of places in his body that although on the face of it he was a handsome bubbly character, yet beneath the surface lay the wreckage of a body. They were running out of places to redirect his lifeblood. He had gotten slower and slower physically over the few years we'd known him, and although I did not want to admit it, he was right, he was running out of time. Fast.

I went into the office later in the morning, and the journey was brilliant, I'd forgotten how fascinating the ride was, a train from South Croydon to East Croydon, then a train to Victoria Station and then the underground to Leicester Square. Walk up the stairs, and you're in the heart of London. The office was a ten-second walk away. If only circumstances had been different, I would have loved this part of my life. I met Phill on the stairs up, and he noticed something strange about me.
'What's happened?' He said.
'You look...Happy?'
'I told Trish all about it last night' I beamed.
His eyes lit up. 'And..'
"What do you think?' I said.

'I bloody well told you she'd stand by you, you Muppet,' he said laughing.

'I know' I said. 'But it's easy viewing from the outside'.

'I guess so' he said.

'So what are your plans?'

I'd like to finish off those little jobs for you and then head home in the next few days if that's OK?'

'Of course,' he said.

'It'll be sad to see you leaving, but I'm sure it's for the best'.

'Yeah, I'll be sad as well, it's been great being pals again, and if circumstances had been different it would have been a blast'.

A day or two later, I packed my stuff up from Phill's place and headed back to Croydon. There were a couple of tiny bits of work that would bring in a hundred pounds or so and even though I was farting against a tornado, it still counted. I could pay the petrol money back home. I was now looking at money in a completely different light. What you could do with a certain sum, how it would mean that designing a quick logo equated to buying food for a few days, everything had changed.

I told Steve and Sandi that I'd be leaving by the end of the week. I could no longer bear the weight of their generous hospitality. They had never said a word against me, had fed and sheltered me and given me a chance to escape from what was in my mind, Hell.

As the years went by, Steve became more and more frail. Not so much that you'd notice until he had to start using a walking stick. That's when it really hit home for me.

I went down to see them late in the year, and by this time, Steve was hardly even able to talk. His energy was virtually depleted, and Sandi was utterly shattered, having to care for him. I was devastated. I had been expecting him to deteriorate, but the speed caught me entirely by surprise.

I'd hoped he still had years of fun and banter, but that was completely gone. When it came to mealtime, he had to have help eating. I mourned that lovely man even though, physically he was still with us.

By this time, Trish and I had managed to get down to see him and Sandi for the last time. Steve, by this time, was not present. Sure, he was there physically, there was a shell, and occasionally you'd see glimpses of him trying to reach the surface, but it never materialised.

Steve died early the following year. I was genuinely honoured that Sandi and their son Michael asked me to design the order of service. As we couldn't make it down to his funeral, we said a silent prayer in his honour.

The Hare

I WAS DRIVING ALONG the Edinburgh City bypass, heading to the gym to meet up with Trish who'd gone there directly from work. I was a beautiful warm autumn evening, I remember distinctly how the colours of the season had made me feel happy and energised.

The sun was setting over the Pentlands hills to the south, and I looked over the fields to the magic that was happening in the sky. As I watched, I spotted a big hare sitting in the middle of a field adjacent to the road. It was beautiful, sitting back on its hind legs chewing on some kind of vegetation and visibly enjoying it. The sun cascaded over the field and the hare was lit up with the golden rays. I remember thinking I wished I had my camera with me.

As I was taking in the scene, the hare stood bolt upright. It had spotted some danger. As I drove along taking in everything and still concentrating on the road, I saw a Range Rover speed into the field, the dust from the summer crop sprayed up around the tyres as it sped in. It headed unwittingly towards the hare. The hare bolted and was heading towards me on the bypass. I watched the scene unfold in my head and hoped it would not develop the way I'd seen it. About thirty seconds later, it had run a mazy distance trying to avoid the vehicle. My exit was coming up, and I slowed down, hoping to see the hare escape to freedom. It was getting closer and closer to the road, and my heart was in my mouth.

It disappeared from view, and I breathed a sigh of relief. It was a wasted sigh as it suddenly appeared on the grass verge on the side of the road right next to me, and as I pressed

Thunder At One AM

my brake, it ran out. The car in front of mine mashed it into oblivion. The driver didn't even see it.

I was devastated. How quickly life changes. It was one of the saddest things I've ever experienced. From beauty, peace and tranquillity to a pulp in the blink of an eye and with no rhyme nor reason for it.

Sticky Knickers

AS USUAL, I WAS last minute dot com in the morning. Trish had been up for an hour and had showered, had her breakfast and ironed her clothes for the day. I jumped out of my kip and headed straight to the shower.

'Fancy putting some porridge on for me?' I shouted.

'Sure but you better hurry I've got a meeting at nine'.

It was just before eight, I reckoned I had ten minutes to get ready and get out of the door. I dried myself and hurried through to the spare room where the iron lived. I grabbed a shirt from the top of the clean washing basket and gave it a smooth over. I grabbed the jeans from the floor and stuck them on.

'Are you remembering you're at Barry tonight,' she shouted.

'Of course dear,' although I'd completely forgotten.

Trish and I still trained with a personal fitness instructor once a week to give us that kick up the arse that we needed to keep our fitness from slacking.

I took my training bag from the cupboard and filled it with a T-shirt, shorts, socks from the washing basket and popped my training shoes in.

After work that night I went to the gym. Our locker room was pretty good, not too pokey and relatively clean. I got changed and headed up to the gym. I generally wear a black t-shirt as it hides the sweat more than most colours. As I walked up the stairs, I passed a couple of girls who I hadn't met. I heard them sniggering so looked around. They laughed and ran off. I honestly thought they were shy and maybe fancied me. I headed in through the main door, and the music blared, there were a lot of people in tonight. I headed to the mats and started warming up, stretching off from head to toe, generally about fifteen minutes. As I was doing this, I could

Thunder At One AM

see folk looking over at me. This was not normal, I looked around to see if I'd put my t-shirt on back to front, or inside out, which had happened a few times before. Nope, all was in order. What was it they were seeing? I didn't feel particularly handsome or ugly that night. I was scoobied. I looked around for clues but only spotted a lot of smiling faces.

After warming up, I headed to the treadmills. Trying to ignore the looks. I started running and felt OK, quite good, in fact. I had the earphones in so could only hear the music. After my play-list stopped, I heard laughing behind me. People were pointing at me, I could see them in the wall-length mirror. I had to do something. I walked to the toilet. As I opened the cubicle door, a white flash caught my attention as I passed the mirror. I stood in front of it and angled my back to see around. There were a pair of Tricia's knickers sticking there. Presenting themselves to the world at my expense. 'What the..' I said to myself. I took the t-shirt off, and the knickers were still so full of static that I got a shock.

They must have been sitting in the washing basket when I grabbed the t-shirt. I stayed in the loo for a while waiting for the memory of those who had witnessed my embarrassment to fade. An hour later, I left and was still confident that a cheer might go up.

STICKY TICKETS

WHAT A DAY. BLOODY parking and bloody parking tickets.

I had arranged to meet Trish for a bite to eat at the Mexican place in Fountainbridge before we went to the cinema. I locked the car, put the hazard lights on, indicating to the shark-like circling wardens, that I would be back soon. I ran up the four flights of stairs as quickly as I could, the downstairs machine wasn't working. As I stood at the machine Trish rung me on my mobile to tell me she was going to be half an hour late, I'd just put the last of my money in the bloody machine as she rang, seven quid for four hours, I wasn't too happy I can tell you.

I waited on the machine to print my ticket, and as I was about to grab it from the slot, the phone went again, and I instinctively put it to my ear. The ticket flopped out of the machine and floated behind the automatic sliding double doors at the entrance to the cinema and wedged itself behind them.

'I'll have to call you back' I said. I put the phone in my pocket and went to pick the ticket up, as I got a few feet from the doors they automatically opened up, trapping the ticket between them. I tried another angle, sidled up to the door from the wall side, trying to avoid the sensor. As I got close enough to put my hand out to try to grab it, somebody from outside walked in. The doors opened again. I had to snatch my hand away as it would've been taken off by the force of the doors. Twenty minutes passed, and I was still no closer to getting the bloody ticket, I was also conscious that the wardens would be hovering around my car waiting to pounce if they hadn't already.

I looked around the cinema complex and spotted a door, looked like a broom cupboard in a corner. I abandoned my ticket for the time-being and walked over to the closet. I opened the door and took a mop from the plastic bucket and made my way back over to the automatic doors. I lay on the floor, out of the sensors range and stretched my arm out, shoving the handle of the mop behind the doors. Success, they never opened. The only problem was I could not get the ticket to come back the way, I needed something for the ticket to stick onto. I ran over to the sweets kiosk and nicked a ball of chewing gum from the pick n mix, I knew nobody would notice. I quickly chewed the strawberry globe until it was a gooey, sticky mass and stuck it onto the end of the mop, by this time the cinema was getting pretty busy and the doors were constantly opening and closing with people coming and going.

As I lay there, almost everyone that came in had a look at me lying on the floor with the mop, and my arm stretched out as far as it could go. After many attempts, I managed to force the ticket against the side of the door frame and nail it with the gum. I carefully pulled the mop from behind the doors, removed the ticket, part of it stuck to the gum, but mostly it was OK. The main thing was the date and time were still visible.

I Threw The Mop Down And bolted downstairs to the car, I could see a warden hovering about with his camera and log book. I shouted over to him, and he looked around.

'This your car sir?'

'Yes,' I said, sorry but I've had a nightmare getting this ticket'.

'Nightmare?' He said.

'It's an automatic machine? Anybody can operate one of them?'

'I know' I said, 'but this was an accident, my ticket fell behind the doors....' He put his hand up.

'Don't sweat it' he said. 'I haven't issued you a ticket, you were lucky though, I'm just about to go off duty'.

'Cheers pal' I said, 'really appreciate it'.

'No worries, next time maybe you can get some old lady to help you get your ticket' he said and wandered off thinking he was a comedian.

I got into the car, peeled the backing paper off the ticket and stuck it to the side window. What to do now? I thought. Trish got in touch to say she was still going to be at least another thirty minutes. I sat in the car, thinking about my next move. I was suddenly startled by a knock on the window and pressed the window button down, to my horror as the window sunk into the door frame, the ticket went with it into the door recess as the window slid all the way down. Another warden was standing there.

'I noticed you had your hazards on and came along to see what was going on,' he said, 'looks like you don't have a ticket'.

I rolled the window back up, and there were only sticky remnants on the window, he knocked again, must have thought I was trying to ignore him. I was about to explain but just couldn't be bothered with the whole story again. I was furious. With him and my own stupidity. I could feel the anger rising.

'Ach just FUCK OFF.' I shouted. And drove like a demon to the first speed bump.

The guy stood there scratching his head as I drove off.

Thunder At One AM

Valentine Gladhouse

I WAS UNDER MY car up to my knees in mud. I'd only nipped out for a last-minute Valentine's day gift for Trish. We never usually do anything for Valentine's Day, but this time I'd promised to take her somewhere special. I remember she'd raised her eyebrows at that one.

She was out with her pals for the afternoon as I told her we'd be going out for a slap-up meal around seven. Earlier on I thought I'd surprise her, get her a small extra Valentine's gift, a show of love and all that. I looked at my watch, it was 4pm. 'Shops shut around 5 so that should give me a good hour,' I said out loud. I jumped in the car, had decided Peebles was the best place to pick something semi-special up. I took the back roads from Newtongrange, past the little farms and reservoirs, it was a beautiful run in the car. By the time I got into Peebles, it was 4.50, and most of the shops had closed.

After running up and down the High Street a couple of times, noticing that shops were shutting as I passed them, I was left with no option. Sugar Mountain, the sweet shop was the only one left open. I loved that shop, home-made sweets and treats to make your eyes and mouth water. The problem was though that there was nothing that Trish liked. She was more into classy chocolates. I opted for a quarter of Butternuts, American hard gums and some white mice for Trish. The first two were for me. I must admit I did leave the shop feeling a bit underwhelmed at my gift but thought she'd appreciate the gesture.

I looked desperately around to see if I could get a win from somewhere, but the shutters were down all over town.
I headed back to the car and started the engine. The car

incidentally was a brand new Mercedes C Class, black, glossy and great to drive. I'd taken it on a three-year lease as business was good at the time. It made me feel like a million dollars when I drove it. As I drove back along the slow, windy roads the sun was setting, a fantastic orange glow was emanating from the direction I was heading in, as I approached Gladhouse reservoir the sun was getting more and more orange, it looked incredible. I decided to have a quick look from the water's edge and knew of a little spot that I'd be able to park in. I took a right turn off the main road, over the wee bridge to Moorfoot and I quickly got the car parked. I ran down to the water's edge and stood there, almost slipping on some ice, shivering in the cold but admiring in awe the picture that was unfolding before me.

I stood there for ages, just watching, eventually looked at my phone to see the time, but the power had gone, I walked back to the car and realised that it was 6 o'clock, it was semi-dark, and I realised I'd better be heading home. By this time my shoes were covered in mud, I'd been sinking at the side of the reservoir without realising it, only up to my ankles, so it wasn't too bad. I started the car and stuck it in reverse. The wheels spun furiously, but I moved not one inch. 'I'd no idea what was going on. I got out of the car and couldn't believe my eyes, the wheels were a good three or four inches under the mud. I'd parked on frozen grass that had melted a bit while I was standing there like an 'artiste' watching the sunset. 'Fuck.' I shouted. I knew the situation I was in was not good, but as I began to look at my options, there were no outstanding ones.

It was getting darker, I had no power on my phone, no torch and was a good 15 miles from home.

I paced around a bit, and a thought came into my head. I'd watched a programme a while ago which was about rescuing yourself in such situations, It might have been Top Gear, but

I can't be sure. In a case like mine, you had to gather tree branches, stick them under the rear wheels and use them as a launchpad to get you going. I looked around for loose branches, but there were none available. I looked around at the trees, and there were a couple that would be ideal for snapping branches from. This turned out to be a lot harder than I anticipated. By the time I had a couple of decent branches, I also had three or four cuts, two on my face after being whipped unexpectedly by the resistance of the trees and another couple on my arms and legs. I positioned them under the back wheels and started the car again, As I put it into reverse, both branches flew into the distance. I fetched them and had a thought. If I rocked the car out of the holes, the wheels had made? I placed the branches in position and got back into the car. I left the door open and had my right leg out of the car to give me a bit of purchase. I revved very slowly and put all of my might into rocking the vehicle slightly, it seemed to be working, I was ecstatic. I rolled and rocked but eventually ran out of energy, my foot slipped, and I fell under the car, thankfully the engine had cut out by this point. I tried another two or three times and was only sinking the car deeper into the mud. I was exhausted, covered in mud and starving. I sat in the driver's seat and scoffed all the sweets I'd bought for myself and all of Tricia's white mice.

What was I going to do?

As darkness turned to blackness, I spotted some lights way in the distance. Ah. I remembered. There was a wee hamlet of farmhouses a mile or two into the hills.

I locked the car and headed towards the lights. I checked my phone as I realised it must be getting pretty close to dinner time, it was dead. I looked at the clock on the dashboard, and in another world, Trish and I would be sitting down tucking into steak and chips. I knew she wouldn't be too upset at my plans going wrong as I was absolutely crap at organising things. One of the worst was when we were first married. I'd left it pretty late to get an anniversary present. We were heading up to Aberdeen to meet up with my cousin Drew. I bluffed my way into making her believe I'd planned something special. All I was really doing was buying time to try to organise something on the hoof. I kept looking for opportunities, but none arose. The shops were shut when we got there, and the only thing that was open was a corner shop. I had a look at their card selection, and the only thing that remotely resembled anything to do with love was a card with a hammer with a smiley face on a spring bouncing around. It had one word on it. 'GREETINGS' It was the closest thing I'd get to an anniversary card that night, so I had no choice but to go with it.

'What about this big surprise?' She said.

'It didn't work out,' I said, 'Sorry'.

By the time I reached the cottages, my feet were aching, stomach was rumbling, and I was knackered. There were three houses, two of them had a light on so I decided on the nearest. I walked up to one of the windows and looked in. There was a guy, a woman and a kid in a high chair sitting around a wooden dining table, looked they were halfway through Sunday dinner. It seemed so warm and cosy, I half thought about not disturbing the tranquillity of the situation, but my stomach rumbled again, and the decision was made for me. I knocked three times in succession and stood down from the step. There was no answer, so I knocked again. This time a guy appeared too quickly as if he'd been unexpectedly disturbed. He had a fork with a half-eaten roast potato on it. I could see the steam rise from it and really wanted to grab it and run, but I resisted.

'Yeah?' He said.

'Apologies for interrupting you during your dinner but

would there be any chance of pulling me out of the mud at Gladhouse reservoir?' I asked.

He looked towards the darkness in the general direction of the reservoir as if weighing it up.

'What have you got?' He said.

I fumbled in my pocket for my wallet and pulled out a crumpled five-pound note. Held it up to him.

He put the fork to his mouth and chewed the remaining bit of roast spud.

He said something, but I couldn't understand, bits of potato shrapnel flew towards me.

'He gulped hard, getting the hot powdery loveliness over his throat.

'No. What kind of car have you got?'

I felt like a right twat, slid the fiver back into my pocket hoping he'd missed the episode.

'A Merc. C Class' I said.

'He cleaned his teeth with his tongue, licked the fork.

'I'll be there in half an hour. See you there,' he said and shut the door.

I winced and shuffled my way back to the sunken car. My heels and stomach were aching, I was covered in mud and felt like someone had sucked the life-force from me.

As I walked back and was almost at the car, I heard a massive splashing noise coming from pretty close to me. For some reason, the hairs on the back of my neck stood up, I was covered in goose pimples. Something was freaking me, but I had no idea what it was. It was some kind of frightening base instinct. I inched my way towards the noise, shaking uncontrollably. The intensity ramped up as I took a step or two forwards. There was nothing there. I ran back to the car and sat shaking in the lovely heated leather seat. I had no idea what the hell was out there, but it scared the living shit out of me. I thought it might be a deer, but there was nothing. I slid down into the well of the car and just sat there, shaking until the heat calmed me.

True to his word, the boy turned up bang on half an hour later. In a big blue tractor.

I went straight back to my tenth birthday. My Granny had bought me a scale model of a Massey Ferguson tractor. I wasn't really into cars and things, but as soon as I got it out of the box, I loved it. There was something so special about it. I think it was something to do with the freedom of the countryside and my idealistic impressions about the carefree life of a farmer. I was away in another world when he spoke. 'You awright?'

'Yeah, sorry, I was miles away. Nice tea then?' I said. I didn't want to mention that something had scared me.

'Was OK. Take this and attach it to the caravan header'.

He handed me a thick rope with a metal hook on it, I went to the back of the car, pretending that I knew where or what, the caravan header was. I didn't even know if I had one.

'It's at the front, he said, under the manifold.

I kind of knew where the manifold was from my year as an exhaust fitter in Leith. I slid under the front of the car, but it was too dark to see anything.

'Hold on a second' the boy said.

He went back into the cab of his tractor and put the full beam lights on.

There was very little room between the bottom of the car and the ground as the mud had risen so much. I felt around and found something hard that I could hook the rope onto. I really didn't care if it was the caravan head or not. It would do. I got back into the car, gave the boy a thumbs up and he reversed slowly. The vehicle glided out of the mud as if on rails, I was so happy.

He pulled me onto the main path and jumped out of the cab.

'That OK pal?'

'Yeah perfect, thank you so much, what do you like to drink?'
'Beer?' He said. Jumping up into his cab.
I took the rope from under the car, shook his hand and handed the rope to him.
'Thanks pal, I really appreciate your help.' I said and headed off home.
I always meant to take a few cans round to his house but somehow never got round to it.
Forty minutes later, I got back to Nitten. I opened the back gates and drove the filthy car into the garden.
I got out, shook as much dried mud as I could from my clothes and headed into the house. Trish was sitting in her leather armchair in a lovely dress, done up like she was going to a ball.
She took one look at me, covered in mud, from head to toe and burst out laughing, almost spat some of her wine over me. 'What the..'
'I held my hand up, sorry Trish, I'll explain later,' I said and headed to the bathroom for a shower.

Where to now?

SO. HERE WE ARE. Many years down the line and where am I? Ironically I'm precisely back where I started. No job, depending on my creativity to bring some pennies in the door and still looking for that big break. If nothing else I guess I'm a trier. I remember sitting in the BB hallway back at a presentation ceremony. My name was called out when there was a trophy being presented. Jim Divine - The guy who tries harder than anyone despite not being the most gifted. The latter part of the award was totally ignored by me. I shook like a banana jelly in an earthquake as I walked to the front of the room. This was the first acknowledgement I'd ever had that I even existed, never mind anything else. All I remember was heading up to the front of the room and clasping that trophy in my hands. Everything else echoed and blurred into oblivion. Me and that beautiful little silver cup bonded at a level I'd never experienced in my life. I still have it to this day. I was probably supposed to hand it back the following year, but there was never any chance of that happening.

Since that bloody recession, my life had changed. I'd gone to London to follow a dream, in all honesty, it was me clutching at straws, I'd gone past the desperation stage and was now in a state of abject delusion/optimism. I'm a dreamer. Always have been. But it's those dreams that have kept me going, kept me hopeful, enthusiastic, optimistic and really believing that there are way too many great people in this world for me to fail. Karma has always been my biggest ally, even before I knew she/he even existed. I always believed that if you were a good person, then things would balance out, still do. After I got back from London, I had nowhere to go. I had a massive overdraft to pay back and had no option but to pay everyone I owed money to. Trish and I agreed that this was the only way forward. I'd heard about people passing the buck and blaming other circumstances on why they couldn't pay their debts, but for us, this was the only possible option. It was incredibly painful. After some advice from my mate, we decided to go for a ten-year plan to pay back everyone. This meant that Trish had to pay around seventy to eighty per cent of her salary directly to our deal. I hated it. We had no flexibility, and it looked like she was tied to her job for the foreseeable. We looked at ways in which we could save money. Everything non-essential was cut. Sky TV, holidays, going out for meals and drinks, presents, expensive foods and so on. I felt so guilty. Many times I was unable to speak to her as I knew that this was my fault.

A couple of days after David had given us warning to call in a liquidation team, I was up in the attic, where my studio was. There was a loud knock at the door. This was a very experienced and severe knock. Whoever it was, knew how to knock a door. They'd been to the school of hard knocks, no question about that.

I climbed down the Ramsay ladder and opened the inner door. Two guys were standing on the top step. Both dressed in black, both wearing the whole threatening black outfits including the black cowboy hats. I approached the front door and could see the older guy had a big A4 sized envelope in his hand. I turned the key and opened the door.

'Mr James Dean Divine?' The older one said.

'Who's asking?' I said.

'HMRC,' he said.

'He tried to hand me the envelope, but I pulled away.

'I'm not accepting that' I said.

In my head, it was like an American cop programme where the unsuspecting morns are duped into taking a subpoena and while doing so are liable for the consequences.

'Take it or leave it' he said. 'Makes no difference to me'.

'In that case, I'll leave it,' I said.

The envelope flopped to the ground, well, it fell onto the top step but just lay there. All three of us looked at it. I was in a position of semi-positivity. David had informed me that someone would turn up at the door demanding payment. I honestly never expected it to happen so quickly.

As we stood there looking at this envelope, the main man said.

'You owe us a lot of money, but I'll do you a favour and only ask for 75% of it now. We can discuss the rest later'. He said.

My heart ramped like I was climbing Everest with an SAS backpack. I literally shit myself. My mind was doing somersaults. I couldn't think straight. Was he right? Was David's advice right? Were we going to lose the house? Shit. I slammed the door on their faces and ran back up the Ramsay ladder. I was straight on the phone to David. Shaking again like I'd never shook before. Fuck. This was tense. All that work to establish a career, a business, a life, a marriage. Had I fucked it all up again? David picked the phone up on the third ring.

I explained what was happening at the front door.

'Are these guys allowed to ask me for money? Can they force that letter on me?....'

'JIM.

Calm down.' He said.

The process of liquidation has begun and has been approved. These guys can't touch you'.

'Are you sure?' I asked.

'100%.

Tell them to go away, and when they get back to their office they've to call me'.

'David?' I said.

'Thank you. You've no idea what an incredible saviour you've been to me.' I said.

'Only helping a good friend,' he said. And rang off.

I went downstairs, incredibly relieved. The guys were still on the top stair.

'You can take your envelope with you and put it wherever you want' I said.

'I'm now in the hands of a liquidator,' I felt so positive.

The older guy picked up the envelope, and the two of them headed back to their car, defeated.

I felt like I'd just won something.

'David, you are a fucking superhero' I said.

The process of paying off our (my) debt was long and tedious. I felt so guilty using Trish to bail me out of the horrible situation. But I had no choice. I had no job and no money coming in. I wrote to a lot of companies for a job, tried many applications for all types of jobs but found that my skill-set was not of the desirable kind. After many months looking I got onto a roster of freelancers. Eventually, I was able to secure some freelance work. A day or two at a time. The pay wasn't great, but with our new found poverty, we looked at money differently. If I got a couple of day's work, it meant that we could buy food for the week or fill the car with petrol, or perhaps go to the pictures. In a way, it was a real eye-opener. When your salary is paid straight into your bank account every month, it becomes invisible. A series of numbers that are a means to an end. It's just there, taken-for-granted like the air that we breathe. As soon as you realise how valuable it actually is, it has a different perspective. We were at the stage where we'd go to Tesco on a particular night and time. The bargain shelf was filled with food that was close to its sell-by date. The prices were reduced dramatically, and it meant that if you were quick enough, you could eat good food for a fraction of the cost.

At these times, I felt like absolute shit. I married this

wonderful girl with the brightest of futures, I promised her the earth, happiness and love, all the way to those pearly gates and here I was at the sliding doors of a bloody supermarket waiting for cast off's. I hated myself.

I knew that if I was on my own, I could cope with this no problem. I'd spent my childhood being hungry and poor, and it would be easy enough to slip back into that way of life. A life without. You just got on with it.

But I'd married this innocent, beautiful young woman and I would rather die than subject her to what I'd been through.

I spent a lot of time going over where I'd gone wrong, what could I have done better, but it was all a useless waste of energy and emotion. There was no going back. We were where we were, and Trish was with me all the way.

One of the worst moments for me was coming home from another failed day where I hadn't managed to find work. It was a Tuesday night. Trish had decided to do the Lottery, believing that it could be us. I told her the bad news about no work, and she headed to the computer to check her numbers. I could see from her body language that the Lottery was not for us that night. I stood in the kitchen as her shoulders shook, she put her hand up to wipe away the tears. I really felt like karma had abandoned us.

That was a real low point. It only encouraged me to get my finger out a bit more. Eventually, I managed to get some good freelance work, two or three days a week. Things were starting to look good. I'd met a guy called Steve Johnstone a while back at some networking event, he was part of a group who looked for freelancers and sourced work for them. I met up with him, and he introduced me to his colleagues, Matt and Dan. They were brilliant. Within a few days, they'd got me regular work and well paid at that. Things were looking up. The debt was being paid, and our lives were getting back into a good rhythm.

We hadn't been on holiday for a couple of years as finances were so tight. One day we were invited out by our good friends Chris and Rona, and they'd just bought a house in the South of France.

'How would you guys fancy coming out to join us for a week's break at our new place?' Chris said.

'No charge, of course. We've bought you a couple of airline tickets so you'd better say yes' he said.

'Why would you do that?' Trish said it's so generous'.

'We know things are pretty tough for you and it's not a problem for us, plus we really enjoy your company. And Jim's, at times,' he said laughing.

It was a brilliant break, just what we needed. Chris's brother Jim also lived in the same village as them. Laroque D Alberes. Jim and his wife Lynne came over for a meal one evening. As we were sitting, Jim asked me what I did for a living.

I just happened to have a presentation on my laptop, I did a presentation of my work, and he was impressed. So was Chris. Chris hadn't ever appreciated what I did until that moment.

'You know something Jim?' He said.

'I think you could be just the person we're looking for'.

Chris had worked for the Forestry Commission since he left school.

'Let's talk about this when we get home'.

We did. It ended up with me getting an eighteen-month contract which helped to pay off a good bit of our ten-year debt a lot quicker than we'd anticipated. What a fantastic bit of luck that was. Thank you karma.

After the project was completed, I was again thrown into the unknown, but this time, I had a bit of a cushion behind me for the first time ever.

I went back to Steve, Dan and Matt and was able to secure wee bits of work here and there. One day I was approached by a small man asking about my availability. I was in the position where I was making some money, it was intermittent, and there was no guarantee I'd be getting any more. He offered me a decent salary to come and work with him. I'd be the Creative Director of his company and have the autonomy to push creativity in any direction I chose. He'd been following my recent career and liked the cut of my jib. It was the offer of a consistent wage for the first time in years. That stability would allow us to build for the future. Get a bit of the debt paid off and perhaps even save a wee bit here and there. After a couple of meetings with him, I accepted. There were reservations in my mind though. Every time we met up before I took the job, we never met in his office. It was always in a coffee shop. In fact, I never set foot in the office until the day I started the job. Something was niggling inside of me. Without going too much into it, I managed to stay there for almost a year, but by that time, I was ready to lose my cool and use my fists. It was time to get out before I did any damage. The only good thing about it was I met a lot of really lovely people, and a great friendship was created.

Hibs

HIBS HAVE BEEN PART of my life for most of my life. I was never one of those football fans who couldn't see past their own team, I was always very well balanced as I loved the game more than I loved my team. And I loved my team. Every time they got beat it hurt, it hurt a lot. I'd spend hours when I should have been sleeping, wrestling with the what-ifs when I replayed a game in my mind. That passion is impossible to explain to anyone who is not a lover of sport. Sometimes it was so bad that Trish and I didn't talk. I'd conned her into becoming a Hibee and sometimes the guilt of me doing that hurt so bad, she used to follow Aberdeen, but after we got married and moved into Easter Road I convinced her that this would be a wise move, I'd regretted it many times, and one particular game stands out.

Shortly after we moved into our flat, it so happened that Hibs were playing Aberdeen at home. One of Aberdeen's star players was Paul Kane, or Kano as he was known when he was Hibs Capitan, a few years previously. It so happened that Trish was training with Kano regularly as he was trying to improve his speed and as Trish was one of the top sprinters at Meadowbank and he lived not far from there it made perfect sense. Trish and I went along to the game and took our usual place in the old stand at the East end, 'the Cowshed,' an old guy was sitting on the benches right next to us singing Kano's praises.

'Why did ye ever leave us, Kano?'

Every time he won the ball, this old guy would jump up between Trish and I and offer the same diatribe,

'Why did you go tae they sheep shagger's Kano?'

As the game went on, Aberdeen were in complete control, although it was still nil-nil they were the more likely team to score. Shortly before half time, Kano won the ball from one of our sleeping mid-fielders, sent it rocketing towards his centre forward who easily knocked it into the net.

The old boy changed his tune then.

'Kano ya fuckin traitor', Ah'm glad ye went tae the sheep shagger's, yer fuckin shite, always huv been. ' He was distraught.

As the game went on Kano got better and better, by this time the old boy had a mouth as frothy as if he'd tipped a whole tin of Cremola Foam into his gob.

'He was popping his head between Trish and me with a whole list of profanities that would make a Leith docker shudder with embarrassment.

'Kano, yer nuthin but a fuckin traitor, fuck off back tae yer sheep shagging hame in the highlands ya useless cunt'.

Trish and I looked at each other and headed home as the fifth goal hit the net. Five-nil?

'Sorry about that doll,' I said. I really was sorry. We stayed a couple of minutes walk from Easter Road Stadium, so we got home in no time.

As the years went on, Hibs had their ups and downs, mostly downs it has to be said. Tony Mowbray was the only bright spark over the past few years. The football his team played was excellent. It got Trish and me back to buying a season ticket. Every second Saturday we'd be there looking forward to a great football game, and sometimes it didn't even matter if we won or not, the entertainment value was so high, it was brilliant. By this time, her Aberdonian days were well behind, and she was loving being a Hibee. As the seasons came and went, things got a bit worse until we were relegated from the top tier of Scottish Football, down to the second tier, the Championship. Watching at times was hard. As well as that predicament it was also now 114 years since we'd won the Scottish Cup, despite being arguably one of the four best teams in Scotland for that period. Every year it was the same old chants from our derby rivals Hearts. 'Another year of pain'. It was hard to take at times yet within a year we'd win the Scottish Cup and the Championship, that year was 2016.

It was amazing. We'd been to the League Cup final in March 2016 against a team who'd never been in a senior cup final before, Ross County from the Highlands. Surely this would be our day? Having said that, Ross County had unbelievably beaten Celtic 3-0 in the semi-final. They went one-nil up before half an hour was up, but we managed to equalise on the stroke of half time. Things were looking good. We missed so many chances and should have won comfortably but we 'Hibsed' it. They scored with the last kick of the ball. Trish and I, and many thousands of others headed home dejected, as usual at cup finals. A few weeks later Trish decided to run the world's biggest half-marathon. She'd already run the world's biggest marathon in New York. The biggest half marathon was in Gothenburg where our friends Nina and Jerry lived. This would give us a great excuse to go and visit them. As the half marathon date drew closer, Hibs were winning their way through to the Scottish Cup. Eventually getting to the final again. We'd lost the last 10 Scottish Cup finals we'd been in so why should this be any different? After that last trip to Hampden, we were not going to bother, just as well because the final was on the same day and the same start time as the Gothenburg Half Marathon.
As you'd expect, Hibs reached the Scottish Cup Final, it was against Rangers, so again, there was no way we were going to win. That's just how it goes.
I'd taken my kilt out to Gothenburg as Jerry, myself and some of the Swedish Hibs fans were going to watch the final in the pub while Trish ran the half with our pal Mick. As it turned out, it was incredible. Hibs went one-nil up in the first couple

of minutes and were really playing some great stuff, but as usual, Rangers came back into it, and by the hour mark they were two one up. We all resigned ourselves to the usual, another year without winning it. Amazingly on the 80th minute, we equalised. Everyone in the pub was going mental, this was going to extra time, we still had a chance. Then to clinch it all we scored with the very last kick (or header) of the ball. It was insane. We were jumping about all over the place. The Swedes in the pub who were not football fans looked a bit dazed. Jerry and I were going ballistic. We never thought this could happen. In the meantime, Trish and Mick had finished the half and were desperately looking for their phones in the baggage area to see what had happened. As it turned out, they got to them just as Hibs equalised. They got their stuff and started to run to the pub, but as they were leaving, they saw that Hibs had scored in the final minute. Trish said the two of them were hugging each other and shouting, jumping about like lunatics while all the other runners stood there looking at them, wondering what the hell was going on. It has to be said, I remember them both coming into the pub to loud cheers, and from there, the rest is a blur. Back in Edinburgh, it was mayhem. The open-top bus tour went all through the city, grown men were openly weeping in each other's arms. What a fantastic game it is at times. The following day they reckon there were over a quarter of a million Hibs fans in Leith celebrating. We missed it all.

Hibs were worth following again. Trish and I had been to quite a few matches during the season, and they really were entertaining again. In the Championship we were the best team by miles. We'd almost wrapped the title up early on, and by the time the final game of the season arrived, we had won the title. It's the first time in all the years of following Hibs that I've known we were going to pick up a trophy before the game even kicked off. One of our friends D- Mac was in charge of the marketing and promotion of the Championship on behalf of Ladbrokes betting. He'd been in touch with Trish a couple of weeks before to tell her to keep the last day of the season free. I knew nothing about it until a couple of days before.

'D-Mac's invited us to Easter Road for the final day of the season,' she said.

I was so chuffed. I knew he'd get us a really great table and probably get us to meet the team as well. I was so made up. What a climax to the most incredible year.

'Where are your ties?' She said to me on the day before the game.

'I don't have any. In fact, I do, but only one. It's that orange, brown and cream one, the nylon one I bought from the second-hand shop.

'There's no way you're wearing that,' she said.

We nipped down to her mum and dad's and borrowed Eric's green Hibs tie.

The next day we turned up at Easter Road as VIPs, I was dressed up like never before. I looked more like the Hibs manager than Neil Lennon did, I felt great.

We got to our table where David and his wife Allison were sitting. We'd known them a few years and always had a great laugh.

'This is so kind of you D-Mac' I said.

He'd read my autobiography 'The Lost Tornado' and loved it. In it, I talked about my dream of playing for Hibs, but that never happened.

'Well you might never have played for Hibs' he said.

'But after today you can say you presented them with their medals'.

I was shocked. What a day this was turning into. After all these years I'd finally get to step onto that hallowed Easter Road turf in front of a full house.

We had a great meal and a few drinks, the whole place was buzzing, we were on our way back to the big time, the Premier League. We'd just won the Scottish Cup after all those years of pain and had at long last silenced our bleating neighbours. The Jambo's could no longer taunt us.

D-Mac and I headed downstairs as the game reached its conclusion. It ended a draw with St Mirren, but in all honesty, all we wanted was the end of the game. I'd been told to go into the trophy room, as I walked in the Championship trophy was sitting there on a table. It was beautiful. It had all of the great names of the league winners. This used to be the big league trophy before the new Premiership had been created and had the great teams, like Celtic and Rangers nine league wins in a row, Aberdeen's glory days where Alex Ferguson had led them to dominate Scottish football.

I was mesmerised and help it aloft while nobody was looking. Pretending I was the Hibs Captain.

The players all ran from the pitch, past us and into the changing rooms. They emerged minutes later with the clean, fresh kit on, T-shirts proclaiming they were Scottish Champions and Scottish Cup Winners.

The presentation was getting closer. I was so excited. I'd dreamed of walking onto that pitch forever, hopefully, to kick a ball, but at this point, it didn't matter. D-Mac nodded to me, we left the room and headed to the tunnel. As we walked out, I could hear the roaring of the crowd. The announcer introduced us, and as soon as they saw a couple of suits walk out of the tunnel with the trophy, there was booing all around. I laughed out loud at the irony of the situation, I'd have done exactly the same. I looked around for some pals, and I could see them laughing in the main stand. They knew how long I'd waited to do this. I loved every minute of the experience. I stood on the pitch taking in the atmosphere, and when we left a good twenty minutes later, I felt so fulfilled. Not just for me, but for my team, Trish and all my pals. It was the most fantastic end to a season I could have hoped for.

And to top it all, when we got back to the table for a few drinks D-Mac handed me a little box.

'What's this?' I said.

'Open it'.

As I opened it, I was gobsmacked.

'Is this for me?' I said.

'Yip, I kept one back, especially for you,' he said.

It was a championship medal. So even though I'd never achieved my dream of playing for Hibs, I'd been on the pitch, presented the trophy and got myself a medal in the best season we'd ever had. What a day.

So

AFTER ALL MY TRIALS and tribulations, jobs that brought me many awards, friends, heartaches, tensions, pressures, laughs, tears and everything else that comes with a life lived, where am I now?

To be honest, I'm not sure. Am I happy? Am I more satisfied than I was when I was a kid? More content than when I got my first job? Happier than when I got married?

I honestly can't say.

Life still has many pressures. I spent around eighteen months re-branding a company, I was sure that's where I'd end my career, but after the project was complete, so was my use to them. Even at this advanced age, with all that experience, I once again found myself out of a job. No income to speak of and after a wasted trip to the Job Centre, I didn't even qualify for the most basic help.

There are though, a few things that I am delighted with: Trish and I are still as close and happy as we've ever been, that's been over thirty years married. I keep telling folk that I hypnotise her every night and tell her that she's married to the most incredibly handsome, witty guy. I really do feel lucky to have her at times, at other times I wish her Mum and Dad would take her back, but that's a rarity. I'm the sort of person that thinks about doing things, getting in touch with people, sending flowers or a card when they're down or up. But I never get around to actually doing it, Trish does all this for us both. My friends are still incredible. In some instances, I may not have been in touch with them for years, maybe ten or fifteen years but they're still there if I need them with no animosity or anything other than smiles when we finally meet up. I've always believed in keeping positive and although it's been so hard to do that at times, I know I'll always come out

Thunder At One AM

of that tunnel raring to go, wherever I'm going.

Despite me getting older and apparently wiser, I'm still getting into bother as you'd expect, I guess that naivety will never leave me. Relatively recently I'd spent a few days of the Isle of Skye, shooting the Old Man of Storr (This is a mountain rather than an actual old man). I wasn't sure how long I'd be up there, I reckoned an hour or so and didn't bother taking up my heavy-duty weatherproof gear, just took a lightish jacket. I ended up staying there waiting for the sunset for six hours, the light looked like it was going to be spectacular, hence me waiting and waiting, freezing my bollocks off. In the end, it fizzled out like a damp squib. By the time I had gone back down the mountain to the car, I was freezing. The next morning I woke up and my ribs were aching. I'd been shivering so much that I'd bruised the bloody things. I told Trish about this, and she decided she was going to buy me a real man's winter, weatherproof jacket. It was brilliant, and I know it cost her a bit of cash. Like most items of clothing and footwear that I enjoy wearing, I wore them everywhere. One time I was in Dalkeith for a haircut, I had to go to the building society to withdraw a thousand pounds in cash. I can't remember who it was for now. Anyway, I got the money and put it into the secure zipped inside pocket of my new jacket. I hung it on the coats-stand and headed to the barber's chair. There was hardly anyone in as it was early on Saturday morning. I chatted away with my hairdresser, as usual, shooting the breeze and talking football. When he'd finished, I got up from the chair and headed to the coat-stand. As I approached it, I saw my jacket had been moved slightly, and the inside pocket was wide open. I shit myself. I grabbed the coat from the stand and checked the pockets. My car keys were there but the plastic envelope with the money in, it was gone, the zipped pocket was empty. I immediately went to the door, closed it and locked it.

'Right, nobody move' I shouted. As if I was in reservoir dogs or something.

There were only about another three customers in, and three hairdressers. Everyone looked at me. Puzzled.

'Right, somebody's nicked my money from the inside pocket of my jacket,' I said.

'I had a thousand pounds in there, and I want it back now'.

I had the jacket on at this point, just to allow me to go through the pockets quickly, I did this over and over again, still no money.

An oldish woman was sitting on the leather sofa, waiting to be taken, she was clutching a big carpetbag close to her chest. In my mind she had stolen the money, I was absolutely 100% confident that she was the culprit. I walked over to her.

'Right, I know it was you that stole my money, hand me the bag'.

I held my hand out, she was looking quite sheepish, but to be honest so was everyone else. I stood there looking at her.

'Here you are son' she said, handing the bag over to me. I had a quick check to see if she'd moved the money from the bag onto her person. I took the bag and searched through it. There was no sign of my money.

'Right, stand up, I think you've hidden it somewhere else'.

She stood up and did a twirl. As she did this, a young apprentice hairdresser behind the counter caught my eye. He looked really suspicious.

I handed the bag back to the woman and went over to him.

'Right you, empty your pockets,' I said.

'What are you on about' he said.

'Empty your pockets. Nobody's leaving this shop until I've got my money back,' I said.

'You're not searching me,' he said.

As I was about to grab him, somebody said

'Are you sure it's your jacket?'

'Of course, it's my bloody jacket' I said.

'It's really expensive and a fairly new design, I'm sure not many people in Dalkeith would have one of these. Look, It's got my car keys in it,' I held them up to show the audience.

I now had a half per cent bit of doubt in my mind.

I wandered slowly over to the coat-stand, walking backwards, keeping an on my suspects, making sure that I'd be onto them if they tried to bolt through the door. As I got to the coat-stand I looked at it, there with the only other coat on the stand was another jacket, identical to mine. It was right at the back of the stand. Exactly where I'd left it.

I grabbed it, and sure enough, the inside pocket was firmly zipped shut, I opened it up and pulled out the plastic envelope with the money in it.

My face temperature increased by about a thousand per cent. I could feel the blood rush up there, turning my face into a crimson red that was not going to go away quickly.

I looked in the main pocket and pulled out my actual car keys, I looked at the ones in my had, and they were similar to, but not mine. I took the jacket off slowly and placed it back on the coat-stand, slipped the other keys back into the pocket. I stood there with my back to everyone and put my jacket on, taking a moment to figure out exactly what I was going to say to these people who were standing aghast, staring at me.

I turned around and smiled at them all. Put my hand's palms up and said 'What can I say? Sorry, I guess?'

I walked over to the woman and said 'I am so, so sorry for offending and accusing you, but you looked really suspicious, I was convinced, especially the way you were holding onto that bag.'

'Don't worry about it son' she said.

'We all make mistakes'.

'I really appreciate that, thank you,' I said.

I held my hands up to the rest of the people, including the guy who had the exact same jacket, which fit me exactly the same. He was sitting in the barber's chair sniggering, as were the hairdressers, and who could blame them.

I did a low bow to them all and said again how sorry I was.

I got out of there as quickly as I could and headed around to meet Trish at the opticians.

As I got there, she was on her way out.

'You look a bit flustered, are you OK?' She said.

I told her exactly what had happened, and she burst out laughing.

'How come these things only happen to you?' She said.

We had to walk back, past the barbers to get to our car.

'Do you want to walk on the other side of the road?' She said.

'No, the damage has been done, I'll walk past with my head held high.'

As we walked past, everyone in the shop was engaged in chat. I'm sure I know what they were talking about.

Another thing that's keeping me excited is my photography. It's improved so much over the past few years and is incredibly rewarding. I've been all over the country and especially enjoy getting great shots of Scotland. I'm out and about a hell of a lot and spend days walking around, waiting for the perfect light. In Summer I can be out from three in the morning until half ten at night. This gave me a lot of opportunities to go away for the weekend on photography shoots. Mostly on my own but occasionally with my photography Mates Paul and Alan.

I'd recently been to Glencoe in the Scottish Highlands with Alan where we'd got snowed in at our hotel for a few days. I was brilliant being snowed in at such a fantastic location, but throughout the three days, we only managed to get about forty minutes photography in as the weather was so bad. I was fortunate enough to get one of my best ever shots as the snow closed in. The good part about it was that our cars were going nowhere for a few days so we could sit and have a beer or two with the other residents who were also snowed in. On the Saturday night, we got talking to a young English couple, they worked for the BBC and had just arrived here after completing the filming for the Nature-watch programme. We got on really well. As we yakked away, there were to older guys sitting at a table next to us downing a lot of whisky. After a few more, they asked if they could join us.

'Yeah sure, no problem,' I said.

The young English couple could hardly understand what the guys were saying, they were from Glasgow and had really strong accents.

'They're inviting us over to their lodge, they're part of a Scottish Mountain Climbing club and want to show us their new lodge'.

The six of us got our big jackets and gloves on and trailed over the knee-deep snow, only a hundred yards or so. The biggest guy opened the door and invited us in. It was beautiful, a log fire was burning in the middle of the room, and there were chairs positioned all around it, incredibly cosy and unexpected. We sat there for a good hour while they regaled us of their mountain stories, which I was relaying to the young couple. As the night went on and their whisky bottle contents got shorter, the two Glaswegians started to become aggressive. They thought the English couple were taking the piss by not understanding them.

'Whae dae you's think ye fuckin are?'

The big one was saying.

By this time, I reckoned they'd downed at least a bottle and a half of full-strength Lagavulin. They were getting out of order, and the big guy was trying to pick a fight with the young English guy. Alan and I were mortified. As the Glaswegians headed through to the kitchen for more drink, I suggested the four of us run out of the place. We grabbed our stuff and legged it back to the hotel. We sat looking for them to head back over but thankfully there was no sign of them. The next morning the snow was beginning to melt, everyone was out scraping their cars, getting ready to leave. I saw the two Glaswegians heading over to me and braced myself for the fallout. I looked the big one right in the eye, and he obviously remembered nothing. Close shave.

I was sure that Alan and I could've taken them on easily, but it's not the kind of thing you want to do on a relaxing weekend.

There was another time when I was really to go radio rental on a guy though. Again, Trish was in full training mode for a marathon, and I'd decided to go away up north to Ullapool. It's a brilliant wee town and has some real characters, especially in the pubs and bars of an evening. I'd been a couple of years before and loved the location and feel of the place. This time I looked at the accommodation and felt I deserved something a bit special rather than go to the usual two or three-star accommodation I regularly used. As I said earlier, in summer, I can be out and about for up to nineteen hours in a day. In summer in Scotland the sun comes up at three-thirty in the morning and sometimes doesn't go down until at least ten PM. This can make for a long day, especially if you're in such a remote place that you can't get a hot meal or a coffee. Summer in Scotland is not always a hot affair. Much of the time it's as cold as Autumn or Spring, and as wet. You can plan all you want as far as a great location, brilliant scenery and the most incredible setup. But with photography, it's all about the light. The quality of light is what makes the image you're trying to capture. I've seen myself waiting for hours on end to see if a shaft of light will fall on a mountain or into a valley, only to be disappointed as the heavy clouds roll in to ruin your day. It really is a waiting game, I remember Trish once saying to me.

'Why do you go back to the same places, time and time again?'

Everything is different every single time you go back to these places. But it's mainly the light. I also have a few months more experience under my belt every time I go back. To me, photography is like fishing. You can have all the right gear, the right knowledge, the right pitch and the patience. In this case, the fish is the light. When it goes right, it's amazing, truly. The feeling you get when you've got the shot in the bag is like nothing else. Again, like fishing, you've captured your raw material, it's now up to you to decide what this is going to be cooked into. Post-processing (the part of photography where you put your files onto your computer to work on, similar to when photographers used to go into their darkrooms to process) is one of the best bits for me.

Anyway, I digress a little. I'd decided to get a nice place for B&B in Ullapool, in fact, when I got there, it was actually a ten-minute drive out of Ullapool, which I wasn't pleased with as they hadn't mentioned this on their website. I was heading up Friday morning and planning to stay until Sunday, two night's accommodation. On the Friday morning, I dropped Trish off at work and headed for a coffee and to sit and check the route I was going to take. I looked at the weather forecast, and it looked like heavy snow was due in the western Highlands later in the afternoon, in fact, it was due to hit as I arrived, around four o'clock. I drank my coffee, planned my route and decided to get up there before the really heavy snow came. It was a good decision, as I drove past the Glengarry Pass and into Ullapool the snow was getting thicker and thicker, making driving tricky. I hit the town centre looking for the B&B. After a while, my satnav took me back out of the town and up the long driveway of the B&B ten minutes away. I'd arrived an hour before I was due to check in but would rather be there than stuck up a mountain pass. I parked the car and had a look around, it was charming, very tastefully done. I thought I'd wander into the house to let them know I'd arrived.

There were two lovely houses, identical but one was for guests and the other for the owners. It wasn't apparent to me, which was which. Inadvertently I'd stumbled into the wrong house. I knocked on the door, but there was no answer, I did this a few times then turned the handle, it was open. I proceeded to wander through the house, looking for signs of life. As I walked around a corner, a woman screamed. And virtually shit herself.

'What are you doing in here?' She said.

'Jim Divine' I said. Extending my hand, looking to shake hers. 'I'm booked in for two nights but had to get here early to avoid the snow'.

She completely blanked my handshake attempt.

I put my hand in my pocket.

'You're in the wrong house' she said.

'Guests are over there, and you're way too early.'

I was taken aback. I'd just explained to the snooty cow why I got here early.

'You can't check-in for another hour' she said.

'That's fine, I was only making sure I was in the right place, I'm heading up to Ullapool to hopefully get sunset at Stac Pollaidh,' I was really annoyed by this old bat.

'I suppose that since you're here, I'd better show you your room,' she said.

'Is it ready?' I asked.

'You're the only one staying tonight' She said.

I don't know if she heard me, but I think I growled a bit at that. For fuck's sake, I thought. All that pish and hassle and the room was ready, and there was nobody else staying. She was obviously just after a moan.

The room was really wonderful. The decor was very tasteful, the room was big and spacious, and the whole house was like a show-home. It felt like I was the first person to stay there; it was so pristine. I'd have to make sure I wiped my arse properly to ensure that I didn't get any marks on the white sheets, as I sleep naked most of the time. As she showed me around and gave me instructions on what I could and couldn't do, I was liking her less and less.

'I guess you might as well bring your stuff in now' She said.

'Thanks' was all I could muster.

She left, and I sat on the chair at the side of the bed and considered my stay. The place felt dead, lonely. I stuck the kettle on and sat and had some tea, made sure I ate all of the biscuits they'd put out. I wandered down to the lounge area, and again, it was lifeless. I like to go to places where I can meet new people, sit and chat about all kinds of nonsense, here there was no chance. The place felt depressing. It is the only place where I've stayed and absolutely hated from the first moment. I'd decided I was only going to stay the one night even though I'd committed to two. I was happy to take the hit as long as I could get a room in the main town.

I got my heavy weather gear on and headed downstairs. It was still relatively light, I'd have time to go over to the mountains and hopefully get a decent sunset. I waited downstairs to let her know I was heading out, I could hear a couple of voices, presumably her and her husband, they were talking behind a frosted-glass door I could plainly see their silhouettes. I made some noises, but they never came out.

'Fuck you, ya arrogant, ignorant bastards' I thought.

I slammed the door on my way out. As it turned out, it was not a bad sunset but nothing special.

By this time, I was getting famished. At lunchtime, I'd stopped for a bite to eat at a wee cafe in Pitlochry, two sausage rolls (with plenty of brown sauce), a pot of tea and a chocolate eclair overflowing with fresh cream. Delicious. I couldn't remember if I'd paid for dinner, bed and breakfast or just bed and breakfast. Decided to phone the miserable bastards to ask, I was going to lose a night's accommodation and wanted to cut my losses.

I called.

'Hi, It's Jim Divine here,' I said.

'Who?' A man's voice said.

'Jim Divine. I'm staying with you for two nights'.

'Oh Yes,' he said.

'How can I help you?'

'Can you tell me if I've paid for dinner tonight or just bed and breakfast.'

'Just bed and breakfast' he said flatly.

'Do you want dinner?'

'What is it?' I asked.

'Hold on, let me know your mobile number, and I'll forward a menu onto you'.

A few minutes later, a text arrived with a menu attached.

I thought some of my mates were having a laugh with me. Or maybe they'd got in touch with the B&B to try to wind me up. Everything on the menu was onion-based. All of my friends and colleagues knew that onions were my mortal enemy, I hated them, I called them the Devil's Vegetable.

I sent a text back to him, asking if that was all there was to choose from.

'Yes,' came the text reply.

'Thanks but I'll give it a miss' I said.

'No answer'.

I was incredibly hungry now and pretty cold as I'd spent hours up at Stac Polaidh and Sullivan mountain range. I headed on to Ullapool and found a warm, cosy little pub that served fish and chips, and as it was Friday, you got it half price. What a result. It was just what the doctor ordered. Filled and warmed a hole superbly. As I sat there eating and having a low alcohol beer, I went onto Facebook and told my friends about the dinner menu. It was a hoot, and they all took the piss out of me. There was a lot of banter and laughs at my expense. After I finished I went off to look for accommodation for the following night, as I said, I'd decided to leave that crummy place first thing in the morning, I'd get as much breakfast into my belly as possible to try to make up for the fact that I'd be paying for not staying there another night. As it wasn't the height of tourist season I was able to get accommodation pretty quickly, I opted for the Ferry Boat Inn. It didn't have any stars as the owner was happy to be unconventional and stick to what he liked to do. It was perfect. And very reasonably priced.

After I'd secured my bed for the following night, I got into the car, had a small drive around the harbour admiring the lights and enjoying the soft sounds of the waves.

I got back to the B&B around ten or ten-thirty. There were a couple of lights on. I got my room key ready and headed in. I could see the shape of someone standing behind the inner frosted-glass door, he looked like he was pacing. I say he because if there were only two of them in, he was the bigger shape.

I was about to put my key into the door when the handle turned for me, and the door opened.

My first thought was 'wow, that's really nice, I've only texted and spoken to the guy so he must have waited up to introduce himself to me. Perhaps I was a bit hasty organising another room for tomorrow, maybe he'll be OK, despite his wife being a little arsehole. As I got over the threshold, I stuck my hand out to shake his. Like his wife had done earlier, he ignored it. 'For fuck's sake,' I thought, what the hell have I done to deserve this treatment'.

The door closed behind me, and the guy squared up to me.

He was a good six inches shorter than me and a lot skinnier,
I could pound this little cunt into the ground if I wanted but
being a non-violent, gentle type of guy I decided to take a
deep breath and wait to see what unfolded.

'How much do you think it costs us to get a meal to you?' He
said.

'Eh?' I said. I was baffled. It was like I'd been thrown into
some kind of show where everyone knew what was going on
except me.

'What are you on about?' I said. I was aware that I'd contorted
my face into a mask of total and absolute confusion.

'One pound sixty-five,' he said.

'What are you on about' I said. My mind was racing at a
hundred miles an hour, trying desperately to catch up with
whatever was going on.

'One pound sixty-five is all we make from your meal,' he said.
Holding his hands out, palms up in front of him, some weird
gesture I had no way of deciphering.

'Excuse me, can you hold on a minute' I said.

'I have absolutely no clue what you are actually talking about.'

'You were slagging us on Facebook,' he said.

'What?' I said. 'How do you know I was on Facebook?'

'We do a check up on all of our guests to make sure they're
worthy of staying with us. We don't want trouble makers,' he
said.

'You were spying on me on Facebook?' I said. 'What the fuck
is that about?'

I never swear or lose my temper, but this little twat had really
boiled my piss. I could feel my fists balling but again, took
a couple of deep breaths to lower my heart rate and regain
control.

'One pound sixty fi...'

'Stop' I said.

'You're missing the point. Do you think I was slagging the

price of your food?'

'Of course, you were,' he said.

'No I wasn't, as I said, you're missing the point. All of my friends and family know that I HATE onions, and if you look at the menu you sent to me, everything is onion based'.

'Do you know we have to order that food in specifically for our guests?' He said.

'We get a chef to cook it in Aviemore and get special transport to bring it over. Do you think a profit of one pound sixty-five is worth it?' He said.

'That's your problem' I said.

'Why were you spying on me?'

'I told you, we like to know a bit about the folk who are staying with us'.

'Well I can tell you this pal, there's no way I'm staying tomorrow. I know I've paid for my room for two nights, but I'm leaving first thing. You can keep the money and buy yourself an onion quiche from Aviemore'.

I left him standing there and headed up to my room. If these arseholes were spying on people on Facebook, God knows what they were doing in the rooms. I checked the place for hidden cameras. I felt so uneasy. I knew I'd insulted the little twat, but he deserved it. I got the impression that he was so furious that he'd come into the room in the middle of the night with a carving knife to sort me out. I was ready for him, I put my camera bag in front of the door so that if he did come in, he'd trip over it and this would give me time to sort the little fucker out. I slept very uneasily that night. All the way through I was on the point of storming out of their bloody shit B&B to make a stand, but it was early morning by this time, and I'd have nowhere else to go. I eventually fell into some kind of sleep, lighter than I hoped but enough to replenish the energy I needed for the next day, I made sure I squirmed on those pristine white sheets. I woke up early and had a quick wash and a cuppa in my room. I'd decided during the night that I wouldn't lower myself to taking breakfast from them. It was the first time in all those years of photography and staying in accommodation that I'd fallen out with the owners after only meeting them face to face for less than a couple of minutes. I got my shit together, making as much noise as I could. It then dawned on me that if they owned the house next door, why the hell were they staying in this house? I banged and scraped my way downstairs, ensuring that they knew I was angry. I slammed the front door as I left. There was something quietly satisfying about doing that.

I got into the car and headed to the Ferry Boat Inn, where I was greeted warmly and had a full Scottish breakfast.

That day I got some absolutely stunning shots, even if I do say so myself. I travelled away up north and headed to some great places: Achiltibuie, the Summer Isles, Dornoch. It was brilliant, and I still remember the pleasure I had to this day. I got back to Ullapool late and decided to have fish & chips again as it was so good last night. This time I was able to have a few beers as my bed was only a short walk away. As I sat there, I again went onto Facebook, and the banter was brilliant, I was laughing out loud at some of the comments and must have looked like a weirdo to the locals as I sat sniggering my way through dinner.

As I was doing this, a text alert pinged onto my screen. It was from my previous B&B man. A simple message.

'I want you to take that Facebook post down'.

'No,' I replied. Keep it nice and simple, I said to myself.

He sent another text

'You'd better take it down, it's detrimental to our business, and if you don't I'll get my lawyer onto you'?'

I was tempted to write back 'Fuck off' but went with 'Nope, it's staying there for eternity'.

'If you take it down I'll refund your money as you're not

staying with us tonight'.

'Nope,' I said. 'When I put things up on Facebook, or I post anything on Social media, it's well-considered and put there for a reason, there's no way I'm going to take it down and more to the point, if you look at the comments there are absolutely none that are detrimental to your business.'

'You'd better take it down. I'll be watching you,' he said.

I decided to end it with a polite message...

'If you ever attempt to get in touch with me in any way you'll regret it you little shit. You may have thought you were dealing with some poncey, photographer sap, but I guarantee you, if I hear from you again, you'll pay for it. I know people that would be delighted to come to visit you, and believe me, if they step over your threshold you'll wish you'd never been born. If you're in any doubt look up Pilton and Claremont Court on Google.

I'm presuming this is the last I'll hear from you?
I'd love to say it's been a pleasure, but in actual fact, you and your wife are two of the most miserable, soor-pussed, unwelcoming, angry little bastards I've ever had the misfortune to come across in my life, now go away and wilt in some dark corner of your swampy overgrown garden.'

Jim Divine - Photographer.

What now?

I DON'T KNOW IF I'm any happier, but I can tell you this without a single iota of doubt. I love my life and everyone in my life.

I've no idea what the next chapter holds for me, but I can say with absolute certainty, it's been a hell of a ride so far. Perhaps I'll be lucky enough to write a third chapter to my life, but we'll have to wait and see.

I'm pretty sure that before I shuffle off this mortal coil, I'll get into more trouble.

Something I'm looking forward to with great enthusiasm.

Jim Divine is an Award Winning
Graphic Designer and Photographer.
He lives in the old Mining Village of Newtongrange
with his Wife Trish.

For more information visit: www.TheLostTornado.com
or Email: Jimdivine@21nine.co.uk

Printed in Great Britain
by Amazon